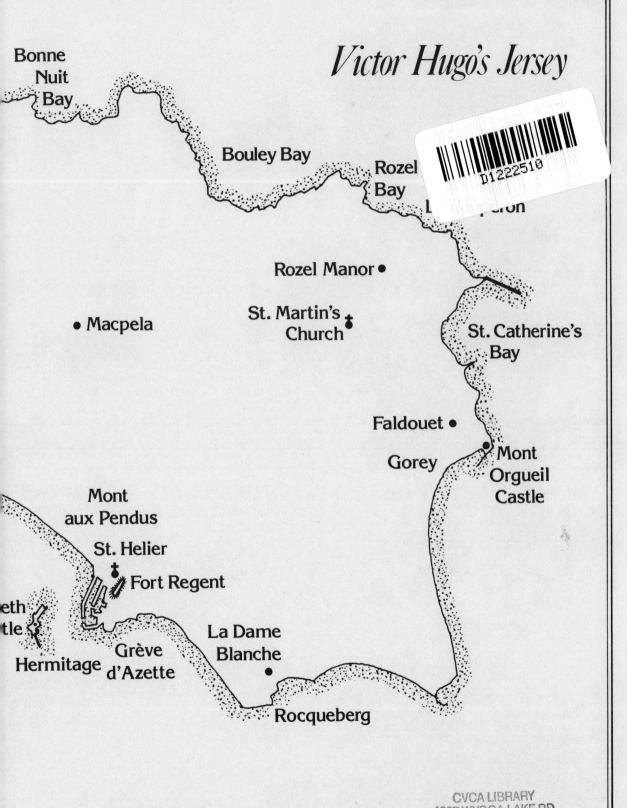

Victor Hugo's Jersey

Bonne
Nuit
Bay

Bouley Bay

Rozel
Bay

Rozel Manor ●

St. Martin's
Church ✝

Macpela ●

St. Catherine's
Bay

Faldouet ●

Gorey

Mont
Orgueil
Castle

Mont
aux Pendus

St. Helier ✝

Fort Regent

...eth
...tle

Hermitage

Grève
d'Azette

La Dame
Blanche

Rocqueberg

VICTOR HUGO IN JERSEY

VICTOR HUGO IN JERSEY

Philip Stevens

Phillimore

1985

Published by
PHILLIMORE & CO. LTD.
Shopwyke Hall, Chichester, Sussex

ISBN 0 85033 560 4

Printed and bound in Great Britain by
REDWOOD BURN, LTD.
Trowbridge, Wiltshire

Contents

LIST OF PLATES

(between pages 38 and 39)

The author would like to thank the following for permission to reproduce photographs: Bulloz (Collection de la Maison de Victor Hugo) for numbers 1, 3, 8, 11, 13, 16, 17 and 21; Bibliothèque Nationale, Paris for numbers 2, 4, 5, 6, 9, 10, 12, 14, 18, 19 and 20; Ulster Museum for number 15.

Acknowledgements and Preface

I am most grateful, as anyone studying this period of Hugo's life must be, to the late Professor Frances Vernor Guille, who worked for many years in America and France to collate, decipher and edit the Journal of Adèle Hugo which has so illuminated Hugo's exile in Jersey. One can only regret that the two final volumes, covering 1855 and 1856, have not yet been published. I would also like to thank those who have helped me directly: Mme. Ecalle and Mlle. Lafargue of La Maison de Victor Hugo in Paris for allowing me to consult the Hugo family correspondence in their care; Mme. Oppenheim of 'La Durande' and Mme. Goguet of La Maison de Jersey in Paris; Miss Dorothy Vincent of Jersey Public Library for showing me the newspapers of the period; Mr. Robin Cox for his help with the maps; and Mr. Ian Monins for his great help and encouragement.

This is not a rash attempt to describe the evolution of Hugo's thought and writing during his exile in Jersey, something on which there is a vast literature, but rather a day to day account of the life of the Hugos and the proscrits in Jersey. It is intended to show that Victor Hugo bore no grudge for being expelled from the island when he honourably refused to disown a facetious letter attacking Queen Victoria, although he disapproved of its style and tone. Too often one hears that Hugo was expelled for 'writing an insulting letter to Queen Victoria'.

This book also describes and records Hugo's deep and genuine love for Jersey. It is perhaps time, on this centenary of his death, for Jersey to reciprocate, possibly by erecting a statue to France's greatest poet who was arguably the greatest man ever to set foot on the island.

Philip Stevens

39 Starfield Road
London W12

Jersey

JERSEY dort dans les flots, ces éternels grondeurs;
Et dans sa petitesse elle a les deux grandeurs;
Île, elle a l'océan; roche, elle est la montagne.
Par le sud Normandie et par le nord Bretagne,
Elle est pour nous la France, et, dans son lit de fleurs,
Elle en a le sourire et quelquefois les pleurs.

Pour la troisième fois j'y vois les pommes mûres.
Terre d'exil, que mord la vague aux sourds murmures,
Sois bénie, île verte, amour du flot profond!
Ce coin de terre, ou l'âme à l'infini se fond,
S'il était mon pays, serait ce que j'envie.
Là, le lutteur serein, naufragé de la vie,
Pense, et, sous l'oeil de Dieu, sur cet écueil vermeil,
Laisse blanchir son âme ainsi que le soleil
Blanchit sur le gazon les linges des laveuses.

Les rocs semblent frappés d'attitudes reveuses;
Dans leurs antres, ainsi qu'aux fentes d'un pressoir,
L'écume à flots bouillone et luit; quand vient le soir,
La forêt jette au vent des notes sibyllines;
Le dolmen monstrueux songe sur les collines;
L'obscure nuit l'ébauche en spectre; et dans le bloc
La lune blême fait apparaître Moloch.

A cause du vent d'ouest, tout le long de la plage,
Dans tous les coins de roche où se groupe un village,
Sur les vieux toits tremblants des pêcheurs riverains,
Le chaume est retenu par des câbles marins
Pendant les long des murs avec des grosses pierres;
La nourrice au sein nu qui baisse les paupières
Chante à l'enfant qui tette un chant de matelot;
Le bateau dès qu'il rentre est tiré hors du flot;
Et les prés sont charmants.

    Salut, terre sacrée!
Le seuil des maisons rit comme une aube dorée.
Phares, salut! amis que le péril connait!
Salut, clochers où vient nicher le martinet;
Pauvres autels sculptés par des sculpteurs de proues;
Chemins que dans les bois emplit le bruit des roues;
Jardins de laurier rose et d'hortensia bleu;
Etangs près de la mer, sagesses près de Dieu!
Salut!

A l'horizon s'envole la frégate;
Le flux mêle aux galets, polis comme l'agate,
Les goëmons, toison du troupeau des récifs;
Et Vénus éblouit les vieux rochers pensifs,
Dans l'ombre, au point du jour, quand, au chant de la grive,
Tenant l'enfant matin par la main, elle arrive.

O bruyères! Plémont qu'évite le steamer!
Vieux palais de Cybèle écroulé dans la mer!
Mont qu'entreint l'océan dans les liquides marbres!
Mugissements de boeufs! doux sommeils sous les arbres!

L'île semble prier comme un religieux;
Tout à l'entour, chantant leur chant prodigieux,
L'abîme et l'océan font leur immense fête;
La nue en passant pleure; et l'écueil, sur son faîte,
Pendant que la mer brise à ses pieds le vaisseau,
Garde un peu d'eau du ciel pour le petit oiseau.

Creux de la Touraille (L'Homme sans Tête)[1]
8 Octobre 1854

Chapter One

A Delightful Island

In the revolutionary year of 1848 Victor Hugo was a right-wing deputy in the Assembly but the logic of his humanitarianism was leading him to the left. He thought he discerned in Prince Louis Napoleon, then in exile in England, a like spirit: had Napoleon not written *Thoughts on the Extinction of Pauperism?* Hugo and his sons, Charles and François-Victor, successfully urged, through their paper *L'Événement*, that the presidency should go to Napoleon. On assuming the post in 1848, Louis Napoleon assured Hugo he would be a Washington rather than a Napoleon.[1]

Yet, once in power, he began to show his displeasure with Hugo's split with the conservatives and his championing of liberal causes. Furthermore, he was attempting to change the constitution, so that he could again be a candidate for the presidency in 1852. On 17 July 1851 Hugo made an eloquent speech in which he compared *Napoléon le Petit* with the great Napoleon, but Louis Napoleon's support was growing and on 2 December he staged a *coup d'état* and dissolved the Assembly. On the 3rd a warrant for Hugo's arrest was issued, but he hid until the 11th and then slipped over the Belgian frontier with a forged passport.

Hugo joined proscribed republicans (*proscrits*) and others in Brussels where he castigated Louis Napoleon's coup in the *Histoire d'un Crime* and the man himself in the shorter *Napoléon le Petit*. The Belgian government, though not antagonistic to Hugo, was concerned about the effect which the impending publication of these works would have on its relations with France. Hugo had anticipated the effect of his polemics and had considered a Portuguese exile: he had friends in Portugal but it was too far from France. He had also thought of London but his son François-Victor persuaded him against the idea: lost among the refugees from the popular risings of 1848 and 1849 he would be compromised. Further, he did not speak English and he knew of the internecine strife between the London proscrits. Mme. Hugo even suggested going to America on the rather doubtful grounds that both London and Belgium could be taken by Louis Napoleon in a few hours. Hugo himself seems to have had no very strong preference for a place of exile. 'What does it matter where', he wrote to the family friend Paul Meurice on 28 January 1852, 'as long as we have freedom. Liberty is our home. We will make a broadside from some island like Jersey and from there we will bombard Bonaparte with ideas.'[2]

Ever conscious of his place in French history and literature, Hugo was aware of his affinities with the great Napoleon who had twice been exiled to an island, and with Chateaubriand, who had taken refuge in Jersey in 1792-3, and whom he had met and long admired. At Granville in 1836, he had gone out in a boat with two boys who spoke of landing in Jersey, but a breath of wind had taken them back into port. That was the closest he had been to the island where he was to spend more than three years.[3]

3

By April he had decided on Jersey, writing to his wife from Brussels 'Jersey is a delightful English island, 17 leagues from the coast of France. They speak French there and one can live well cheaply. All the proscrits say that life is marvellous there '. Mme. Hugo told her daughter Adèle that they would spend 'la belle saison' there and winter in London. Hugo got Jersey addresses from M. de Léliou and information from a work by Achille de Salvandy, from Delhasse and from Théodore-Étienne Mézaise, an ex-suitor of Adèle's who had taken refuge in Jersey. From Mézaise he learned that Jersey was intellectually sterile, but that the climate was healthy and sunny, the island democratic, practically independent and well connected by boat with the coast of France.[4]

The decision made, Hugo wrote to Adèle 'You will see how happy we shall be when we are together. Jersey is a charming place; we shall have the sea, the greenery, nature in its magnificence and, best of all, a home ...' For his son Charles, however, the prospect was gloomy. 'Papa maintains that it will be a delightful stay', he wrote presciently to his mother, 'but I fear that Jersey life will be too contemplative and isolated for Adèle and François-Victor. No doubt there is something sublime about the spectacle of the sea, but it will end by depressing us.'[5]

Hugo had first expected to leave Brussels on 14-15 July, and he wrote to his wife of his plans for getting lodgings in Jersey. In the event he was able to stay in Brussels with Charles until 1 August, so he sent her ahead with these words: 'Go directly to St Helier ... there must be some good hotels there ... install yourself there (having found out the price first) ...'.[6]

Mme. Hugo and Adèle left Paris for Villequier, Le Havre, Southampton and Jersey. They had been joined in France by the faithful family friend, Auguste Vacquerie, whose brother Charles had been drowned at Villequier with his wife Léopoldine, Hugo's daughter, in 1843. On the mail-boat from Southampton, Adèle watched Jersey approach: 'Rocks, then more rocks, and then, in the distance, the shore that is called Jersey '. The tide was low and they had to transfer into a dinghy. Landing at St Helier, which Adèle found clean with elegant houses in deserted streets, they spent the night at the *Pomme d'Or* hotel, which they had been told was the most acceptable to French people. Bed and board cost 5 francs (4 shillings) a day which was reasonable but, to the annoyance of the women, the hotel lacked cupboard space. In the evening they went out for a stroll and found, with difficulty, a space with some trees, presumably Royal Square. The next day was spent looking unsuccessfully for lodgings, and in St Aubin 'une anglaise' shut the door in their faces.[7]

In spite of the representations of the proscrits in Brussels, Hugo had left Belgium. He told them why. 'I understand that the moment I publish ... *Napoléon le Petit*, my presence will be an embarrassment, even a peril for Belgium ... I am going to Jersey in an England which has the greatness of being able to grant asylum with impunity.' Going to Antwerp and then London, where he met Mazzini, Louis Blanc and Schoelcher and confirmed his impressions that the London proscrits were at odds, Hugo and Charles took the *Dispatch* (Captain Babot), from Southampton, with Juliette Drouet, Hugo's devoted mistress, among the other passengers. The French Vice-Consul and spy in Jersey, Laurent, informed the French police that a woman had arrived on the same boat whom many recognised as George Sand, but who was travelling incognito. Juliette went to the *Caledonia Hotel du Commerce*. Hugo and his party had arrived on 5 August, the very day that *Napoléon le Petit* appeared in Brussels.[8]

He was greeted on the quay by a crowd of Jersey and English people and by most of the proscrits, one of them waving a red flag. Hugo claimed that 'the whole island was there to greet him' but Laurent reported that there were about 60 proscrits and added that there was no demonstration. In his oration at the *Pomme d'Or*, Hugo said that he had left France on the quay at Antwerp and found it again on the jetty of St Helier, and he ended 'Would that, one day, it could be said of Jersey and of France: it is this little island which has delivered that great nation. Vive la République!'.[9]

He was impressed by the demonstration of support and this led him to exaggerate its extent among the people of the island. 'The inhabitants of St Helier are ardently sympathetic to the republican proscrits', he wrote to Madier de Montjau. Vacquerie, writing, it is true, long after the welcome had turned sour, sounded a more bitter if realistic note, in saying that the impecunious proscrits were treated much less well than the anti-revolutionary gentlemen and priests who took refuge in 1792. It was as a poet, rather than as a politician, still less as a peer of France, as Hugo claimed, that he was welcomed to Jersey.[10]

That evening, he read some pages of *Napoléon le Petit* to his nearly complete household: Mme. Hugo, their children Adèle and Charles, and Auguste Vacquerie. His younger son, François-Victor, recently released from the prison of La Conciergerie, was still detained in France by an actress. Hugo and Charles both seemed to Mme. Hugo to have put on weight since she last saw them.[11]

The next day, 6 August 1852, the search for lodging began anew. They were keen to move as they found life at the *Pomme d'Or* disagreeable. Hugo wanted to live by the sea 'the proscrits' country', and so, like George Eliot five years later, they looked in St Aubin and then Gorey. Hugo was determined to find somewhere in Gorey, of which he wrote 'After Le Tréport, Le Passage[12] and Éntretat ... the most beautiful place I have seen' but the next day found them looking at 'a beautiful house with a terrace'. If this was Marine Terrace, it is possible that they rented it on the spot, but at Charles' insistence they went back to Gorey and found an admirably situated house. Hugo's dream, even then, was to live in Guernsey in a room overlooking the sea, but here in Jersey he set his heart on Gorey. Mme. Hugo and Adèle, however, were in favour of the house with the terrace because, as Vacquerie explains, it was nearer to St Helier and Adèle wanted distractions. Charles wanted to live on some wooded height, while Vacquerie pompously stated that he attached no importance to material things. Adèle concluded 'Victor Hugo acceded to my choice'. He later explained that this unprepossessing house, Marine Terrace, was taken because they all wanted to leave the hotel as soon as possible, and, as bad luck would have it, this was the first rented house they saw.[13]

On about 19 August the Hugos moved into No. 3 Marine Terrace, the western and left half of the building. It has recently been demolished, but it stood in St Clement's parish, nearly on the St Helier parish line. The Hugos referred to the area as St Luke's, Georgetown or Grève d'Azette. The house was rented furnished for 1,500 francs (£60) a year from Thomas Rose, who had painted and papered the interior. Rose lived next door in No. 2, or at least he owned the property along with much else in St Clement, St Brelade and Middlesex. He was a friend of J. M. W. Turner, and was an original and enterprising man about whom too little is known. Hugo referred to him as 'the excellent M. Rose', and the Roses and the Hugos must have had many contacts, though we know little of them.[14]

Hugo later described Marine Terrace in some detail. 'The flat-roofed house was rectilinear, correct, square, freshly distempered, quite white. It was built methodism. Nothing is as glacial as this English whiteness. It seems to offer you the hospitality of snow. One dreams, with a heavy heart, of the old wooden peasant hovels of France, happy and dark, with vines ... This house, a heavy white cube ... was shaped like a tomb ... the smallness of the windows added to the brevity of daylight ... and aggravated the crepuscular sadness of the house ...'[15]

The entrance was a corridor leading from the street at the back to a barely-furnished drawing room and darkroom and thence to the conservatory. On the first floor were Mme. Hugo's and Adèle's bedrooms, a visitors' room and the dining room facing the sea. On the second floor were the rooms of François-Victor and Charles, with Victor Hugo's, of course, facing the sea.[16]

'The Prince of modern poets', reported the Jersey paper L'Impartial, 'who has so admirably sung of the sea, could not have chosen a habitation more suited to his tastes.' On the day they moved in Hugo wrote to Luthereau that he had rented a 'pretty little house' by the sea, but his abiding distaste for it was soon established. Three days later he was writing more soberly to van Hesselt 'I'm set up in a little niche by the sea that the island papers call "A superb house on the Grève d'Azette". It's a cabin ...' He was to refer to it again as a 'hut' and a 'shed'. For Mme. Hugo the house was 'comfortable and neat like all English houses' but, though fully furnished by Mr. Rose, it contained no linen.[17]

From Marine Terrace a treeless garden opened onto a sloping area of 50 by 40 feet, which was surrounded by walls and broken up by granite steps and parapets. The garden was covered with tufts of marigold. A grassy rising, with nettles and a large hemlock, hid the beach from the garden, but one could discern from the house a tower, reputed to be haunted, in a small wood on top of a hill to the right. On the left was the dike. This was a stone pier lined with large tree trunks planted in the sand, whitened, dessicated, gnawed away, with knots, stiff joints and knee-caps, looking like a row of bones: the careful description is Hugo's.[18]

At the end of the terrace was La Grève d'Azette and the sea, invisible from the ground floor. Vacquerie describes the scene for us: 'At low tide, there was only a sandy beach whose flatness extended as far as the eye can see, bespattered with innumerable small chocolate-coloured rocks which would make one believe that an untidy Gargantua had passed by. But, when the tide rose ... the view was truly beautiful. The sea threw itself violently against the trembling wall and shook the terrace; it piled up in an angle made by the dike ... and a strong rock which jutted out in the sand as if to shield us; it attacked the wood and the granite terribly; it was a battle between water and earth; the ocean writhed, roared, swirled; the whole dripping rock disappeared momentarily; the wood of the dike took revenge for shipwrecks by breaking up the exasperated wave.'[19]

When the tide fell, peace returned. In Hugo's words:

> One hears afar
> The creaking of a capstan as the anchor rises
> Horses on the beach ...
> Pull carts loaded with seaweed;
> Women turning over sand and silt;

> Pass, hoop-nets in hand, prowling bare-legged;
> Great white birds come and go in the skies.
> On the horizon, the sea, bottomless as night.[20]

Juliette Drouet, meanwhile, had found lodgings nearby. She had originally intended to stay at the *Auberge du Commerce*, but she found it expensive, and the proximity of tradespeople and farmers proved insupportable. On 12 August she and her maid Suzanne moved into lodgings at Nelson Hall, Havre des Pas, for 8 shillings a week and 2 shillings a day board, which was fairly cheap for a holiday flat by the sea. Nelson Hall was a few paces from the sea, but separated from it by a plank fence surrounding a boat-yard, so at the end of September Juliette moved upstairs for a sea-view: in fact, a marine panorama that streched from the battery of Fort Regent round to the rocks of St Clement. On a clear day she could see the reefs of Les Minquiers on the horizon. At the back and north of Nelson Hall there were small unkempt gardens full of vast cauliflowers gone to seed. To the west was the signal mast of Fort Regent on which they hoisted a white flag to announce the arrival of the mail-boat with letters and newspapers. At the bottom of Fort Regent there was a 'suburb' of St Helier with a cemetery (Green Street) with a monument to *Centenier* George le Cronier, murdered in 1846 while arresting a prostitute. On the east there were charming hills broken by small woods and scattered with villas and cottages.[21]

But Juliette soon became fed up with her landlady who got shamelessly drunk with the other neighbourhood gossips who would, she said, have been more than a match for the rag-pickers of Paris. On 6 February 1853, she left Nelson Hall and moved next door to the *Green Pigeon*, Richard Landhatherland's public house. In 1854 she moved again, to Maison du Heaume nearby.[22]

While the Hugos were setting up in Marine Terrace, François-Victor remained in France wrestling between filial piety and his passion for a Vaudeville actress, Anaïs Liévenne. She was in the last stages of consumption, living in luxury and debt. Alexandre Dumas the younger, who had himself been Anaïs' lover and whose heroine La Dame aux Camélias she so much resembled, called her a courtesan in love, 'just a stock figure of romantic drama'. François-Victor could hardly indulge Anaïs' expensive tastes as he depended on loans from Paul Meurice or occasional subsidies from his impecunious father, who severely disapproved of Mlle. Liévenne. She had written to Hugo to ask him to let François-Victor stay in France, promising that they would both come to see him in Jersey.[23]

François-Victor lacked the funds to get to Jersey. On 17 August we find him in Dieppe writing to Meurice for a loan to be reimbursed by Hugo. He must have borrowed the money, though he did not get to Jersey until 22 September. But he missed Anaïs and so went back to France on 14 October. Hugo was sad to see him go:

> My child, I followed right to the end the smoke
> Of the boat fleeing on these seas, my prison,
> And I felt my soul, scattered to the four winds,
> Going with you into the gloomy horizon ...[24]

In Caen, François-Victor's luggage was searched for seditious literature but a disgruntled Bonapartist functionary told him how to get to Paris avoiding the agents who had been forewarned of his route. Once in Paris in mid-October he continued to dissipate, on gambling and Anaïs, what little he had but, following an invitation from his father, brought her to Jersey for a stay of some weeks. François-Victor knew that if she was prepared to leave the theatre and live on what he could earn with his pen, Hugo would consent to their marriage.[25]

During this stay François-Victor may have started to plan his further literary career, for Hugo records this melodramatic conversation between them:

> One morning at the end of November ... the father and the youngest son were sitting in the lower room. They were silent like shipwrecked sailors, thinking. Outside it was raining, the wind blew, the house was as though deafened by this roaring outside. Both were dreaming, absorbed, perhaps by the coincidence of both winter and exile. Suddenly the son raised his voice and asked the father:
> 'What do you think of this exile?'
> 'That it will be long.'
> 'How will you fill it?'
> The father replied:
> 'I shall contemplate the Ocean.'
> There was silence. The father went on:
> 'What about you?'
> 'I', said the son, 'I shall translate Shakespeare.'[26]

But François-Victor was not quite ready for Shakespeare, and he left Jersey with Anaïs to continue their old life. Some time later, on 13 December, Mme. Hugo and Auguste Vacquerie followed them to Paris. At the same time Hugo wrote to him: 'Something serious has happened. I cannot write it. Your mother will tell you ... your coming here is absolutely essential ... Do not waste a minute '. In a further letter a week later, Hugo gave a hint of what was wrong. 'I do not, perhaps, have much time ahead of me ... Come, come immediately, I demand it, my poor Victor. If necessary, I order you.' At the same time he wrote to his wife in Paris: 'Our poor child has lost his reason. It is essential to tear him away from Paris, or he is lost. He admits himself that he gives this woman 500 francs a month. Where will he get it? 6,000 francs a year!'. Hugo authorised his wife to pay François-Victor's debts of 1,547 francs. Mme. Hugo learnt from Alfred Asseline that Anaïs was also consorting with a M. de Waresquiel, and that the French government would be only too glad to see the Hugos' name dragged through the mud.[27]

Mme. Hugo and Vacquerie managed to drag François-Victor and Anaïs back to Jersey on 30 December. For three days Victor Hugo begged Anaïs to leave, painting exile in the gloomiest colours. On 31 December Charles and Vacquerie waited in an adjoining room for a fainting fit or suicide attempt by Anaïs, while François-Victor languished in his room. At 3 p.m. he left Anaïs, swearing he would be back at 5 p.m., but he never saw her again.[28]

The next day Hugo, just like M. Duval in *La Dame aux Camélias*, made Anaïs a 'generous proposition', presumably a bribe to leave, and the following day François-Victor managed to get a letter and photograph through to her, while she bribed Catherine, the cook, to give him his passport and tried to get a letter through to him telling him to flee.[29] But on 3 January 1853, after a breakfast of cutlets, wine and tea at the *Pomme d'Or*, Anaïs was escorted back to France by Charles, though not before she had written a letter, full of reproachful anger, to François-Victor, saying that she would never return. The letter was suppressed by Hugo, so that his son remained in a fool's paradise. Even while Charles and Anaïs were sailing to St Malo, François-Victor was roaring with laughter. He went to the theatre that evening, and at midnight Vacquerie was woken by shouts of laughter lasting three-quarters of an hour. The next morning they talked cheerfully of this and that, which made

Vacquerie anxious about François-Victor's false sense of security, which would be even less well founded once Anaïs was out of their sight. From St Malo she managed to get a letter through Catherine, the cook, to François-Victor, telling him how to escape, but that too was intercepted by the family. François-Victor now realised what Anaïs really thought of him. Mme. Hugo found a cache of clandestine letters which he admitted were his and, 'full of courage and reason', he surrendered his passport to his mother.[30]

François-Victor was well out of it. On the boat to St Malo Anaïs chatted with M. de Bressé and made fun of the young John Rose who was consumed with love for his teasing and indifferent neighbour Adèle Hugo. No doubt Anaïs found surcease for her own wounded pride in mocking John Rose, and Charles found her remarks lacking in pity. He wrote to his father from Paris to say that Anaïs had been light-hearted and amiable, eating well twice a day and ordering tea at all the hotels on the way. In short, 'a few sighs, no tears, a few laughs and a good appetite'. Charles returned to Jersey by way of England and a very rough Channel crossing from Southampton. Some days later Anaïs in Paris went off with a young naval officer.[31]

She was relieved to have escaped from the sombre Hugo household. 'I felt myself too weak to say goodbye to the light-hearted world and enter such a serious one', she admitted honestly to Janin. Yet she did not blame François-Victor for having loved her too much. 'He was young and in love, two reasons for seeing only the present moment. And then, is he to blame, when he and his family offered to share the bread of exile with me, as he would have shared with me the happiness that was coming to him?'[32] After several weeks of harrowing grief François-Victor regained his former happiness, thanked all who had opened his eyes to his folly, and never again spoke of his former amourette. Like Gibbon, he had sighed as a lover, obeyed as a son.[33]

The Hugo household was completed by Fanny, the chambermaid, Catherine, the cook, and two other servants, Marie and Julie. Léon Daudet tells us that Mme. Hugo bickered with her servants so much that Hugo would escape to Juliette Drouet's, and that the cook was dismissed for stealing. Juliette's maid Suzanne also helped at Marine Terrace until 1854 when she left, while the Hungarian proscrit Sandor Teleki would try his hand at cooking, so the Hugos were well cared for.[34]

Chapter Two

A Regular Life

Daily life in this unusual household was nonetheless quite humdrum. Hugo had told his family that as long as exile lasted, they would live for thought, nature and the family.

Hugo himself would get up at dawn (his windows had no curtains) and sit on his bed writing until midday. Jules Laurens, a painter who sketched Hugo's room in 1855, described it as a Bluebeard's cell: small, bare and whitish, with a map on the walls and, above the bed-head, the famous drawing of a gibbet; on the rough table between the windows, piles of books pell-mell; the complete wardrobe of the occupant, including a soft black felt hat, was draped on a church pew; and the low, simple bed was covered with goose-quills, ink and notebooks.[1]

'We emerge for lunch at 11 o'clock', wrote Mme. Hugo to her sister Julie two months after arrival, 'we chat, Charles makes a thousand more or less amusing jokes; Auguste, impassive, is no less fond of drollery. My husband silences the young by talking of serious matters which he develops and sums up like the man of genius he is ... an hour and a half after entering (the dining room) Charles goes out to smoke on the terrace, Auguste walks about thinking of the play he has written or will write ... Adèle goes to her room ... my husband goes down to the drawing-room where visitors await him ... at seven we gather again ... Fanny, our chambermaid, appears with the candlesticks which she majestically places on the table ... that means she wants to go to bed. Conversation often goes on late. My husband talks about his past, the production of *Hernani*, his struggles at the theatre, his difficulties in entering the Academy.'[2]

Their social circle was widening a little, Mme. Hugo told Mme. Meurice. They were asked to a sumptuous dinner by a charming Englishwoman and her niece, who sang at the piano. 'I have never heard such a discordant voice sing such monotonous airs', she complained. On getting up from the table, Victor Hugo tried to follow his wife but his way was barred by a servant, because women were expected to take their coffee in the drawing room while men remained in the dining room, a separation of the sexes which Hugo did not find entertaining.[3]

Mme. Hugo, 'with a foot in low society and another in fashion', as she put it, would take François-Victor and Adèle to dances. She told her uncle Asseline: 'Here they dance a lot – stupidly – but they dance'. For her sister Julie she described one of these 'dancing routs':

> The day before yesterday I took Adèle to a Jersey ball. It was good enough, pleasant and elegant; there were some delicious faces, pale ones surrounded with curls and set on slender or on plump shoulders. The house was strewn with flowers ... we had beautiful bouquets ourselves. A gallant gentleman, knowing that we were to go to the ball, sent them to us. You must believe me that the menfolk in our house did not give us them: they are incapable, the savages! Toto (François-

Victor) came with us ... Adèle, dressed completely in white with her snow-white bouquet and her individual bearing, made a great effect although surrounded by these English beauties. Imagine, my dear, I received some personal compliments, unbelievably; it is so long since this happened, that I must seem the most flippant creature alive, I on whom all misfortunes have fallen and left their marks...[4]

Then in 1854, a Grand Fancy Dress Ball was announced for 22 February in the Queen's Assembly Rooms. Mme. Hugo wrote to Julie that Adèle was going in Louis XV costume, foreshadowing old age by pomading her long black hair. An account in the paper after the event, however, said that Mme. and Mlle. Hugo were in evening dress, along with uniformed officers from the French war-steamer *Ariel* and the English cutter *Dasher*, with Mr. Rose as Charlemagne and Colonel Le Couteur, the Vicomte, as Attoharho, chief of the Black Eagles.[5]

While François-Victor, the dandy, would go to costume balls when he could afford it, Charles seems to have avoided them. Charles had been followed to Jersey by Augustine Allix, and though she was quite often at Marine Terrace, we have little idea about his love life. François-Victor's seems to have been under a curse: he had just lost Anaïs, who was dying of consumption anyway; he may well have been keen on Margaret Allen, an English girl living in Jersey, but she was to die of scarlet fever in January 1855; and later his Guernsey fiancée, Emily de Putron, was to die of tuberculosis. Perhaps significantly, it was François-Victor of the two sons who was closer to his father and who never married. Whether the Jerseywoman Josephine Nicolle, or 'Miss Joss', as they called her, was involved with Charles or François-Victor is not clear, but she was attached to the family and indeed followed them to Guernsey.[6]

But it was Adèle who was the main emotional casualty, for she did not need what her mother called 'this heroic remedy'. Adèle had been in love with Auguste Vacquerie after their first 'intoxicating kisses' in 1846, and at one time it seemed only right that they should marry as his brother Charles and her sister Léopoldine had been happily married. Now in 1852, though Vacquerie loved Adèle still, her love for him, as she said, 'had not developed'. She was aware that their neighbour's son, John Rose, was pining for her; she would go next door, dressed to kill, and flirt with the Rose brothers, John, Thomas and the 16 year old G[eorge]. Adèle was flattered by John's attentions but, after he stole a furtive kiss, she remembered Balzac's words that one leads to another, and feared that if she gave him any encouragement she would become 'his mistress and his wife'. Yet she still resolved to 'be loved without loving' and she teased him by appearing at the window and by giving him her picture. The Roses wrongly assumed that Adèle was rebuffing John because of Vacquerie, an impression Adèle fostered. When, six months later, she learned that John Rose had died, she wrote in her diary: 'I was not madly in love; just a bit taken with him '.[7]

Adèle was spending her time playing the piano, painting and learning English, but she was not moving in the direction of marriage. Mme. Hugo despaired of any of her children marrying; she liked having them around the house, but thought that marriage 'completes one's destiny'. She could not understand why her beautiful daughter would refuse suitor after suitor, and feared that she was being infected by the freedom English girls enjoyed. Mme. Hugo wanted Julie's help in forcing Adèle into marriage and wrote: 'Adèle reigns among our islanders, for you know that young girls have precedence here over married women who have swarms of children and scarcely move from their hearths. And so Adèle finds the life of a girl preferable to that of a woman; she politely dismissed a suitor who offered 400,000 francs (£16,000) and his hand. My daughter found the hand a little wrinkled, as the suitor was 45. Yesterday this young beauty received a basket full of flowers. We ask ourselves if it was from the suitor. I will keep you up to date with this business, for we will get to the bottom of it.'[8]

Three months later nothing has changed: 'What distresses me is (Adèle's) resistance to marriage. "Lose my name", she says, "and give myself a master, I who am so proud to call myself Mlle Hugo, I who am free, so calm and happy in my house!" A marriage other than the one I spoke of appeared on the horizon. A white bouquet mixed with a spray of orange flowers was sent her; she immediately gave the gallant knight the cold shoulder ... The marriage would have had some advantageous aspects.'[9]

When Adèle had written that she was not madly in love with John Rose she added 'Besides, there was the Other'. It may be that he was Albert Pinson, a feckless English officer who had joined the West Yorkshire militia to avoid the debtors' prison, for on 28 December 1852 the Roses asked Adèle to wait with them for 'P' who was 'in love with her'. If Pinson was not already in Jersey in 1852, he was certainly there by 1854 when he attended at least six table-turning seances at Marine Terrace. Adèle described their first encounter: 'He saw me for the first time on the bench on the terrace in Jersey. I was sitting down reading; I was absorbed in my book and I didn't see him. But he saw me and from that day he loved me ...'. This was only perhaps wishful thinking, for Pinson seems either to have been indifferent to Adèle as a woman, or to have gone off her quickly. This no doubt flamed her lifelong passion for him and made Vacquerie hideously jealous. 'I declare, I am not like you', said Vacquerie, 'I do not take pride in not loving; I am proud of loving. It is I who am the more loving. For eight years I, who am a man of genius, have deployed my talents to make you love me. I give up. I cannot do the impossible: Pygmalion had only one love, his marble statue; I, Galatea, have more to do: I have to animate you. It is not I who am deserting you: you are deserting me.'[10]

Like François-Victor, Vacquerie seems to have been fond of Margaret Allen, who spoke French, 'already a comfort in our suffering' as Vacquerie wrote when she died a few months later. But now he merely flirted with Margaret to make Adèle jealous. To his fury, Adèle did not respond. He hit her; then he apologised and tried to embrace and hug her. Then he insulted her: 'You are thinner than I thought; a skinny girl indeed. You give yourself away; your arms are like spindles. I don't think you want them to be seen.' He spat in her face and kicked her backside though they were out on the terrace. 'Auguste is making my life impossible', wrote Adèle, 'God cannot have meant anyone to put up with what I endure.'

So Adèle consulted the turning tables. How could she cool Vacquerie off and stop Pinson from leaving Jersey? The spirit of the table, which seemed to speak with Léopoldine's voice, suggested sexual entanglement. Then Adèle broke off the seance to see Vacquerie: she found him burning some verses which he had written attacking her. Adèle smoothed his mattress, remembering that she had once loved him. She sat on his bed and sobbed.

'Léopoldine' now advised her to make Pinson jealous so that he would resign his commission, and she must have been tempted to make up to Vacquerie (just as he was doing to Margaret Allen in order to make Adèle jealous), but she no doubt realised how unfair on Vacquerie this would be; and another spirit said that jealousy was useless. The table advised her to become pregnant and tell Pinson 'I shall die if I am abandoned and have a child'. Vacquerie did not know whether to be angry or resigned. 'You wait ten years', he warned Adèle, 'in ten years you will pay for this'. Now the table started counselling Adèle to show Vacquerie the door. 'Why do you tell me to throw Auguste out right now when Albert loves me so little and does not mean to come back to me? Will you answer that question?', she asked piteously. The table fell silent. Then Adèle thought it would be all right if Vacquerie stayed, and left her alone, while she hid her liaison with Pinson. When she told her mother, who was on Vacquerie's side, she was heart-broken, but could only say that Vacquerie's sudden departure would provoke comment. Now another spirit was telling Adèle to make Auguste a happy man, and let Pinson go.

By the end of December 1854 Adèle thought, or rather hoped, that Pinson was getting jealous of Jules Allix who was paying court to her. She drafted a letter in code to Pinson, putting all her cards on the table. 'I must use grand means. I have two: my death and jealousy.' The real letter would have been carried by Margaret Allen, the go-between, but it could scarcely have helped Adèle if it had been delivered. Pinson, who had fobbed her off with excuses about his having no money, would have been a disastrous husband, though whether she could ever have been happy with Vacquerie, who found it difficult to 'reconcile woman's charm and her emancipation', is doubtful.

The tragic sequel to this story, with the demented Adèle leaving Guernsey in 1863 to follow Pinson to Nova Scotia and Barbados, has been recounted by Guille and filmed by François Truffaut in *L'Histoire d'Adèle H*. It was as though Vacquerie's warning had become a prediction and a curse.

Life was flat and unchanging for the two other women in Hugo's life: his wife and his mistress. 'Our life is always regulated', Mme. Hugo had written two months after arrival. Now, two years later, a bitter and resigned note creeps in. 'Our lives do not change; exile is impious, it is monotonous.' Mme. Hugo was beginning to look old and fat and she had lost the sight in one eye.[12] She was also hard up, trying to economise. When Victor Hugo arrived in Jersey he had 13,000 francs (£520) from the sale of furniture in Paris and an annuity of 7,400 francs (£296). The French courts had decided that he could not receive royalties, so he had to work hard to support his family of five, Vacquerie, Juliette and several servants. He was particularly short of money in 1853 and 1854, and his burdens were increased by the fact that he kept open house. 'Every day someone shares our leg of mutton', Mme. Hugo complained, and she reckoned that they were spending £480 to £600 a year, of which £200 was for food and drink alone. The proscrits found that they could also get free meals from Juliette whose maid Suzanne kept an excellent table.[13]

The Hugos might lay on a lavish meal for a visitor like Jules Laurens, but their fare was, by previous standards, frugal. They had wine only at festivities, cider for small reunions and beer otherwise. Hugo preferred grog. Mme. Hugo complained that in two years at Marine Terrace she had bought only two dresses, at 25 francs (£1) each.[14]

It seems that in 1853 Victor Hugo had made her an allowance of 450 francs (£18) a month. Some time later she estimated that 80 francs (£3) covered her and Adèle's keep, 25 francs (£1) the servants' wages, and 205 francs (£8) the dry groceries, candles, laundry etc. What was left, 130 francs (£5), was just not enough to get the fresh food from the market that was needed to feed seven, especially since prices had increased since the allowance was first made. In addition, she was now hardly touching her personal allowance, and Hugo was trying to make her get by on 395 francs (£16) a month, to pay off her 'debts'.

Their strict economies led their neighbour, the proscrit Pierre Leroux, to complain to George Sand that Hugo was too fond of money. 'Hugo, who has a small family and an income of only 7,500 francs (to say nothing of what he gets from his books) told me the other day that only griefs of the heart really counted as real. That's true and false. I would be really glad to see him like me, in the grip of misery.' Leroux never lost a chance of reminding Hugo how poor he used to be, his coat with a hole at the elbow, and how rich he was now. This was quite absurd from Leroux who, though he kept a household of about 30, was himself a miser and professional sponger. In the same letter to George Sand he had asked her to find a thousand francs for him on the strength of the fact that his son-in-law, Luc Desages, would one day be an inheritor.[16]

Hugo has sometimes been accused by his biographers of meanness, but he gave generously to a fund for the Crimean wounded, to the proscrit Landolphe in Guernsey, and to the man who importuned him on South Hill with a political chat, suddenly asking 'Donnez-moi un sou'. This was at a time when, as he said himself, he needed money 'like the Devil'.[17]

Juliette Drouet was lonely, bored and jealous. Daudet and Barthou have it that Hugo visited her daily at her lodgings, but the truth, revealed by her daily litany of frustrated love, was that his visits were sporadic. His first visit to her took place four days after their arrival on the same boat. On 1 February 1853 she asks him to take her for a walk instead of posing for photographs; on 10 March she complains of his 'longer and longer absences'; on 31 July they do go for a walk, but after 10 days of claustration; and on 24 September she calls herself 'a squirrel in a cage'.[18] She was jealous of her 'sea-wolf' as, in the last days of summer 1852, he sat at his 'observation post' watching the bathers. 'Don't forget that you must go to the theatre tonight to give me a few more minutes in the day. While waiting, I allow you to look above your wall at the more or less naked bathers who are at this moment swarming over the Grève d'Azette ... The whole garrison is bathing at the right hand end, so the *landscape* does not lack its admirers.'[19]

Berret claims that at one stage Juliette asked to live at Marine Terrace. This seems very unlikely, as she had an 'invincible scruple' so that she would never address a word to Hugo, whom she could see from her window, when he was with his wife. Mme. Hugo, Juliette thought, had 'sovereign beauties and saintly qualities', and it cannot be supposed that she would have been prepared to make Mme. Hugo's domestic life even less tolerable than it was.[20] Hugo, however, was able to use Juliette's lodgings as a place to entertain the proscrits, escape from his wife's quarrels with her servants, and write. When he returned home, Juliette would accompany him, with her maid Suzanne lighting the way ahead with a lantern.[21] Some proscrits avoided Juliette because they were disgusted at Hugo leaving his wife in the evenings to take his sons to dine with his mistress. Julitte discovered that she was called Hugo's harlot:

'Well, the English called Joan of Arc the Armagnacs' harlot', said Hugo, 'but how did you hear this vile thing?'

'From Suzanne', said Juliette.

'Tell her I wish to speak to her.'

'Master, I heard it in Mme Clarek's greengrocery shop', said Suzanne. 'They were talking about Madame, and a man who is known to be an exile turned to me and said: "Your Madame is Hugo's harlot." Please forgive me for speaking this way, but I swear that I have not invented a word.'[22]

On instructions from Hugo, and in order to fill her day, Juliette began a journal which she kept, unfortunately, for only four weeks but which is full of interesting detail. 'Events are so infrequent in this little island and French papers come only twice a week so ... I will take what lies beneath my gaze and around me.'[23] All Juliette's writing energies were devoted to her twice daily love letter to Hugo. If she missed a letter, she would write a 'restitus' to make three letters the next day. They move in a spiral from adoration through resentment and apology back to adoration. Mme. Hugo is treated with an exaggerated and studied respect, but almost everyone and everything else is dismissed with irritation. She castigates a theatrical troupe for massacring Hugo's *Angelo*, belittles the crazes for photography and table-turning, and denigrates the proscrits and most islanders.[24]

A graphic account of life at Marine Terrace, full of convincing detail, has been left by Jules Laurens, a painter who arrived there in March 1855. When Laurens entered the hall of Marine Terrace he saw on the right the barely furnished drawing room with its photographs of the Hugos and Paul Meurice, and waited in trepidation while the sounds of comings and goings could be heard overhead. Then Hugo appeared. 'He was wearing thick grey trousers, a red English knitted waistcoat and a puce dressing-gown. His greying hair was cut short, but he had no beard yet, and his thin eyebrows looked as though burned, his skin and complexion appreciably flushed.' Laurens had no letter of introduction, but mentioned common friends: Edouard Bertin, Louis Boulanger and Théophile Gautier. Hugo complained they had forgotten him, and the interview was obviously getting somewhat sticky when Laurens opened his portfolio of Normandy and Jersey drawings. 'There's our common language', Hugo burst out.

Hugo said he hoped Laurens would stay for a good long time, and he offered to pose when Laurens drew le Dicq to add a live detail. He even offered to act as his guide round the island and then in other parts of the archipelago. His neglected wife also took to this 'amiable young painter' and Adèle was intrigued by him. Laurens described her as brown in colouring, svelte and delicately, nervously Arabian. Only François-Victor showed no interest, already suffering from the consumption that was to carry him off.

Laurens gives us a glimpse of Hugo's relationship with his wife. At Mme. Hugo's request, Laurens went up to sketch Hugo's room, which was, as we have seen, a cell of monastic austerity. Hugo left his room for a moment and Mme. Hugo, in morning dress, darted in furtively, and thanked Laurens for the opportunity to see the room. While Hugo and Laurens were in the drawing room they heard orders being given to change sheets. Hugo, busy discussing Gothic cathedrals, asked whether they thought Laurens wanted to hear all this. At one point Hugo said: 'I do not expect to return to

France, alive or dead'. 'Oh, you', said Mme. Hugo, 'you never have anything but these dark thoughts.'

Hugo told Laurens that he had satisfied his conscience and achieved public and material success. Pointing to his seascape, he said 'The Good Lord paints me unpublished Rembrandts there' and 'Only fools grow weary before the monotony of the sublime'. Of the scraps of paper scattered all over his room on which he noted his thoughts, he said 'I am the Wandering Jew of literary toil'.[25]

Outside the family and the world of proscrit politics, very little happened. However, on the night of 1 April 1853, as Hugo was going to bed, he felt a trembling as of hundreds of passing carts. It was a violent earthquake: the bells in Marine Terrace rang, the sea sounded like the roaring of animals, and all St Helier was on its feet with three old women outside General Le Flô's house in Colomberie announcing the end of the world.[26]

On the night of 31 May 1854 thieves broke into the conservatory of Marine Terrace. Hugo heard steps below but thought it was Charles or François-Victor. Had the thieves got into the house proper, the *Jersey Times* announced, they would have been met by four well-armed men. The newspapers show that petty thieving, robbery and vandalism was rife at this time. In the absence of night police, assaults and damage to property, including the letter-boxes newly installed at the instance of Anthony Trollope, were seldom detected. On 24 June 1855, as Hugo was bathing, he was hit on the head by a stone. To the amazement of Dr. Gornet he was not knocked down. He found the children who had thrown the stones from the Rocher des Proscrits (Le Rocher Besnard) and told them to use smaller ones next time. Rumours spread around St Helier, and the proscrits, who thought Hugo had been ambushed, came to see him in the evening.[27]

Chapter Three

Music in the Poet's House

Marine Terrace became a sort of writers' colony. The vast table in the dining room was covered with books. Hugo wrote most of *Les Contemplations*, half of *Les Châtiments*, other verse from *Les Quatre Vents de l'Esprit* and *Toute la Lyre* and a play, *La Forêt Mouillée*. Mme. Hugo started her account of Hugo's life, *Victor Hugo raconté par un témoin de sa vie*. François-Victor began *La Normandie Inconnue* and his translation of Shakespeare, 'one of the best produced by our 19th Century', in the opinion of Hazard. Vacquerie and Charles wrote dramas, while Adèle continued her journal of exile. Hugo kept up his commonplace book, *Choses Vues*, and everyone wrote letters to friends in France. 'The amount of Art produced by this house born of Politics is incredible', wrote Vacquerie.

There was also to be a family effort, an account of Jersey illustrated with photographs, and by mid-1854 Charles, François-Victor and Vacquerie were all involved. Hugo would complement their work with verse and perhaps drawings, and it would be called *Jersey et les Iles de la Manche* or just *Vues de Jersey*. 'I have finished my third', wrote Vacquerie to Meurice, 'I have done the invasions: it is amusing as a pile of tall stories. It's better written than the subject calls for. Charles and Toto are completing their part.' They all hoped that the book would ease their financial worries, and they delayed going on to Spain until it was produced. The problem was to find a publisher. Vacquerie thought of Hetzel, though he was 'no bookseller'. It was offered to *La Presse* and *Le Siècle* but, as Meurice told them, no one in France would print a book that brought together the words Hugo and Jersey. Hugo suggested offering it to Grant, an English publisher.

By 1855 the joint work had still not appeared, and it never did. What remains of it is to be found in Vacquerie's *Les Miettes de l'Histoire*, Hugo's *L'Archipel de la Manche* and *Les Contemplations* and François-Victor's *La Normandie Inconnue*. This was presumably the work which was inspired by the 'admirable marine panorama' between Marine Terrace and St Helier, of which Adèle speaks. The photographs are found in various collections.[1]

Industrious though they all were, the Hugos did not have to work for salaries and they had servants. So there was time for conversation, like letter-writing one of the vanishing arts of the 19th century. It seems that, like Boswell, Adèle made a running transcription of conversations, for example:

Victor Hugo ... But the English cavalry, who have the finest uniforms in England, tend their horses and do nothing else, and do it so well that ...
Adèle (to a servant) Can I have some eggs?
Mme. Hugo Ask for them later: write down what's being said.
Victor Hugo ... so well that the English infantry used to insult the cavalry and the foot-soldiers told the mounted men they were fine soldiers, required only to look after horses ...

By far the commonest visitors at Marine Terrace were General Le Flô, Charles Ribeyrolles, Hennet de Kesler and Sandor Teleki, all aristocratic or bourgeois and politically moderate. One might think that Leroux was welcome as he was so often with the Hugos. They called him Pieuvre (Octopus) Leroux and they found him very tiresome. He kept calling Hugo a rich man and expounding his socialism. Once Charles cut him short with 'Monsieur Leroux, your humanity bores us'. One can only assume that Hugo liked his company, as he was intellectually a cut above many of the proscrits. Hugo's eventual departure from Jersey, Leroux wrote later, 'afflicts my heart'.

There were the usual family quarrels and laughter. Hugo would tell his sons not to interrupt or tease Vacquerie about his age. Mme. Hugo would ask them to stop talking about ghosts. Once, in 1855, François-Victor was reading out of the papers and talking about the Crimea and the poor harvests in France. Hugo was brooding over the badly arranged asparagus: tips and ends mixed up. Charles failed to get any political reactions from Hugo who said that he was more interested in the asparagus than in the eternal battles at Malakoff and the harvest. 'Explosion générale', Adèle records.

Much of the talk, however, was about the great political events since 1848, especially the coup d'état, and about people they had known. But philosophy, religion, spirits, literature and crime were not forgotten. Nor were more everyday matters: sea-sickness, toothache and the speed of light; dreams, faux pas and suicide; the lack of bearded Englishmen, false lace and Beau Brummel's dressing habits.

Hugo would expound his views of reincarnation and the ladder of perfectability which stretches from inert matter to apes; deny warmly that theirs was a time of decadence; or describe how he decided whether or not to read a book (by opening it at three random places and seeing if the page said anything to him). He attacked Communism in this way: 'the distribution of land will be useless when the world's riches are multiplied tenfold. But that will come from the exploitation of the earth, and by the thousand discoveries that industry will make and is making every day '. He claimed that the sun was inhabited by giants 500 feet tall, but thought space travel impossible:

> *Victor Hugo* ... Earth has a thick and heavy atmosphere, necessary for human lungs: the moon's atmosphere is light, and no good for men who would die there.
> *Adèle* In a hundred years, in two hundred years, three, four, five hundred years, who can tell me that a scientist, and there have been some, will not make a discovery, like so many that have been made, and won't discover the secret of holding on to the atmosphere, thus making it heavy, and going to the stars?
> *Victor Hugo* Because what is possible is possible, what is impossible, impossible. Everything discovered up to now lies within human grasp, and has not undermined the laws of nature; but what you suggest undermines and upsets all the laws of nature.
> *Adèle* Didn't they say that about printing; that electricity, steam, chloroform, photography and even the turning tables would undermine and upset nature? ... You believe in progress to the limits of the possible, I to the limits of the impossible.

Adèle was absolutely right, but even she would have been astonished to know that the space age would begin barely 40 years after her death. In this conversation with the old conservative Le Flô, it is Hugo who discerns the future:

> *Le Flô* ... Can you imagine women voting, rushing about in public, mixing with men? It's madness. One realises woman's charms so much in quite another way, at home, as the angel of the family and hearth, obliging, made to delight and please us, and to be respected as our mother and the mother of our children.

Charles Why can't you have both? Instead of going to a dance, a woman can vote; why is it more fitting to buy ribbons than to vote? You say mixing the sexes is awkward. Why can't you have separate groups?
Victor Hugo Now look, Le Flô, you would allow women political rights when these rights would harm them: if a woman steals, she is put in prison; if she murders, she is guillotined: but she can't vote or take part in politics. In short, you give her all the rights that can harm her, none that can do her good.
Le Flô This discussion has carried us too far. For my part, I repeat, I cannot conceive women except in the family where, thank God, there is quite enough strife without adding more.
Victor Hugo (smiling) Does Mme. Le Flô have political views? Is she not completely royalist, more so than you? Why shouldn't she have the right to vote, even for her King, like you? Doesn't one see women managing and guiding men all the time, especially in politics?

Here the talk is of English literature:

Ede Remenyi (to Paul Meurice) Do you speak German?
Paul Meurice Ja.
Adèle (to Hugo) German must be very like English.
Victor Hugo English is a German dialect. English is poor German.
François-Victor This poor German produced Shakespeare, Milton, Byron and Walter Scott.
Victor Hugo Shakespeare is a wonderful rose in a dunghill. Byron is great, but he is well below Shakespeare.
François-Victor I find Byron as good as Shakespeare.
Victor Hugo No. Shakespeare is the Babylonian Tower of English Art; after him comes Byron. As for Milton, he is a very great poet.
Charles Very boring. Can something be beautiful and tedious?
Victor Hugo Yes, Corneille proves it. Corneille and Milton are like the Champagne, full of steppes and arid roads, but where one finds a wonderful marvel, a masterpiece: Notre Dame de Lépine. There are very beautiful things in Milton: the wind of the abyss, and demons using cannon which made Voltaire laugh so much ...

Sometimes discussion lasted too long into the night. Once Hugo had been talking of Shakespeare and Racine. 'It was nearly midnight', Adèle wrote, '[Charles] Asplet the grocer was asleep, and the paper-maker [Philippe Asplet] also made a poor listener; Victor Hugo stopped talking and everyone went to bed.'[2]

The Hugos took pleasure in going to the theatre and concerts. On their arrival in Jersey the director of the Royal Crescent Theatre put the Governor's box at their disposal. At a play on 19 August 1852 Sidney, the lead actor, came forward and thanked Hugo for coming. Adèle noted that the men smoked and the actors spoke English, but she does not say what play was being performed. In October a French troupe arrived and played *Notre Dame de Paris*, possibly in front of the author, and on 26 November he witnessed what Juliette called a 'long drawn-out massacre' of his *Angelo* by M. Alexandre's troupe, and she commended his 'heroic impassivity in the face of savage profanation'.

Perhaps this experience led them to avoid the theatre which is not mentioned until late 1853 when they watched Mlle. Grave in *Midi à Quattorze Heures*, *La Grande Dame* and *La Marraine*, and as Marguerite in *La Dame aux Camélias*. Hugo sent the servant Julie to see the piece, and this is how she described it: 'In the first act they dined and danced but Marguerite didn't dance much. In the middle, it is the father who makes Marguerite go out on one side and the gentleman on the other. In the last act Marguerite is in bed; a gentleman gives her a tisane, and she doesn't have her maid '.

A month later Hugo saw *Louise de Lignerolles*, and in January 1854 he was rehearsing the roles of Ruy Blas and the Queen with M. Besombes and Mlle. Grave. M. Besombes told Hugo: 'Sir, if you had wished to be an actor, you would have been the greatest actor of our times'. As Hugo entered the theatre he was greeted with a salvo of applause. The *Jersey Times* reported that 'several of its passages were seized on by the exiles present, as applicable to the present state of things in France and were greeted with acclamations'. When Ruy Blas recalled the shame of Spain, a proscrit shouted 'and France'. Was it at this performance of *Ruy Blas* also that Vacquerie was so annoyed by the whistling applause of a Jerseyman 'who thought he understood the play'?[3]

Vacquerie thought, however, that Jersey people had the keenest of passions for music, and the newspapers show a succession of concerts, of which some were given by proscrits like Charles Benezit, and some given to raise funds for the proscrits, like that of Signor Fumarola.

The Hugos had known many composers, including Rossini, Berlioz, Chopin and Liszt, but Hugo himself used to send singers away and never wished to hear a pianist. He called the piano a 'wooden brute' and an 'infamous instrument'. When, at Marine Terrace, Augustine Allix sang Schubert's Serenade, Hugo said it was charming, but what really gave him pleasure was the line 'L'oeil téméraire d'un tyran jaloux'. But something had happened in Jersey to mollify him, perhaps its 'majestic calming effect'. 'Music and *dogs* in the poet's house, you'll be amazed to hear', wrote Mme. Hugo to Julie. 'Music, neglected in Place Royale, despised in rue de la Tour d'Auvergne, is now received with open arms at Marine Terrace', records Adèle who was a good pianist and spent many hours practising on the infamous instrument. Already by the end of 1853 there were frequent musical soirées at Marine Terrace: Ede Remenyi played the violin, Colfavru or Augustine Allix performed songs by Pierre Dupont, or Xavier-Durrieu sang in Spanish.

In November 1853 Mme. Hugo was present at one concert by the singer Géraldy, and Victor Hugo at another. Géraldy visited Hugo who, however, soon turned the conversation away from music. Then on 11 September 1854 we find Hugo and Pierre Leroux clapping loudly for a performance by Augustine Allix. Another concert was arranged for her on 11 October. Mme. Hugo wrote about it to her sister Julie:

> (She) has a very beautiful voice, an excellent technique. She is one of Del Sarte's best pupils. It was a question of getting her known; the best way was to get the good Jersey people to listen to her. It was a risk. The best room in the island was hired, and programmes were issued. Alone she was not enough to make a concert. It happened that one of our friends, the Hungarian proscrit Teleki, was giving hospitality to one of his compatriots, Remingi, a violinist, but one who was hardly comparable with Paganini. Liszt had referred him to Teleki, saying he was the first violinist of Europe. Remingi offered to accompany Mlle Allix at her concert. I don't know how it was done but, with God's help, there was a crowd at the concert, a crowd without patronage, which has never happened in the island. Mlle Allix sang in a way that was infinitely pleasing to the Jersey people. Her success immediately secured her pupils, as we wanted. As for Remingi, he transported the English and Jersey people to the point where our cross-channel neighbours applauded with passion – which is not usual with the cold-blooded.

Mme. Hugo omitted to mention that Augustine Allix and Remenyi played her husband's *Le Papillon et la Fleur*, music by Reber. Remenyi repeated it at another concert on 20 October, when he again played his own *Marche Triomphale*, which was now, at his own request, dedicated to Victor Hugo. There were two more Remenyi concerts, and it seems that he kept in touch with the Hugos as he was later invited to Hauteville House by Mme. Hugo.[4]

There were other ways to spend the time. Hugo and his sons fenced, sometimes with Dulac. On Sunday mornings some proscrits would appear to play billiards;

though the shutters of the house were closed, the islanders could hear the click of the balls and, realising that Hugo was not at Mass, would say that they respected him only six days of the week. The Hugos and their maid would also play Steeplechase. Mme. Hugo described how 12 people would group themselves round the board, letting out amazing cries. When Jules Laurens knocked Hugo out of the game, Hugo called him 'M. Bonaparte'.[5]

The first mention of photography, which was to become something of an obsession, was on 22 November 1852, when Adèle mentions the project for a joint album, *Jersey et les Îles de la Manche*. Charles and Vacquerie would make daguerrotypes of Hugo in a calm mood for *Les Contemplations*, and agitated for *Les Châtiments*. Photography needed patience for the preparation of the collodion plate involved 19 operations over two days. At first they were frustrated by their own lack of skill, as they produced contrastless chocolate tones, and they were very sensitive to criticisms of their work. Hugo was so smitten with the new art that Juliette protested that he should take her out more instead of 'posing interminably in front of the daguerrotype'. Hugo himself was taking pictures of Mme. Hugo's servants:

I didn't know he was occupying himself thus. I put my face to the window and saw him on the terrace making a woman, in a smart bonnet with a melancholic expression, strike attitudes. I was anxious to know whose was this pretty face which had insinuated itself into my house; it was Catherine, my cook, who had left her stove to dress her hair so that my husband could take her picture.

Charles had probably met the Caen photographer, Edmond Bacot, when he came to Jersey with money and goods from the republicans of Caen in December 1852. In the middle of March 1853 Charles went to see Bacot, and from Caen he wrote that Bacot had shown him all he knew, and that he would return with French chemicals which were much cheaper than those in Jersey. Charles saw the Château de Fontaine Henry and a production of *Uncle Tom's Cabin*. It was snowing at the time. In Caen he was denounced as a member of a secret service, and thoroughly searched. The same thing happened on 2 April, when details of Bacot's processing method were impounded by the police. Charles was prevented from leaving St Malo and had to return to Caen, and he was nearly stopped from re-embarking at Port-Bail. Not surprisingly, he had had to borrow money from Bacot. On 14 July Charles wrote to Bacot from Jersey for more details of processing and for more chemicals. His enthusiasm landed Bacot in trouble for his letter was assumed to be an order to a secret society, and Bacot was put on trial.

Hugo tried to help Charles make a living from photography. He sent Hetzel a copy of his own portrait, and asked if he would like to order them by the hundred. Hetzel agreed to take a hundred, but it is doubtful if Charles and Vacquerie made much out of photography. They have, however, left us with many interesting pictures – of the family, of the proscrits and scenes of Jersey.[6]

The garden of Marine Terrace when the Hugos first arrived was a treeless wilderness of tamarisk, marigolds, daisies and nettles, inhabited by Mr. Rose's chickens. That was how Hugo liked it, but two proscrits, Le Flô and Teleki, shamed Mme. Hugo into having it tidied into a neat 'jardin anglais' of compartments, lozenges, zigzags and Ss. 'Imagine compartments like geometrical figures and winding paths between them', she wrote to Julie.

We have a superb turf bank, shaded from behind by a rare shrub and scattered with pink daisies which decorate it attractively. In the morning we have spades, rakes and shears in hand; we prune, we hoe, we water – it is a pleasure to see; only my husband objects and jokes about our work. He claims that we are depriving him of his right to criticise the bourgeoisie, with our puny paths laid out straight and all our scraping ...

In fact Hugo told Leroux that he found this over-organised English garden, like England itself, annoying.

The gardening craze must have lasted, for a month later Mme. Hugo told Julie, who was planning to come to Jersey, that she would be made to rake and hoe the garden. But a year later, in May 1854, Hugo records that the garden is so full of cauliflowers gone to seed that he can see nothing but their yellow flowers and the sea. Laurens, visiting Marine Terrace a year later, described the garden as very bleak: Mr. Rose's chickens, which would make a meal of the Hugos' peas and beans until chased away by them, seem to have reclaimed it.[7]

It was as well that Marine Terrace had a large garden because the house was alive with dogs and cats. There was Ponto, a black spaniel, of whom Hugo wrote:

I say to my black dog 'Come, Ponto, let's go'
And I go through the woods, dressed like a peasant ...
My dog Ponto follows me. A dog is virtue
Which, unable to become human, becomes a beast
And Ponto looks at me with his honest eye.

They got a mate for Ponto, a grey bitch called Chougna. Together they would kill Mr. Rose's chickens until Catherine, the cook, told Chougna not to. Chougna obeyed and even bit Ponto when he went after the chickens. Le Flô had given a piebald greyhound, Lux, to Charles, and there were two other dogs, Dech and Triboulet, Vacquerie's grey terrier. Grise was a cat, born in La Conciergerie; Agneau her descendant; Mouche a black and white cat, and Carton, a wild black cat, particularly attached to Hugo.[8]

Beyond the garden was the sea, where François-Victor and his mother swam frequently. Hugo determined to swim as much as all the others put together, and in the summer of 1853 he was caught by the tide and nearly dragged away. Vacquerie, like Renoir later in Guernsey, was surprised in this puritanical land by the bathers' lack of modesty. A wheeled changing cabin is dragged to the water by horse but, if the tide is falling, you may have to return to your cabin 'as naked as truth'. Bathing costumes being struck from the dictionary as obscene, 'modesty consists in bathing naked'. Vacquerie was exaggerating, and a more plausible account comes from Juliette:

The two sexes, without positively mixing, are close enough to each other. English customs are against the wearing of bathing costumes. Some French people who insisted on wearing these summary garments in the water were booed and almost stoned ... Women dress and undress in the open air ... and their bathing costume generally consists of a decollete shift or a linen dress which when wet clings to the body showing up all the shapes as though one were naked ... it is not only the women of the people and the bourgeoisie from the town who show themselves with such ease, but also women of the world and young misses.[9]

The beaches here and at St Aubin and the dunes at St Ouen were also used for riding by the Hugos or their visitors, and by other better off proscrits like Teleki and Colfavru. Hugo took riding lessons at the school of the proscrit Felix Bony, and he indulged his passion for riding and jumping vigorous horses. 'If you come ... you will find us galloping along the sea', he wrote to Mme. de Girardin. Some political meetings took place on horseback. Sanders, the Metropolitan detective who had been sent to spy on the proscrits, found their tracks in the sand half a mile below the hot sea-baths at St Clement's, and he concluded that Hugo must have harangued them as they rode round him in a circle. Sanders also thought that Hugo hired horses to avoid the 'lower class' of proscrit, but it may be that he did not like flaunting his relative wealth among the poorer exiles for, when Bony died, Hugo renounced riding for good.[10]

Chapter Four

Cythera of the Celts

In the first few months the Hugos got to know the coast and bays by taking trips round the island by omnibus or on the sea, and in the afternoons they would go for walks across the fields or on the cliffs. Juliette would walk alone or with Hugo who believed in exercise after eating (*mille passus post prandium*) and would often take the opportunity to post letters.[1]

We have seen how impressed they were with Mont Orgueil Castle and Gorey, 'one of the most beautiful places in the world', as Adèle called it. On 26 August they returned with the Meurices and saw a procession of school children; on another occasion a man recognised Hugo at Gorey with 'How happy I am to see the greatest poet of our time'. On 17 June 1853 the family made a 'grand promenade' to Gorey with Le Flô and Teleki. The men climbed the castle to take photographs and joined the women to drink (in milk) to their return to France. Later Mme. de Girardin was taken there, as were Vacquerie's mother and sister.[2]

In August 1852 they saw Grève de Lecq and Boulay Bay with an omnibus party of English people. Adèle thought the best view of Boulay Bay was from a 'funnel of hills with the sea at the bottom'. It was probably from here that Hugo wrote 'J'ai cueilli cette fleur pour toi sur la colline ...' for Juliette, for he goes on to describe 'some roofs, visible at the bottom of a funnel'.[3]

They admired the coast from the *Rose* steamer on 1 September 1852. It left Albert Pier and passed St Brelade, Gros Nez, Plemont and Grève de Lecq, arriving at Rozel at midday for a musical fete. Juliette had excused herself, as she feared to be recognised, nor could she afford the entry fee (one shilling) and she did not want to be forced to glance surreptitiously at Hugo in the crowd. From Rozel Harbour the Hugos proceeded up the 'Norman road' to the fete and bazaar which was being held in aid of St Martin's parish school in the deer park of Rozel Manor. The band was conducted by Mr. Hartung, and the scattered crowd of elegant English people stared at Hugo. At 5 p.m. they embarked again and saw the fine beaches of St Martin, the great harbour works of St Catherine, Mont Orgueil and Marine Terrace.[4]

Perhaps it was this trip which inspired the couplet:

> O heathlands! Plemont, from which the steamship steers wide
> Ancient palace of Cybele fallen in the sea

as well as the passage of the *Claymore*, going in reverse sense, in *Quatre-Vingt Treize*:

The *Claymore*, dexterously piloted, skirted the long north escarpment of Jersey, unseen in the mist, hugging the coast because of the redoubtable reef of the Pierres de Lecq in the middle of the sea between Jersey and Sark. Gacquoil, standing at the helm, pointed out Grève de Lecq, Gros Nez and Plemont, making the corvette slip between this succession of reefs ... They reached La Grande Etape [L'Étacq?]: the mist was so thick that one could scarcely distinguish the high silhouette of the Pinnacle. One could hear the belfry at St Ouen sound 10 o'clock, a sign that the wind remained before. All remained well; the sea became agitated because of the proximity of la Corbière.[5]

If they did not already know of the beauties of Plemont, this sea journey must have prompted their many visits there. Hugo compared it with Étretat in Normandy, and said he would be buried there if he never returned to France. For Adèle the caves of Plemont were:

> one of the marvels of the world ... Imagine immense carved rocks in the form of a cathedral, or in mysterious caves of cataracts and torrents ... carved by the Great Sculptor who is God. At the entrance there is a rock on which a stone monk appears to be sitting and reading. The opening of one cave is screened by a waterfall; a nearby cave lets those who dare enter hear admirable music produced by wind whistling between the stones. Another cave is completely red or reddish. One wonders whether it is reddened by blood rather than wine. It is in a haunt like this that Job in *Les Burgraves* must have waited for the spectre of Donato.

On 2 September Hugo tried to go down the steep slope that leads to Plemont beach, but came back up with vertigo, unlike the 'goatlike English' who, Vacquerie records, 'threw themselves running down the path'.[6]

Like Gorey, Plemont was to be a favourite excursion for visitors. From Plemont one could go to Gros Nez castle, the 'ancient Gothic arch'. They decided to photograph St Ouen's Manor, which is not far from Plemont and Gros Nez, and found it 'one of the most curious architectural antiquities of the island'. An enormous Frenchwoman appeared from the deserted manor and admitted the Hugos with some English people who had been waiting. Hugo and Le Flô admired the view from the old drawing room lined with portraits and saw the boots of an ancient de Carteret 'duke'. Le Flô asked the Frenchwoman for some milk which she refused. 'There is the face of a man (*le nez d'un homme*)' said Hugo pointing to a portrait, 'who would be bound to refuse a glass of milk to anyone with sense (*à quiconque a le nez bon*).' 'You are impertinent', replied the Frenchwoman, but as she showed them off the property she recognised them and exclaimed: 'Oh, you are the great French rebels', a remark which Hugo later claimed as proof that the islanders did not really know why he had left France. The party then went on to Grève de Lecq where Vacquerie astonished a group of English people by drawing a shell along the beach with a string of seaweed.[7]

Hugo remembered Rozel Manor, which he later compared to Stolzenfelz, but it was to Rozel Bay that he would return to write poetry. 'Nous nous promenions parmi les décombres a Rozel Tower', 'Ibo', 'Un spectre m'attendait' and 'Ce que dit la Bouche de l'Ombre' were all written there:

> I was wandering close to the dolmen which dominates Rozel
> At the place where the cape lengthens into a peninsula
> The spectre was waiting for me ...[8]

Other dolmens (prehistoric stone tables) are mentioned in *Les Contemplations*; Corbière Dolmen (La Table des Marthes?), the Dolmen de la Tour Blanche, and the Dolmen de Faldouët. In *Les Mages* he writes of 'The dark cromlech, scattered in the grass ... on the silent hill', and he thought that the Dolmen de la Ville, which was given to a Governor of Jersey, Conway, and re-erected at Henley, had been one of the marvels of the island, being the only circular cromlech. When Charles declared that Jersey could not inspire an interesting book, Hugo disagreed, mentioning only the Bastion at Mont Orgueil, Plemont and the 'Druidic' monuments. He wrote:

> The Channel Islands do not have the temple of Astypaleus, but they have their cromlechs ... You will find Caliban but not Venus there: you will never see the Parthenon. But sometimes, at

nightfall, some great shadowy table placed on cloudy uprights and surrounded by misty blocks will, in the livid light of dusk, form the outline of an immense and monstrous cromlech.[9]

Hugo refers briefly to other points on the coast: St Catherine's, St Brelade's church, Noirmont with its dangerous currents, and the 'little deserted bay of Bonne Nuit'. An ink wash design shows he also visited the Hermitage of St Helier on 3 September 1855. St Brelade's Bay, 'surrounded by jagged hills and rocks', was a favourite place for excursions, and the Fort de St Brelade was used more than once as a dining room. The bay was also the scene of a nocturnal conclave of proscrits which so alarmed the French vice-consul, Laurent.[10]

On 21 July 1854 they went for a picnic to Portelet Bay. Hugo described Janvrin's Tomb, which sits on a rock in the bay, with minute attention:

Low round tower, slightly sloping walls, not very old (Louis XVI), on an islet topped with greenery and a granite base. At low tide, a sandy isthmus joins the islet to the land. In the grass by the tomb picked flowers which are enclosed here. No door to the tower-tomb. Two square windows, one facing east, the other west. Interior like a muddy hovel. Dust. Dead flies. Walls covered with broken plaster. No roof. Beams of a collapsed ceiling, through which the sky was visible, as through the bars of a gigantic prison window. On the ground in the tower, an old superannuated cannon. On the wall facing the western window could be read the word: HUMPHRIES. The wind, the mist, the rain entered the tomb, and so did the sun. Among the rocks of the islet there is a bottomless gully. Whoever bathes there, drowns. The granite is covered with a plant used for making what the English call pickles.[11]

Descriptions of places inland are far more rare than those of the coast. He refers to a *Cour de Fief* held in the house of a Mr. Malzard on 22 May 1854 at which the prévot swore to uphold the seigneur and seigneurie of Morville with the words 'Je l'jurons'. The Vallée des Vaux, which equals Tempé, Gemenos and Val-Suzon, he calls the place where all the consumptives are sent. St Martin's he describes as 'a country church, full of character'.[12]

Like George Eliot only three years later, he was accustomed to visit Queen's Valley. In *Pasteurs et Tropeaux* he compares 'the valley where I go every day ...' with the promontory of La Corbière, the 'herdsman of the waves'. It was probably also Queen's Valley that he had in mind in *Entrée dans l'Exil*:

J'ai fait en arrivant dans l'île connaissance
Avec un frais vallon plein d'ombre et innocence.[13]

During the Jersey exile (1852-5) it seems that Hugo seldom crossed the seas, unlike in the Guernsey period when he made lengthy annual trips abroad. On 24 June 1853 he went to see the proscrit Landolphe in Guernsey, and he went to Sark which he had already described as 'a fairy castle, full of wonders', at least twice, in 1853 and 1854. He planned to visit the Ecréhou reefs and islets and the Pater Noster rocks (Pierres de Lecq) in 1854, to the alarm of the French vice-consul, but unfortunately he never got there: what descriptions he might have left us.[14]

Jersey had whetted his appetite for the other islands, and he told his visitor Laurens in 1855:

When you have seen the bay of St Aubin (the second of the island), the admirable granite cliffs of the north, Grève de Lecq with its tunnel traversable at low tide, the cape of Mont Orgueil; when you are sufficiently amazed by the southern appearance of certain plants, holm-oaks, fig-trees, due to the effect, even at this latitude, of the warm currents of the Gulf Stream, but with an underlying freshness always in the air, well, why don't we go to Guernsey, the archipelago of Alderney, Sark, Herm, Jethou, in the full roughness of the Ocean? Terrible and sublime equinoctial effects are found there in particular.[15]

The Hugos felt, especially in the Jersey countryside, that they had never left France. Hugo often alluded to the fact that the island was once joined to Normandy, and for him it was a morsel of France stolen or gathered up by England. 'In its rocks (it) is like Brittany, in its fields ... like Normandy', say both Adèle and Vacquerie, and Hugo was probably the source of these similes for we find him saying: 'Normandy in the South, Brittany in the North, for us (Jersey) is France'. Both Jersey and Guernsey have 'pleasant interiors and harsh, brooding coasts, but Jersey is neater than Guernsey, prettier but less beautiful. In Jersey the forest has become a garden, in Guernsey the cliffs stand colossal. More grace here, more majesty there '. Jersey, where all is scent, sunshine and pleasantness, is an 'idyll in the midst of the sea'.[16]

But if the Channel Islands are part of France, they are also the Aegean Islands of the West, with Jersey as Lemnos. 'God made the same island twice', wrote Hugo. 'He gave one to the Greeks, the other to the Celts.' Jersey he also compared with Cythera, and the Channel Islands with the Cyclades (which do not include either Lemnos or Cythera) and with the Iles d'Hyères.[17]

For Adèle, Jersey held an exquisite and unique beauty. 'It is a garden in flower, bathed by the sea ... a bouquet of flowers wetted by the ocean, with the scent of roses and the bitterness of the waves.' For Hugo, likewise, it is 'the savage and the smiling married in the beautiful medium of the sea in a bed of greenery'. To Luthereau he wrote: 'Everything is beautiful or charming. One goes from a wood to a group of rocks, from a garden to a reef, from a field to the sea.' Mme. Hugo also caught the mood: 'Jersey is a charming island. Imagine an immense garden with neat houses and the sea beyond.' To Mme. Meurice she wrote: 'We have visited the surroundings of St Helier ... it is a park.'[18]

Vacquerie's dislike of travelling and solitude led him to see the paradise of Jersey as a purgatory. 'This charming wooded island, full of running streams, this Eden', he wrote to Meurice, 'appeared as a pile of arid and burnt rocks; we looked in vain for a leaf; St Helier looked furiously like St Helena.' He later recollected:

I had been promised a verdant island, a scented garden and the bouquet of the Ocean: I had in front of me a steep, sharp rock, without a tree or blade of grass. Not a house; the town hides itself in an angle of the cliff ... A cannon and a gallows were the flowers that Jersey showed us when we disembarked. I have said that the town hides itself: with reason. It is difficult to imagine anything more abominable than St Helier. A flat, grey, monotonous town; houses all the same, square, cold, the richest of them separated from the road by three or four feet where dejected plants agonise behind a railing, each house with its own inscription: Trafalgar Place, Victoria Terrace, Wellington Square etc. ... Oh, a hovel on the continent rather than a palace in an island ... I hate islands.

If Vacquerie was splenetic about the town, all was different in the 'real Jersey of verdure and granite'. When you go out into the fertile fields nature is as beautiful as the town is horrible. 'From St Aubin to Gorey, the woods abound; the ears of corn that England buys for seed shine in the sun and the grass supports the cows which win prizes for milk at Paris exhibitions.' The ivy is beautiful, aloes grow in the open ground, the cabbages are like shrubs and the camellias like trees. The south of Jersey is a garden, nearly every house having its conservatory.[19]

Chapter Five

Frenchmen Without Knowing It

The country may have been a fragment of France, but it was the Englishness of the islands, especially Jersey, that struck the exiles. 'Jersey is actually French, but English by law', says Adèle. 'In the superb upkeep of its roads, the tidy cleanliness of its cottages and the aristocratic elegance of its inhabitants, Jersey is English.' Hugo sums up the complexity of the insular character: 'Jerseymen and Guernseymen are certainly not English without wanting to be, but they are French without knowing it.'[1]

Vacquerie, disconcerted to find that in the land of 'gin and boxing' the streets bore the names of Englishmen responsible for the defeats of Napoleon, lamented the anglicisation of the island. 'Jersey today ... does everything it can to become English, it speaks English, it changes its Norman road names into Saxon ones, it is the humble servant of the Queen's lieutenant.' He is contemptuous of the 'low Norman-cum-English' they speak believing it to be French, so that they can refer to Victor Hugo as 'one of our muses'.[2]

Hugo, always more subtle than Vacquerie, had a high regard for the ancestral form of French in the islands, especially as spoken formerly by mariners. 'The patois (is) a true language, not to be despised. It is idiomatic, very rich and singular. It illuminates, with its obscure but deep light, the origins of the French language.' Although he claimed that 'the Archipelago speaks French with variants', he knew that it was being superseded by English. The poet Béranger told Mme. Hugo that 'he was distressed to learn that French is no longer spoken in Jersey ... you are all going to be reduced to speaking English'.[3]

In recommending the new Institut Français de Jersey to parents, Hugo wrote that among its objects should be to 'strengthen the precious link of the French language which ties the commercial and material interests of the island to our coast and which, at this moment, is breaking; to prevent the young of the future from becoming exclusively English to the prejudice of their nationality ...' (As a charming vignette: when Hugo paid an unexpected visit to the Institut a pupil was in the middle of reciting one of his poems. The boy saw Hugo and was unable to go on.)[4]

François-Victor, though he had only half-understood the Jersey-French of St Ouen, 'the wildest and most Norman of the parishes', regretted its loss because it was the mother tongue of Wace, 'the first Norman trouvère and first French poet'.[5] In a celebrated purple patch he exhorts the islanders not to be ashamed of their tongue:

> Brave Normans of the Channel Islands, who blush to speak as your forefathers did and who teach your children English, who replace old French road names by English ones, who zealously turn the thatched house of your ancestors into a Saxon cottage, know that your patois is venerable and sacred, because it is from your patois that came, like a flower from a root, that French language which tomorrow will be the language of Europe ... Your fathers from Normandy died to propagate

your patois in England, Sicily, Judea, London, Naples and up to the tomb of Christ ... It is here that ... French poetry took its first steps and uttered its first cry.[6]

The Hugos' attitude to English was both cause and effect of their lack of contact with English people. Hugo, though by no means an Anglophobe, reputedly said to Lady Diana Beauclerk in Guernsey that 'when England wishes to talk to me, she will learn my language '. It seems that Mme. Hugo, Charles and Vacquerie spoke no English, while Adèle was making half-hearted attempts to learn it. Only François-Victor, who planned to translate Shakespeare, knew the language. Conversation with English neighbours who did not speak French, like the Roses, was stilted.

They realised that Jersey and English people formed separate groups, though it is not clear that they always assigned people to the right category. Yet their contact with Jersey people, like the Asplets, the Picots and Josephine Nicolle, who would all have been able to speak French, was also limited. Thus we cannot attribute their lack of mixing with local society to the lack of a common tongue. It is rather that they found their own company, and that of the proscrits, enough. Further, they found, or imagined, that the 'English' coolness was off-putting. 'The inhabitants are obliging, attentive even, but cold', says Mme. Hugo. 'It seems that the English are like this.' Hugo produces a variant of what is mere prejudice when discussing the women of the islands, who are 'remarkable for a pure and exquisite beauty. Their complexion is a combination of the Saxon fairness, with the proverbial ruddiness of the Norman people – rosy cheeks and blue eyes; but the eyes want brilliancy. The English training dulls them.'[7]

Vacquerie, far more prejudiced, was quite honest in describing their lack of contact: 'We had made acquaintance with the island – but we did not know the islanders: but that did not worry us ... We did not make inquiries about Jersey people and we learned from them only what one sees without looking.' Like Vacquerie, Hugo was glad to be left alone: 'English hospitality, we do not fault it, we feel it is good the way it is, we would not want it otherwise – we can come here and die here.'[8]

In a discarded fragment we find a hint of what Hugo really thought about some local people:

The people here

Wait, if you come, to feel over your life
A black swarming of chatter, and the tooth
Of gossip nibbling at the hem of your private life
Slander, that will pass a rainy day
Scrutinise the passers-by, that's good when one is bored
What they don't know, they invent; they turn
This idiotic occupation into a fine art
They don't know you – subject of their prattle
Name, country, money, age
They rummage into all this; they are divided into two camps
They know nothing of history, but dance the can-can
They are unaware of the 2nd of December
But they know the thickness of your curtains.[9]

Hugo is taxing the provincial mind (though one suspects that he had Juliette's landlady particularly in mind) with more interest in local politics, the two 'camps' being the liberal *Rose* and conservative *Laurel* factions, than in the politics of France.

Hugo later remembered with a smile that, if he was treated with any respect in Jersey, it was as a peer of France, not a poet, and he had to ask shopkeepers to stop calling him 'My Lord'. There was, it is true, a first flourish of welcome to 'one of our most distinguished muses', but his rather irregular family life and his supposed atheism caused suspicion and, with the increasingly pro-Bonaparte mood, even hostility. On 11 June 1855 he found written on the front door 'Hugo is a bad man'. John Stuart Mill, detained by bad weather in Jersey in June 1854, said the inhabitants treated Hugo as a 'half-mad oddity'. Once, bathing with Vacquerie, he noticed a group of English misses staring at them through lorgnettes. It transpired that a Bonapartist newspaper had repeated Heinrich Heine's assertion that a writer so fond of morally and physically deformed characters must himself be a hunchback like Quasimodo. Vacquerie, ever the clown, placed himself in front of the staring group and asked them the time: they slowly moved off. On another occasion an importunate woman friend of the Roses burst into their room to see the man who had created Esmeralda, and had to be led away by a doctor.[10]

In a perceptive piece dating probably from 1854 Hugo sums up the common view of himself:

> To the English I am *shocking, excentric, improper.* My tie is awry. I am shaved by the barber on the corner ... which gives me the look of a workman ... I hit out at cant; I attack the death penalty, which is not respectable; I say *Mr* to a lord which is blasphemous; I am not a Catholic, not an Anglican; not a Lutheran; not a Calvinist; not a Jew, not a Methodist, not a Wesleyan; not a Mormon; therefore an atheist. Moreover French which is odious; republican, which is abominable; proscrit, which is repulsive; defeated, which is unspeakable. To cap it all, a poet. So, little popularity. If it were still fashionable to refer to oneself in the third person, as Jean-Jacques readily did, I would say: The English have received Hugo in the manner in which they drove out Byron.[11]

Hugo had some hard things to say, immediately after his expulsion, about Jersey, but his gratitude for its hospitality was never in doubt. He also admired the enterprise, intelligence and love of freedom of the islanders. There is no inconsistency here with his views of them as narrow-minded and suspicious; rather the compliments have been turned, for are not the hospitable gossips and the self-reliant provincial? Perhaps the fullest account of his views we find in *L'Archipel de la Manche* which is a descriptive pendant to his great imaginative novel about Guernsey, *Les Travailleurs de la Mer*. They both contain, it is true, inaccuracies, hyperbole and generalisation, and the sense of place, though strong, is not exactly that of the Channel Islands. Yet this is the fullest account of the islands in French at the time, and it repays study.

Hugo felt the heavy hand of puritanism everywhere. The Queen of England, he was surprised to find, was censured for using chloroform during her confinements, and when she arrived in Guernsey on a Sunday, she was referred to as 'that woman', and no one save Hugo bared his head. Sunday is the only flaw in the islands' love of liberty and it is the tyrant which takes them away from money-making. Everything is closed and the man who works faces censure for not being 'respectable', or even prison. Churches and chapels are everywhere. Every sect is represented – in Jersey there is even a Mormon chapel. Mme. Hugo also railed against Sunday: 'Today is Sunday, the town is very sad. The day is devoted to God: the women go to church and stay at home to read the Bible. A woman who would amuse herself or dance on Sunday thinks she has committed a profanation.' For Vacquerie it was a source of amusement. Once, finding Adèle tapping away at the Asplet's broken-down piano, he whispered in her ear: 'You fool! You are playing the piano. Have you forgotten it's Sunday? It is *shocking*. If people hear you, Asplet will lose his customers.'[12]

The English notions of aristocracy and caste, Hugo found, still prevailed in the islands. A de Carteret is a waggoner in Sark, a de Gruchy, claiming to be a cousin of Napoleon's Marshal Grouchy, a draper. They have, by working, lost but not forgotten their ancient nobility. The people are conscious of the past, ruled by custom, conservative.[13]

For all that, the islands are a human anthill: the climate is designed for idleness, but the population made for work. To industry is added 'an intelligence at once solid, active, alert and quick ... Jerseymen ... could be, if they wished, admirable Frenchmen'. Jersey is the seventh port of England with sophisticated traders and financiers. The population is well-informed:

> Imagine a desert island: the day after his arrival Robinson [Crusoe] starts a paper and Man Friday subscribes to it. Placards and posters keep the population up to date. You speak in the streets of St Helier or St Peter Port to an irreproachable passerby, dressed in black, severely buttoned, his linen very white, and he is talking of John Brown or telling you about Garibaldi. Is he a clergyman? No, a cowman.

Again, when Hugo arrived in Jersey he found his complete works, bound and in a tall wide bookcase, surmounted by a bust of Homer, in a grocer's house. (One might question how typical the cowman, or the grocer, who was in fact Charles Asplet, actually were.)[14]

He liked the minimal use of government in the island:

> As a government and as proof of the application of government, what better example is there than Jersey? There is only the authority of the police. Roads are lit, streets paved, citizens protected, thieves arrested, and that's all the authority there is.

Mme. Hugo agreed:

> The government here is benign, or rather it does not exist. Luggage is not searched, and never a question of passports; the police, if there are any, do not appear and no constables patrol. In spite of this lack of authority, the town is marvellously well-kept, theft is exceptional and murder unknown.[15]

Above all, the islands were progressive. 'St Helier is as civilised as Dieppe, St Peter Port is worth L'Orient', wrote Hugo. 'Thanks to progress, thanks to the admirable spirit of initiative of this valiant little island people, all has changed in the last 40 years in the Channel Islands. Where there was darkness, there is light.' He repeats: 'It is a noble little people, big-hearted. It has the spirit of the sea. These men are a race apart ...' and he ends with an unexpected twist, 'a day will come when Paris brings these islands up to date and makes their fortune.'[16]

Chapter Six

The Prophetic Isle

Having exiled himself to Jersey, Hugo began to miss his friends and the life of Paris. He wrote to Mme. de Girardin, Hetzel, Esquiros, Hippolyte Lucas and Coppens, praising Jersey fulsomely, and asking them to come to stay with him. Surveillance of his mail was such that he had to use complicated subterfuges to get it through. For example, he sent a package to Mr. Savage of 52, Milton Street, Dorset Square, London. Inside was a letter to Gustave Flaubert at Croisset, near Rouen; inside that was a third letter addressed to Flaubert's mistress, Louise Colet, in Paris, and inside that a letter to Jules Janin, also in Paris. His correspondents were asked to return letters to Philippe Asplet or Mme. Vin[cent], but one such was intercepted and so George Picot became the post-box.[1]

Most letters from Marine Terrace went out on Sundays, Tuesdays and Thursdays, presumably to catch the tri-weekly mail packets to Southampton. Many of Hugo's letters were to Hetzel in Brussels about the publication of *Napoléon le Petit* and *Les Châtiments*, but he had about 40 other correspondents including George Sand, Alexander Herzen and Dumas.

Some of them did visit the Hugos at Marine Terrace or Hauteville House: the Meurices came three times. Paul Meurice, playwright and formerly on the staff of *L'Événement* had, like the Hugos, done time at La Conciergerie, and when he was released, a ruined man, he became their main link with France. 'There was no letter', writes Hazard, 'which came from Jersey which did not ask for a service ... he had to give a manuscript to the editor, to the printer, correct the proofs, take in textual changes or additions. He must offer a play to a theatre director, busy himself with rehearsals ... Paul Meurice was more than a friend: he was friendship itself.' Vacquerie asks Mme. Meurice for his blue dressing gown, his national guard trousers, his winter clothes and rough paper which is so expensive in Jersey. Mme. Hugo asks for her laundry basket, Adèle for her velvet hat and muffs.[2]

On their first visit, from 23 August to 9 September 1852, the Meurices were shown the island, the Hugos gave a house-warming party and Mme. Meurice's photograph was taken. They left clutching copies of *Napoléon le Petit*. 'Mme Meurice has a double charm for me', wrote Mme. Hugo, 'she is modest and simple and she is fond of me. You know her husband, what a noble character he is, what a rare spirit. Their departure has left a gap which we have filled with work.' They returned in October 1854 and September to October 1855 when they took part in table-turning.[3]

Mme. Hugo's sister Julie, later Mme. Chenay and châtelaine of Hauteville House, came in late summer 1853 and again in 1855. Julie was living a lonely life in France, and Mme. Hugo's letters to her were full of hope and encouragement. She had given Julie's address to three English girls. 'You found my little English girls kind and likeable, one is very pretty, a beauty even. I am touched that you received them at your house and revealed your grace. They will come back and we will talk about you.'[4]

From France came also Mme. Bouclier, probably in 1852, and certainly in October 1855 when she stayed to help the Hugos pack up their belongings and to accompany Adèle and Vacquerie to Guernsey. But by far the most consequential visit was that of Mme. de Girardin, whom Hugo had known at Delphine Gay, an ornament of Charles Nodier's salon. Author of *Lady Tartuffe* and *La Joie fait peur*, a friend of Balzac and Lamartine, Mme. de Girardin did not receive writers 'of the third order', and the only woman writer she accepted was George Sand. Like Hugo, she had nurtured hostility to Napoleon whom she called *Boustrapa* (from Boulogne-Strasbourg-Paris, places where he had tried or succeeded in making coups d'état). Mme. de Girardin came with her maid and stayed for eight days, probably at the *Pomme d'Or*. Like other guests, she was taken to see Mont Orgueil, St Aubin's Bay and Plemont, and her photograph was taken.[5]

Dinner had barely finished on her first day, 6 September 1853, when she got up to announce that she wanted to turn the tables. Since 1850 there had been a craze for table-turning in Paris, and by the middle of 1853 it was a monomania. It had been tried in Jersey, for example by Mme. Engelson, one of Carr's 'romantic exiles', who used a rotating needle in an attempt to contact her husband. That evening, however, Delphine de Girardin failed to move the table because, she explained, it was not round. She tried with Hugo on Wednsday 8th and failed again. On Thursday she bought a circular three-legged table in St Helier, but it did not move either. On Saturday the Godfrays, with whom she was dining, made her interrogate a table which, said Vacquerie, 'proved its intelligence by refusing to reply to the Jersey people'.

But then on Sunday 11 September Mme. de Girardin placed the circular table on top of a large square one and, with Vacquerie opposite, placed hands on the small table. The Hugos, Le Flôs and M. de Tréveneuc watched as the table creaked into motion and began to tap out words: one tap for A or Yes, two for B or No, three for C etc. After some preliminaries General Le Flô asked the table what word was on his mind:

Table Fidelity.
Le Flô Well, I was thinking of my wife; that's curious.*

To be sure that Mme. de Girardin or Vacquerie were not pushing the table, they were replaced by Charles and Le Flô. As Mme. de Girardin asked 'Who are you?', Le Flô asked 'What name am I thinking of?'

Table Daughter.
Hugo (to Le Flô) Are you thinking of your daughter?*
Le Flô No.*
Vacquerie Who am I thinking of?
Table Dead.
Mme. de Girardin (very moved) Dead daughter?
Vacquerie (again) Who am I thinking of?
Table Dead.

Everyone thought of Léopoldine Hugo, drowned at Villequier.

Mme. de Girardin Who are you?
Table Ame soror.
Hugo That is sister in Latin.*

An inexpressible emotion gripped them all; Mme. Hugo was in tears. The table became very agitated, as though wanting to unburden itself.

Hugo Are you happy?
Table Yes.
Hugo (profoundly moved) Where are you?
Table Light ...
Hugo Do you see the suffering of those who love you?
Table Yes.
Mme. de Girardin Will they suffer long?
Table No.
Mme. de Girardin Will they soon return to France?
(no reply)
Hugo Are you pleased when they blend your name with their prayers?
Table Yes ... ('Léopoldine' promised to return soon.)

At first sceptical, Hugo, Charles and Vacquerie soon became avid turners, though Vacquerie at least was worried that too much spiritualism would divert their attention from the proper work: politics. Juliette, who called this turning dangerous and diabolical, complained that Hugo was leaving her alone and bored because of his infatuation with magic.

Seances were to continue for another two years, with over 100 recorded. Mme. de Girardin sent two tables from Paris, a small one with a pencil attached to its foot, and a sort of ouija board with a needle to point to the various letters, but these methods did not work, and the table ordered them to return to the old, laborious tapping routine. Each letter would have taken, on average, about five seconds to tap out, and it could take two hours just to compose a short paragraph. Seances were usually in the evening and often lasted into the early hours. Most took place at Marine Terrace, but some were held at the *Pomme d'Or* or the houses of Edmond Leguevel and the Asplets. François-Victor, at first intrigued, lost interest after a few months, but Charles became a good medium and was sometimes dragged out of bed to magnetise the tables.

Victor Hugo asked many questions and the answers often appeared in his own style though he himself rarely touched the table. On the eve of Mme. de Girardin's departure Louis Napoleon appears cringing before Hugo:

Hugo Are you suffering for your crimes?
L.N. Yes.
Hugo Do you know when you'll die?
L.N. In two years' time ...
Hugo Do you see that I don't hate you, only your crime?
L.N. Yes.
Hugo At this moment, do you regret your crime?
L.N. Yes.
Hugo Do you think *Napoléon le Petit* is a good book?
L.N. I'm afraid ...
Hugo Are you afraid of Victor Hugo?
L.N. Yes.

Later it is Napoleon's uncle, the Great Napoleon, who is summoned:

Hugo What would you do if you were me?
N. Write your verses.
Hugo What do you think of my *Napoléon le Petit*?
N. A great truth, a baptism for the traitor ...

A procession of great spirits moved through Marine Terrace: Dante, Racine, Chenier, Chateaubriand, Hannibal, Mahomet, the Lion of Androcles or the Angel of Death. Towards the end of 1853 enthusiasm began to wane, but early in 1854 amazing results reappeared. Interspersed with other great souls, the voice of Shakespeare was heard. On 22 January 1854 he announced his intention of speaking some lines:

Hugo In English or French?
Shakespeare English is inferior to the French language.

Starting unpromisingly with the 'nether star' addressing the 'upper star' with 'Bonjour, paradis', Shakespeare's drama was rapped out in resounding verse.

As we have seen, Hugo did not usually hold the table, but it often seemed to speak in his style and about his preoccupations. He often remarked that a truth from the table had in fact been announced by him many years before, or that it was confirming a cosmogony, supplanting Christianity as it had supplanted Druidism, which he had been developing for a very long time. But he thought, at least in the beginning, that the words were simply Charles's thoughts amplified by 'magnetism', or that they were produced by spirits pretending to be Joan of Arc, Spartacus, Caesar or Tiberius. Neither explanation seems quite satisfactory, as the dominant partner with his hand on the table often seemed to be pushing it. For example, in June 1854, Albert Pinson joined Charles at the table:

Charles Who is there?
Table Frater tuus.
Charles You are not my brother. Are you Pinson's?
Table Yes, Andrew.

Pinson did have a brother called Andrew who had not been heard of for some time. The table now replied to Pinson's questions in English, although only he spoke it. On 12 June, with Pinson again at the table, 'Walter Scott' produced a good couplet in English:

Vex not the bard: his lyre is broken
His last song sung, his last word spoken.

But the table often 'guessed' the thoughts of those not touching it, which suggests that extra-sensory perception was also at work.

Hugo said that he did not believe in the message of the tables blindly, but he was not perplexed by the phenomenon. The spirits of the table were not supernatural, but quite natural, and he paraphrased Hamlet: 'There are more things under heaven than are dreamt of in man's philosophy.' Mankind was still in its infancy and needed revealed religion, but he did not think that the time was ripe for publishing any account of the seances which would be received with a burst of laughter and used to discredit the democratic movement. There was only one way to prove the message of the tables: ask them secrets – how to cure madness, steer balloons and find gold in Australia – and send the answers to the Academy of Sciences which could verify or falsify them in due course. François-Victor remained incredulous, denying the tables in the name of the rationalism of the times. For this they called him 'Mr. 19th Century' and laughed at his inconsistency when he threw salt over his shoulder.

Hugo wanted not only to talk to the spirits but, so he said, to see them. One night a baker's boy was walking towards St Luke's church which faced Marine Terrace, when he saw a white figure, motionless, at the end of the road. It seemed to be in flames. Terrified, not knowing whether to go forward or back, he took a grip on himself and rushed past it with his eyes closed and his hair on end. When Hugo heard all this he was rather amused, and he told Guérin, who had heard strange shrieks nearby, that he could imagine the apparition emerging from between the knobbled trunks which lined Le Dicq. He now began to hear strange tappings on his walls, and his papers shuffled about in the windless room.

At the end of February 1854, when Charles and François-Victor were returning home at two in the morning, they saw the drawing room windows brilliantly lit up, as though by a blazing hearth and 30 candles. The door was locked and François-Victor went up to bed; Charles failed to find the drawing room key, but went to bed with a certain terror. No candles were found in the drawing room next day. They consulted the tables:

> *Charles* Is there something annoying you?
> *Table* Yes.
> *Charles* What?
> *Table* Your house. If you want to talk to me, come out into the road.
> *Charles* Are you the White Lady the barber told us had been seen near this house?
> *Table* Yes.

The ghostly meeting was arranged for 3 a.m., and the seance turned to Molière's verse comments of *Les Femmes Savantes*. Hugo, meanwhile, was in bed but sleepless; he heard Charles open the door to François-Victor and both of them coming up to bed. The house was asleep except for Hugo who remained drowsy for some time when, at 3 a.m., he clearly heard the front door bell ringing. Cold and probably afraid, he stayed in his room. No one else had heard the bell, but the next evening the White Lady would only sketch her portrait. Hugo admitted that all this and the rapping on his walls filled him with dread, and he wrote of the White Lady in *À celle qui est voilée*, *Horror* and *Dolor*, in verse that is at once placatory and apocalyptic. Vacquerie, Charles and Mme. Hugo were also disturbed by nocturnal tappings and barking dogs, but François-Victor dismissed them. '[17]89 casts out my fears, and I agree with Voltaire on all that.'

The tables told of other spirits associated with La Grève d'Azette: the black birds which made the dogs bark, the headless man, and the three murderesses, one of whom was the White Lady, the others the Grey Lady, a druidess who had sacrificed her father on the altar stone of a dolmen, and the Black Lady, another patricide. Returning home late one night Charles and François-Victor saw the Grey Lady, and early in September 1854 Hugo saw a flame on top of the hill near the Dolmen de la Tour Blanche. He questioned the tables:

> *Hugo* Are you she who appeared at night to me on the beach and demanded verses?
> *Table* I am always she: I am the inconsolable one of the horizon.

The White Lady confirmed that she was everywhere, near the Dolmen de la Tour Blanche, in the flat land north-east of Marine Terrace and at Rocqueberg, but she refused to say anything about the shrouded figure that had been disturbing the inhabitants of Bagot, Georgetown and La Ruelle Pavée for the preceding fortnight.

The White Lady was supposed to be the familiar of a nearby menhir, which stands at Ivy Stone Farm, Samares, and is also called 'The White Lady'. In the Jersey language the term 'La Blanche Danme' can refer either to ghosts or to these menhir. Adèle referred to the White Lady as the familiar demon or guardian angel of Marine Terrace, and in their susceptible mood the family seems half to have believed it.

Hugo was very interested in the prehistoric stones of Jersey, the cromlechs, dolmens and menhirs, which he, like most people of the time, wrongly called Druidic. Some verse was composed near these stones, and at night. At Le Couperon dolmen the Shadow's Mouth (La Bouche d'Ombre) put forth a pantheistic philosophy:

> Sache que tout connaît sa loi, son but, sa route
> Que, de l'astre au ciron, l'immensité s'écoute
> Que tout a conscience en la création ...
> Tout est plein d'âmes.

On 28 December 1854 Mme. Hugo and Charles held the table while Hugo wrote. 'Joshua' spoke:

Man is not a single but a complex ego. Within his skin there are millions of beings ...

At this point Hugo wrote: 'An idea that came to me three days ago'. As he realised that this pantheism owed nothing to the tables in themselves, so the days of turning were numbered, and he was at pains to point out that only two small details in *Les Contemplations* were due to the tables.

There were other reasons for the waning interest in turning. Hugo's doctor advised him to give it up; Vacquerie began to think that it merely articulated the thoughts of those present; Mme. Hugo failed to communicate with Mme. de Girardin who had just died, and the table's welcome statement in 1853 that the Empire and exile would end in two years was clearly not being fulfilled. As the last straw, Jules Allix, an enthusiast for the tables, had gone mad during a seance. He sat immobile on the Hugos' blue sofa for four hours and merely said 'I've seen things', and two days later Augustine, his sister, found him flat on his stomach trying to magnetise a watch so that it stopped at 12 o'clock.

Just after the last seance, Hugo finished writing *À Celle qui est restée en France*, that is, Léopoldine who had started the whole table turning craze two years before, and with it *Les Contemplations*. As an epilogue to his conversations with the Beyond, Hugo wrote:

> Quand j'étais à Jersey, dans l'île fatidique
> Où devant l'Océan l'âme éperdue abdique
> Des syllabes passaient dans les souffles du vent
> Et Dieu resplendissait sous la nature sombre
> Je voyais des clartés sortir des fleurs dans l'ombre
> Une voix me parlait dans le soleil levant.[6]

Anyone studying Hugo's life in Jersey (or Guernsey) is bound to ask himself whether exile suited him, even as it was grinding down his family. He undoubtedly missed France, and in particular Parisian life and letters. 'Every day I sink deeper into oblivion, solitude, dark nature, exile, the oblivion of those who have loved me, and I am alone, my soul wide open ...' he wrote in December 1853. His letters are full of invitations to come and stay at Marine Terrace, or to write back: 'exulibus epistolae dulces'. On the other hand, he had 'thought, nature and the family', as he put it; the presence of Juliette; a great amount of time to think and develop his genius, and to talk with his family and friends, and just enough money. Was his life so bad? Flaubert obviously thought not, and called him 'the Great Crocodile'. But this is unfair; Hugo had given up a great deal in fighting the coup d'état and later in refusing Napoleon's amnesty, and his grief at being separated from France was no less genuine for being partly self-inflicted.

Of course, the exile was the occasion for striking noble poses on the Rocher des Proscrits, and speaking across Le Passage de la Déroute to the tomb of Chateaubriand at St Malo opposite:

> Dans Jersey, l'île anglaise, et seul sur la montagne
> Triste, élevant la voix d'un bord à l'autre bord,
> Ainsi parle, les yeux fixés sur la Bretagne
> Victor Hugo proscrit à Chateaubriand mort.

Furthermore, he seems to be saying that whatever happens is for the good; everything is pleasant or, if unpleasant, ennobling.

(2 September 1852) My joy is in exile ... I feel profoundly calm.
(December 1852) I love you, Exile! Sorrow, I love you!
(29 October 1853) Driven from my country and my home, I smile.
(16 April 1854) ... Envy me ... proscription is fine, and I thank Destiny for it.
(December 1854) I find exile better and better ... I feel at the peak of my powers ... Perhaps I will die in exile, but I will die augmented. All is good.

There is something unconvincing about this defiance, and when he says that exile is a terrible thing, not for the proscrit, but for the proscriber, is he not whistling in the dark? Once having set his face against any return to France while Napoleon was in power ('When Liberty returns, so shall I') he knew that he had to make the most of his exile. In September 1854 he wrote: 'I have never had such faith and hope ... I distinctly see the triumph of the Republic, democracy and civilisation.' He then thought that the Crimean War would bring Napoleon down, but he often said he would never see France again, and would die in Jersey. He must have known that his sentence was an indeterminate one.

One thing is certain, that exile was a wonderful thing for his genius. The influence of Jersey, and particularly the first spring in 1853, on *Les Contemplations*, cannot be over-emphasised. The way in which that exile was brought to an abrupt end is the subject of the rest of this book.[7]

1. Victor Hugo in Jersey.

2. Mme. Hugo in the conservatory at Marine Terrace, photograph by Auguste Vacquerie.

3. Adèle Hugo, the poet's daughter and author of the Journal, in Jersey.

4. Charles Hugo, photographer, writer and medium, photograph by Auguste Vacquerie.

5. François-Victor Hugo, translator of Shakespeare, photograph by Charles Hugo.

6. (*above*) Marine Terrace, the sea-facing facade. The Hugos lived in the left half. Photograph by Charles Hugo.

7. (*below*) A postcard of Marine Terrace from the road. The roof was added later, after the Hugos' exile.

8. Charles, François-Victor and Victor Hugo, photographed by Henry Mullins during their visit to Jersey in 1860.

9. Sandor Teleki (1821-92) in Hungarian peasant costume. A frequent visitor to Marine Terrace, he later joined Garibaldi and the Thousand. The photograph was taken by Charles Hugo in 1853.

10. The Le Flô children, probably Adotic and Caroline. The photograph was taken by Charles Hugo, perhaps in 1853.

11. Charles Le Flô (1804-87), general in Algeria, Orleanist and later, at the fall of the Empire, Minister of War.

12. Charles Ribeyrolles, a journalist who died in Brazil in 1859. The photograph was taken by Auguste Vacquerie in 1853.

13. Ede Remenyi, Hungarian violinist. The photograph may have been taken by Auguste Vacquerie.

14. Une ferme (La Tourelle, St Martin, Jersey). The photograph was taken by Charles Hugo, possibly in 1853.

15. Havre des Pas by James Moore, 1859. 'A village of fishermen', showing the boatyard and La Collette Tower.

16.   (*above*) 'Le dolmen ou m'a parlé la Bouche de l'Ombre.' This drawing by Victor Hugo is probably of Le Couperon dolmen.

17.   (*left*) The Hermitage of St Helier. A wash drawing by Victor Hugo, dated 3 September 1855.

18. Paul Meurice, 'friendship itself', photographed by Auguste Vacquerie.

19. Emile Allix, photographed by Auguste Vacquerie.

20. General Lazare Meszaros (1796-1858), ex-Minister of War in Hungary, photographed by Charles Hugo.

21. Hugo on the Rocher des Proscrits. 'Et s'il n'en reste qu'un, je serai celui-là.'

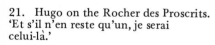

The Raft of the Medusa

When Hugo stepped ashore in Jersey, the island had long been an asylum for refugees. Huguenots had come after St Bartholomew's Day, French nobles after the Revolution. Gabriel de Montgomery and Jean Cavalier had come from France; Charles II, when Prince of Wales, from England. There were some Poles who had fled their country in the wake of the 1830 insurrection and had come to Jersey by way of France and London. A split between radical and more conservative Polish refugees in London, an abiding feature of emigré politics, had led to Polish radicals coming to Jersey in the autumn of 1834. They called themselves the 'Human' commune and numbered only eight; best known among them was Zeno Swieoslawski, later to be printer to the French proscrits. Following the unsuccessful revolution in Pest in 1848 Hungarian reformers had arrived in Jersey, including the former Minister of War, General Lazare Meszaros. There were also a few Germans, Austrians and Italians, but by far the greatest contingent came from France, proscrits who had been 'proscribed' and expelled by Louis Napoleon after his successful coup d'état of 2 December 1851. Some had come direct from France, some, like Hugo, by way of Belgium.

At this time there were about 300 political refugees in Jersey and it has been possible to find the names of most of them and, in many cases, their occupations. Quite a few were doctors and lawyers, while others taught languages, mathematics, science or music. A few seem to have been artisans, manufacturers or shop-keepers, with the occasional photographer, inn-keeper or tailor. Many had to adopt a lesser occupation in Jersey, and it is not clear how they managed to earn even the barest living: the newspapers were full of their advertisements for law, French or phrenology lessons, but their returns would have been very meagre because supply so far exceeded demand, and Jersey already had a complement of professionals.

Some were engaged as journalists, writing mainly for *L'Homme*, the proscrits' house-paper, or printing or distributing it. Comte de Vallerot became a market gardener, Lazare Meszaros tried to grow tobacco, Pierre Leroux experimented with agriculture, developing a grandiose system which he called 'circulus', but which was merely the recycling of sewage. Nonetheless, the proscription was disproportionately middle class, for the Revolution of 1848 had been a revolt of that class against Louis Philippe, and Louis Napoleon's was a counter-revolution. Most proscrits were democrats, some of them liberal, some radical, but one, General Le Flô, was an Orleanist.

The préfets of the neighbouring French coast had been worried by the presence of the proscrits, only a few miles away, almost from the moment of their first arrival in Jersey in January 1852. They had issued a notice that only those with a passport from

39

the French consul or the Lieutenant Governors of Jersey or Guernsey and viséd by the consul would be allowed to land in France. The Lt.-Governor of Jersey, Sir James Reynett, published this in the Jersey papers. The consul in Jersey, however, was a local man, Jean-Pierre Simon, who was trafficking in these passports, and it was said that the 'Reds' themselves held a book of passports and were fomenting a scheme to assassinate Louis Napoleon. The préfet de la Manche suggested that a zealous French agent should be sent to Jersey, if possible disguised with an official title. Thus, on 2 February, the French Foreign Minister announced that Louis Napoleon had agreed to the Frenchman Émile Laurent as French consul in Jersey, and M. Loyeux was to replace the Guernseyman Henry Tupper as French agent in Guernsey. In March, as an added restriction, the cost of passports was increased from three or six pence to five shillings.

The appointment must have come as a blow to John Sullivan, who had made himself a sort of unofficial French agent. In his Jersey militia uniform he had gone to shake hands with Louis Napoleon at a review in France, to cries of 'Vivent les Anglais'. Already in January 1852 he was denouncing the proscrits to Vildieu, the under-inspector of customs in Granville. In June he told the préfet de la Manche that the proscrits were preparing an attack on France, adding that he had personally swayed the Jersey paper *La Patrie* against them. This seems unlikely: *La Patrie* welcomed Hugo and, on 28 August, printed an extract from *Napoléon le Petit*.

The British, meanwhile, were keeping an eye both on the refugees and on the French response to their presence. John Turnbull, British consul at Granville, told the Home Office that French steamers occasionally cruised the coast to intercept any attempt by the exiles, and that 12 or more of the most violent of them had weekly meetings in Jersey. Reynett, writing a month later, in February 1852, could not 'learn that there were weekly meetings' but got the police to watch them.

Laurent, the new consul, was ordered by Turgot, the French Foreign Minister, to draw up a list of all the exiles in Jersey and the other islands, and produce details on their way of life and connections with England and France. Laurent complained that the *connétables* and *centeniers* of the parishes, being elected to office, could not be relied on to undertake the political role of watching and controlling the refugees, and he hoped the new Governor, Frederick Love, would create a salaried police force to watch the refugees, or at least that the post of Inspector of Foreigners could be resuscitated. Love was told by the Home Office that there had never been such a function.

In fact Lord Malmesbury, the British Foreign Minister, was prepared to go only so far to accommodate the French, and he insisted that any communications to Paris about the refugees should be absolutely confidential. This was because the shaky Tory cabinet of Derby and Disraeli wanted to please their liberal wing but depended on the support of the Palmerstonians who approved the coup d'état. London promised to send police agents secretly to Jersey to watch the refugees.

This then was the rather unreal atmosphere of intrigue into which Hugo stepped. Laurent, who admittedly may have been under-reporting, said that only about 60 refugees were there to meet Hugo, though Hugo himself said that 'the whole island was there to receive me'. There is no doubt, however, that there was considerable support for the proscrits in Jersey. It is not surprising that the liberal or 'Rose' papers, like *La Chronique* and *L'Impartial* should have welcomed the 'celebrated poet', 'illustrious author' and 'Prince of modern poets', but even the conservative or 'Laurel' sheet *Le Constitutionnel* was at his feet: 'It seems that the Prince-President , who has found ways of expelling all who make France illustrious by their talents, writing and learning, cannot abide them in countries too close to the one which groans under his government ...'. The paper then goes into a purple passage in the style of Hugo himself:

> May the creator of *Notre Dame de Paris*, the singer of the *Feuilles d'Automne* come among our hospitable population, breathe in the scented air of our free island which has been at all times a sure refuge against all persecutions ... the asylum which you have chosen is sacred for all, and you will be troubled here only by admiration, devotion and friendship.

The editorial a few days later, under the heading 'God save France', called Hugo 'one of the literary glories of France'.

Hugo's speech, *En arrivant à Jersey*, took place not on the quay as was dramatically suggested, but in the more mundane surroundings of the club of the Société Fraternelle of the proscrits, founded a month before. After praising the bravery of the proscrits, and the spectacle of fraternity in practice in Belgium, he added that the same is found 'on all the other rafts of the Medusa, all other places where the shipwrecked proscrits are grouped; it is found particularly in Jersey.' After a forceful plea for unity, he declared that they should have one aim: the liberation by democracy of all oppressed nations.

On the same day, Laurent reported to Drouyn de Lhuys the new French Foreign Minister: 'It is possible that Messrs. Hugo and Vacquerie will profit from the freedom of the Jersey press to publish violent diatribes in the local papers against the French Government; unfortunately there is no legal means of stopping it', and then, with an unwitting false prophecy, 'The Governor can, it is true, expel anyone guilty of a reprehensible act; but it is unlikely that M. Hugo would risk the security of his new asylum by unwise demonstrations.'[1]

Chapter Eight

Terror of a Little Book

Laurent did not delay long in sending reports on Hugo back to France. On 10 August he wrote to Drouyn to say that Hugo, making the most of English freedom of speech at the 'Demagogic Club', was attacking 'Monseigneur the Prince-President' in the most injurious terms. He also told Love that Hugo had called Napoleon 'the Prince of Assassins', and Love passed it on to John Sanders, the detective just sent by Sir Richard Mayne, the London police commissioner, to watch the proscrits for England. Laurent ascribed the tenor of Hugo's speeches to a 'spirit exasperated by domestic woes and the failure of his political dreams', not a wholly inaccurate diagnosis, though the notion that Hugo had been refused a ministry by Napoleon, or (the theory of his critical biographer, Biré) that Hugo had actually wished to be president himself, seems rather far-fetched.

Sanders and Laurent were rivals. Sanders had the advantage that he was on home ground with the support of the police; Laurent that he could understand the proscrits' language. Sanders thought that Laurent was playing a two-faced game, watching the refugees and trying to find proof that the British government was watching refugees and agents like Laurent himself. In fact Laurent had still not discovered about Sanders' arrival by 19 August, for the day before he had written a flattering letter to Love offering to pay for the expenses of a London detective. This suggests that Laurent was not very good at his job of information gathering, and that Love was keeping him at arms' length, telling him very little.

Sanders seems to have been rather more successful. He was keeping an eye on Seigneuret and Bonnet-Duverdier, said to be 'violent' or 'fanatic' proscrits, and on John and Edward Sullivan, who were unofficial French agents. Edward Sullivan, he discovered, was pretending to be a 'Red Republican, Democrat, Socialist etc.' and allowing the refugees to insert opinions in his paper *L'Impartial*, but he was passing information to Laurent who, as part of the disguise, pretended to be strongly opposed to Sullivan. Sanders also discovered that General Le Flô had been looking at fortifications, and that a man of about 40 or 45 with a large black beard and mustachios, of a gentlemanly and military appearance, had been sketching forts and towers, the position of rocks and the movement of tides. This man, who was posing as a proscrit, was either Stoffel or Merliot, and he met Sanders in a billiards room and confided that he was a Bonapartist. He was in touch with the commander of the coast-guard *Le Daim*, Captain Duteilly, who pretended to be looking after the French fisheries, but was in fact observing the great harbour works at St Catherine's, Jersey, and at Alderney.

While the fears in Jersey were that Napoleon was planning to capture the islands, the suggestions were that the proscrits were planning an attack on France. At a meeting on 13 August, Sanders reported, the proscrits were told that the time was ripe for practice drilling, and that they should ready themselves for a landing in small groups and move to a rendezvous near Bayonne. The proscrits were getting more and more excited. 'Victor Hugo and his sons cannot calm them', added Sanders.

A coded telegramme from de Varenne, the French ambassador in Berlin, stated that Mikulowski, the Polish proprietor of the Café de l'Europe, had already made a clandestine visit to the French coast, and had arranged for a landing of 200-300 people near St Malo around 14 August. Hearing this, Love promised Laurent that he would redouble surveillance by the police and by English cruisers in local waters, but he seems to have done little more than direct *centenier* Jean Chevalier to watch Mikulowski. Malmesbury told Walewski, the French Ambassador in London, that he would encourage the refugees to move on to America but could not do more.

On 26 August Laurent warned Drouyn that the Hungarians Lajos Kossuth, Teleki and Meszaros were planning a *coup de main* in the Midi. Malmesbury, it seems, had already briefed his private secretary, George Harris, to call on Napoleon at St Cloud, with the details. Harris was kept waiting for days until he hit on the idea of asking Miss Howard, Napoleon's mistress, for an interview with him. The same evening he received an invitation to accompany Napoleon shooting the next day and dine in the evening. Harris wrote to Malmesbury:

> I got off the shooting and dinner, being too ill for either; but in my interview I told him exactly what you desired me to tell him, viz., the *menées* of the refugees at Jersey, their threats of assassination, their general project, and expectations of help from Mazzini and Kossuth, and, in fact, all the pith of Mr Sanders' reports and General Love's apprehensions, not omitting certain details from reports of the A Division about money and arms; and, finally, letting his Highness know that the Jersey authorities knew what to think of Stoffel and other agents of the French Government.

> The President desired me to thank you most cordially for the intelligence, part of which (viz. the refugees' intention of landing and rendezvous in the South, not far from Bayonne and the frontier), he said was quite new to him. He mentioned that that very morning Manteuffel (Prussian ambassador in Paris) had sent him a warning about the *exilés des Îles Normandes*, that amongst their *projets insensées* they meditated a descent upon the coast of Algeria, where they counted on being able to 'corrupt' two regiments of the line, with which, under Mazzini's orders and inspiration, they were to return to Italy and revolutionize the whole of that country.

Laurent was told by Lord Hardinge, the Master General of the Ordnance, that any refugees who menaced the peace in France would immediately be expelled and that Lord Derby, the Prime Minister, had no sympathy for demagogic and socialist notions. Hardinge, though he shared Derby's views, had come over with an important and numerous suite to make a thorough inspection of the island's defences, and he was gratified by the highly competent drilling of the Jersey militia. Only a week before *Le Daim*, showing no colours, had been ordered off Alderney from where a French agent, Groult, was sending information about the fortifications to France. Northumberland had just ordered another steamer, probably the *Sprightly*, to join the *Dasher* on the Jersey station, and troops were being embarked at Portsmouth for Jersey. British policy was to keep both proscrits and French agents under close surveillance, and try to pre-empt any attack by the proscrits on France, or by France on Jersey.

La Chronique in Jersey truly remarked that *Son Altesse Imperiale* was no more likely to be attacked than the Sublime Sultan, but the French were taking no chances. The préfet de la Manche, Paulze d'Ivoy, reminded travellers that passports must have been viséd before disembarkation in France, and this applied, he told Horace Hammond, British consul in Cherbourg, to British passports too. In September two French families and two Englishmen had to return to Jersey on the *Rose* because their passports had not been viséd by Laurent. 'Passport-tyranny' it was called by the *Jersey Times* which went on to observe that the Prince President 'seems very nervous respecting the Channel Islands, and their French guests and visitors'.

Hugo described this nervousness to Madier de Montjau. In particular, the French authorities were threatening prison to those who carried across *Napoléon le Petit*. This polemic, a frontal attack on Napoleon in the form of a history of December 1848 to April 1852, was also being smuggled across the Belgian, Swiss, Savoyard and Niçoise frontiers. In Jersey it was advertised by Ollivier the booksellers on 28 August, and for 10 days before this the French-language newspapers of the island had been printing extracts. Hugo noted on 29 August that 300 people had come from Granville the week before to buy the book. It was doubtful whether many were republicans, but great profits could be made from reselling the book.'This thirst is a good sign', said Hugo.

Laurent warned the préfets of Manche and Ille-et-Vilaine that a great many copies were to be expected by the day. The edition was no bigger than a pack of cards, and the refugees claimed by about 9 September to have disposed of 4,000 copies. The préfets took Laurent at his word, for on 16 September, as the *Rose* approached the mole at Granville, customs officers noticed people on the shore gesticulating to warn passengers, and in the trousers and boots of one of them, Gustave-Adolphe de la Renaudière, were found fragments of the book. 'Ah, *that* book,' said a gendarme who told Renaudière that he would get five years in prison. In fact he got off lightly with a five franc fine and costs, perhaps because he was not a republican, but a monarchist.

Laurent also wrote to the Granville and St Malo post offices to warn that extracts from the book were being printed on fly-sheets and posted. He was probably thinking of the pamphlet on *Napoléon le Petit* by A. Le Maout, who ran the French pharmacy at 19 Beresford Street. Laurent asked Love to ban these publications and expel the authors; Love refused, but he did order *Sprightly* and *Dasher* to intercept a boat belonging to someone called Aubin on which it was said that 20,000 copies of the book were stowed.

Hugo wrote to Charras that Napoleon 'the imbecile' was 'brandishing bayonets' against the landing of the book. This was true of lesser functionaries like the préfets, but Napoleon himself was not unduly worried. When the book was shown him at St Cloud he took it and examined it for a moment with a smile of contempt on his lips, and then said to his entourage: 'See, gentlemen, here is *Napoléon le Petit* by Victor Hugo le Grand'. Hugo heard about this and responded in a poem *L'Homme a ri*, 'Ah, you will end by howling, you wretch'.

Napoleon would no doubt have agreed with the *Jersey Times* which thought that Hugo had 'proved too much' in the book, and asked how, if Napoleon was so abject, he had been able to wield the powers of Army, Church and people to his own advantage. (Karl Marx, significantly, turned this idea on its head: he thought Hugo had 'made' Napoleon great by attributing so much to him that would have happened anyway.)

The contraband in *Napoléon le Petit* continued for some time. In August 1854 important people in Granville and St Malo petitioned for the extradition of the Jersey refugees when 4,000 copies of the book were seized. This was disturbing the peace, they claimed, and disrupting their commerce with Jersey.

The smuggling of books, pamphlets and newspapers required elaborate means. They were put in watertight lead containers and hidden below the water-line of fishing boats, and then handed over in mid-sea or on deserted beaches in Normandy and Brittany. They were even carried in the entrails of poultry by travellers. The searching of travellers had to match or outdo in ingenuity and thoroughness the devices of smugglers. Vacquerie's apolitical play *Prosperine* was kept by the St Malo customs for four days; children's scribbles were painstakingly examined; linings torn open; wet seaweed carried by vraicking boats and even piles of dry seaweed turned upside down; and a man was arrested because his boots were wrapped up in a copy of *L'Impartial* in which a speech of Hugo's happened to be reported. The wife of a proscrit, Mme. P., was made to strip. 'What are you so keen to find?' she asked the officer. 'Papers, Madame; we know that after Hugo's famous letter there was a reunion of proscrits at your house, and that's not the best thing in Jersey. Besides, you are friends of Victor Hugo, and you must have papers. And anyway, Madame, it is not to see your fair skin that I insist that you take off your underwear.'

The nervousness of the French authorities in late September was to some extent understandable. At 3 a.m. on 3 or 4 September Love was woken by a French refugee warning him that a conspiracy to seize the island was afoot. He had seen a man with a lantern lighting a torch; probably a smuggler signalling the approach of a customs man, suggested Love. It seems, in fact, that the Frenchman had seen a look-out covering a meeting of 300-400 proscrits in St Brelade's Bay, then a deserted place. It is not recorded what they discussed, but the gathering looked sinister. Colonel Le Couteur, the Vicomte, agreed to make enquiries; Laurent asked for more secret agents, and Sanders for another six to eight London police officers.[1]

Chapter Nine

Impotent Rage

General Love had been watching with some alarm as people arrived in every boat from France, looking as though they meant to stay. Ninety-six came on a single boat at the end of August, and by 9 September 700 Frenchmen, mostly 'ill-looking' fellows according to Sanders, had arrived. No one, not even the proscrits, knew which were refugees, which spies and which ordinary workers or travellers.

Love therefore decided, probably on orders from Derby and with prodding from Laurent, to enumerate foreigners in the island. Jean Dupré, the Attorney-General, gave his blessing, resting on the 1635 Order in Council which decreed that if a foreigner spent more than a night in a house the occupant should inform the *connétable* of the parish. On 4 September Love asked the *connétables* for numbers; names; profession, trade or other situation in life; if married, the number in the family, stating whether male or female; time of arrival; date of passport from own country; whether living as servant, journeyman or employee of a Jersey family and, if so, the name of the employer; whether in lodgings or occupying the whole house; with remarks.

The census worried the proscrits and affected Jerseymen who thought it an inquisition. François Godfray, the *connétable* of St Saviour, put a notice in the papers to say that only Frenchmen were to be counted. This suggested, as was obvious anyway, that the census had a political motive, and no doubt was designed to test the authorities. Love promptly admonished him that it was a census of all foreigners. Nonetheless Godfray and Pierre Le Sueur, *connétable* of St Helier, enumerated only Frenchmen.

The proscrits at first said they would send their names not to the *connétables* but to Love, but one of them, Henri Bouillon, wrote an 'impertinent' letter to Love attacking the census. An Italian, Angelo Gonzalez, sent his objections to several papers, to Pierre Le Sueur and to Palmerston who, now in opposition, replied favourably. Gonzalez's argument was that the census was a violation of the right of asylum, a right implicit in the fact that foreigners had seldom been expelled. Dupré, the Attorney-General, commented on this argument:

> The fact that Mr Gonzalez has found few instances of the exercise of that power in the records of the Court, is easily explained. The Governors, in these cases, proceeded by giving an order to the constable, whose business it was to see it obeyed; and the matter was only brought before the court when the individual to be expelled resisted the mandate; but even then the Court never questioned the authority of the Lieutenant Governor but confined its functions to enforcing his order ... It has evidently been the policy of the British Government, in all times, to discourage as far as possible, the settlement of a large French population in this country as being perilous in the event of war. And so rigidly has this policy been pursued, that there is no instance of a declaration of war with France, where the Lieutenant Governor, acting under this law, has not forthwith caused every Frenchman, of whatever position in life, to quit the Island.

Sanders reckoned, not very convincingly, that Gonzalez, in league with Lemoine, Laurent's secretary and editor of *La Patrie*, was a Bonapartist agent trying to stir up the proscrits. But for them, the census question would already have been settled. It is probable, however, that the census was aimed as much against supporters of the French regime seeking the safety of numbers among the proscrits, as against the proscrits themselves. When Laurent asked Love for a list of the French refugees, Spencer Walpole, the Home Secretary, told him to show Laurent nothing.

On 16 September about 40 proscrits, led by Seigneuret, arrived at the Club in Don Street, to oppose sending names even to the Governor. Hugo, who turned up later in the evening with Vacquerie and Pierre Leroux, said that the census would protect them by showing the French authorities that there was nothing to fear, and that if the Seigneuret faction pursued its obstructionist line, he would leave the island. *L'Impartial*, still ostensibly a liberal paper, also supported the census, saying that it would help unmask the agents of Bonaparte.

Hugo's position was helped by the arrival in Jersey on 15 September of Caussidière. Marc Caussidière had been French chief of police in 1848, but had soon sought refuge in England. He was, in Adèle's opinion, a giant who exhaled honesty. He was introduced to Love who immediately ordered wine from him. An agent was sent over from France specially to see what he did, but at a meeting at Don Street he told the proscrits he had only come over to sell wine. He advised them, however, to show by silence their contempt for Napoleon, and to wait for the right moment to strike. He did not mention the census, but he calmed a stormy meeting two days later, which went on till 4 a.m., with this advice:

> I am sorry to see that you all attach so much importance to a measure that appears to me, and to all serious thinking men, simple and just; the Governor or Chief of this island desires to know the number of foreigners here. He does not mention the *refugees* only, but the whole of the foreigners, and instead of sending in your names quietly, you insert, or cause to be inserted, in all the French papers, here and in Guernsey, violent articles that can but only injure the Refugees in general and the Democratic cause. And as I have already told many of the Refugees in London, unfortunately the Refugees fancy themselves of great importance, now I am certain we have none whatever for the English Government, and very little are we thought of or feared on the part of the Despot Louis Napoleon. I do not wish you to send in your names, do as you like, only remember, and remain quiet, that we unfortunately bear a name we do not deserve, that of being turbulent people, opposed to all reasonable measures. Come let us act differently and efface that name. Are you ashamed of your position as refugees, of your names? No, well oppose no longer measures taken for public good, and no doubt taken to benefit you all.

Caussidière tried to arrange for money to be sent from London for poor refugees in Jersey, and for about 60 poor refugees to come from London to Jersey, where the cost of living was low.

By 6 October 240 foreigners, probably nearly all French, had taken Caussidière's advice and registered themselves with the *connétable* of St Helier, the parish where they mostly lived; even so, this must have been an undercount, and it is doubtful what use the census would have been to the British authorities, or what benefit to the proscrits.

Hugo remained a sane and moderating influence on the proscrits, using his personal authority to keep them in touch with reality. On 14 September, for example, he told them that the *Sprightly* might have the task of watching them, but they ought then to thank the English government, for Louis Napoleon would know that rumours of an attempted landing on the French coast were false. Sanders reported that the arrival of the *Sprightly* made the proscrits more cautious. The Bayonne plan was shelved until a move could be made against the government in Paris, but a similar plan seems to have been resuscitated at a meeting on 17 September. Seigneuret, Bonnet-Duverdier and Laflaut, the minority which Sanders called fanatic and violent, planned to form themselves into a secret society and land in France with arms from Kossuth and Mazzini. They said it was 'impossible for so many men to remain exiled from their homes, that they must strike a blow and either die or triumph'. The moderate proscrits rose as a man to object to this threat to the laws of the country which sheltered them, and shouts of 'liars' and 'spies' flew around. The moderates were afraid that the 'violent' faction were Bonapartist spies and agents provocateurs, and made them unwelcome at the Club.

Laurent was so keen to shine that he frequently made a fool of himself. The Paris correspondent of *The Times* reported that 'At a dinner-table in a house in Jersey the fact of the President's assassination was spoken of as certain on the very day it was to have taken place in Marseilles '. It seems that someone present told Laurent who left the next day on the *Sprightly* to tell the préfet. The French Navy sent a war-sloop from Cherbourg to watch the refugees, but Love only allowed it to ride at anchor between tides before ordering it away.[1] The plot culminated in the unsuccessful attempt by Gaillard to turn a multi-barrelled gun on Napoleon while he was making a propaganda tour in Marseilles. Lord Cowley, the new British ambassador in Paris, thought it had all been engineered to win popular support for Napoleon.

If the Paris report meant that some Jersey proscrits knew of the plot, it may have been accurate; Sanders reported that Mme. Seigneuret told the consul at St Malo that Napoleon would not return from the south of France alive. But if it meant that the assassination was plotted in Jersey, then it must have been, as the *Jersey Times* said, a 'fudge', even though the proscrits were daily expecting to be accused of it. *La Chronique* thought the whole story was a fabrication by Laurent to convince the French authorities that there was a threat from Jersey.

An article in the *Daily News* accused the Derby ministry of 'base degrading sympathy with despotism and aggression' by condoning the increase in the costs of passports; and it could indeed be said that by, for example, allowing Laurent to use the *Sprightly*, the British were collaborating with the French. But joint surveillance of the proscrits was negligible, and militarily the two nations were squaring up to each other. Frenchmen were still sketching the forts to which they had been denied entry since August; Cherbourg was being fortified, Granville and St Malo harbours were being improved and there was a suspicious increase in French fishing around the islands. There were reports of 'preparations' in France.

The British government may not have had much sympathy with the refugees, but it was not going to turn them over to the French, still less allow France to attack their sanctuary. Sappers and miners had been in the island for some weeks improving defences, as Hardinge had recommended, and work continued on the harbours at St Catherine's and Alderney. The relatively inconspicuous local militia was increased to 20,000 men. At the same time, the British government did not want to provoke the French by, for example, blatantly constructing more barracks which then housed 800 rather visible British soldiers. The harbours were euphemistically called 'harbours of refuge'. Yet the purpose of the cyclopean works, whatever they were called, cannot have been misunderstood by the French who had many agents in the island, and indeed Cobden, a strong opponent of the Alderney breakwater, thought that it was provocative. The proscrits, for their part, did not have much bearing on the slide towards war. 'The presence of the refugees seems to be rather an advantage than otherwise, since it will be seen as a fair excuse for whatever precautionary measures you might think fit to take', wrote Stanley at the Foreign Office to Jolliffe at the Home Office.

Indeed, the proscrits were not in a position to make any moves against France. Seigneuret could fulminate that he would 'soon let loose a few trained democrats like so many bulldogs or bloodhounds to tear those perjured wretches to pieces', but much of their energy was dissipated in internecine abuse, 'canaille', 'voleur', 'brigand' and 'coquin' being hurled about at meetings which were in a constant state of uproar. The proscrits were deeply divided about what they should do, and the question of how to do it became secondary. Their impotent desperation is epitomised by a proscrit *en blouse*, Doré, throwing a stone at a picture of Napoleon in the window of George Sinel's shop in New Street. 'O, come to my house', said Doré, 'and I will pay you for the glass; but I could not bear to see that blackguard there.'

Sanders thought that all this talk was sound and fury, but he was beginning to be worried about increases in numbers of refugees. Caussidière had already spoken of 60-150 poor ones coming from London to Jersey, but Sanders feared that as many as 1,500 of the 4,590 proscrits in London might come too. Love thought many of them were armed. By mid-October several were arriving by every boat, saying that Jersey would soon be centre of operations. Men like Caillot and Thoré would visit Jersey every month to keep the Jersey proscription awake. Schoelcher, the French Wilberforce, had collected 150,000 francs (£6,000) for a steam printing press to be set up in Jersey.

Schoelcher did manage to establish his press in Jersey, but he soon sold it to Zeno Swietoslawski, a rich Polish exile, who started printing a series of political pamphlets in French, English and Polish, some by Victor Hugo and Alexander Herzen, some by French proscrits in London. Zeno's Universal Printing Establishment, its name written up in several languages, was at 13, Dorset Street with a London depot at Lincoln's Inn Fields.

Zeno published a pamphlet for the *Comité Révolutionnaire des Démocrates Socialistes refugiés à Jersey*, whose principles of liberty, equality, fraternity and solidarity 'would be pursued by all possible means', force not excluded. The Committee, in the opinion of Brock, was made up of the most extreme elements among the exiles, who were left-wing bourgeois radicals rather than revolutionary socialists. In fact, there was no explicit reference in the pamphlet to Napoleon and his regime, and a Home Office official thought it a very harmless document, 'being downright nonsense'. It must have percolated to the Prussian-occupied part of Poland for von Bunsen, the Prussian ambassador in London, sent a copy to Stanley complaining that Zeno had also reprinted extracts from *Ludpolski*, 'The Polish People', a periodical dedicated to the liberation of Poland. Von Bunsen thought that Zeno, who had escaped prosecution for revolutionary activities in Poland, was a major threat and asked the British government to apply laws 'against such persons as abuse the asylum granted to them [by] conspiring against Governts., the allies of Great Britain.'

The British government was no more likely to give in to a Prussian than a French demand to silence the proscrits. In many ways they were less trouble than

Napoleon's agents in the island. The British ambassador in Paris, Lord Cowley, complained to Drouyn about Stoffel and Merliot. Drouyn recognised that these agents had evidently misunderstood 'their duties as well as our intentions, saying things intended to stir up disaffection among the inhabitants against the British Government of Her Majesty, whose subjects they have been for so many centuries '.

Stoffel and Merliot were recalled to France and proceeded to denounce Pierre-Louis Lemoine, French spy and secretary to Laurent, claiming that he was conniving with the proscrits. It may be that they honestly thought that Lemoine, though he had been their paymaster, was a republican, and there are some indications that Laurent himself had doubts on this score. Alternatively, it is possible that Lemoine, who was in contact with the French Embassy in London, was completely reliable, but that Laurent did not take Stoffel and Merliot into his confidence. Perhaps, as Angrand says, they merely wanted revenge on Lemoine.

Sanders who, like the proscrits, called Lemoine the chief of spies, was in no doubt that he, along with Edward Sullivan and Héan of the liberal *L'Impartial*, published the refugees' opinions to gain their confidence, and egged them on so that he could report their sayings to France. There were also various French shopkeepers, Hurel the tobacconist, Mme. Levaillant the grocer, Ollivier the bookseller, Osmond of the Brandy Stores and Auguste Lallour the publican, who would give needy proscrits credit in order to draw them out and report back to Laurent. Nonetheless, when Lallour arrived back in Brittany, he was denounced as a dangerous democrat bound to carry out the threats of the 'Comité de Jersey' against Louis Napoleon.

In this extremely confused picture it is none too clear, even with the hindsight of British and French documents, which of the French people in Jersey were proscrits still opposed to Napoleon, which Bonapartist spies and which merely apolitical. As will be seen, the proscrits themselves did not know, though they were less willing than Sanders to assume that any supposed proscrit who took an extreme or violent line against Napoleon must be an agent provocateur and thus a French agent.[2]

Chapter Ten

The Most Abject Will Reign

Since the beginning of 1852 Napoleon had been hinting of his imperial ambitions. The Senate was assembled on 4 November to amend the constitution and a general plebiscite on the establishment of a new empire was fixed for 21-22 November. The very word 'Empire' reminded the refugees of the first Napoleon and his wars, and seemed to cover an attempt to legitimise the coup d'état, pushing further into the future any prospect of an honourable return to France.

Hugo had already been asked by some democrats in Paris what they should do, and at 8.30 p.m. on 29 October he summoned those in Jersey to decide whether they should vote against Empire or abstain. In a vehement address he said:

> Since the 2nd December, as you know, there have been various polls; what they were and how genuine, that you know also. I used to be member for La Seine, and I have been asked by the electors in Paris what to do about these elections. I have said that ... Republicans should abstain; that absention is a weak word and that Republicans have another duty to fulfil – to rebel. M. Bonaparte is in power. Democracy can only pursue and punish him where it may; more than that is not possible; one can only fold one's arms for the moment, and that line of conduct includes abstention.

Someone suggested that they should vote against Empire. Hugo replied:

> If there is a majority against Empire in a city like Paris or Lyons, will M. Bonaparte, who oversees, counts, controls and announces the ballot let it be known? Will a man who fears candour have enough to publicise his defeat? He will not, as you well know. He will rig the voting. He has already decided in council how many votes he wants. He knows he must announce more than he got on 20 December [1851; 7½ million]. He could not allow people to see the figure go down; that would be a certain sign that his fall had begun ... It is thus useless to vote, to return ballot papers which he will not count ...

Joseph Déjacque, a utopian anarchist who had fought on the barricades in June 1848, said that it was not necessary to address the people who knew only too well what to do, but Hugo replied, 'There are citizens in Paris who brave prison, Cayenne, death ... they cry out for help. And we reply: "You are not the people: the people are those sheep who vote, obey and applaud ...".' No, said Hugo, the true people are those who suffer and fight, and who have the right to tell those who fête the president that they are not the people.

This attack on the inertia and reaction of the common man led Fombertaux to say that the people were forced to subscribe to Napoleon's triumphal arches. Hugo, for all his championing of 'the people', had a Whiggish distaste for demagogic populism. It is significant that he compared the people with that other subject of his study, the sea: both were shifting and fickle. Hugo saw himself as a pilot who needed the people but who feared to be engulfed by them.

After 21 people had spoken, it was agreed that they should record the decision to abstain: but how? In a declaration or a manifesto? Could they speak on behalf of those who had not attended? Pierre Leroux, who had established a pleasant life for himself in Jersey, wanted no part in any struggle, but was for abstention in principle. Finally it was decided by 93 to 3 to make a declaration of absention, and, by another vote, that Victor Hugo, Fombertaux the elder and Philippe Faure should draft it. In fact, Hugo alone wrote the *Declaration à propos de l'Empire*, tried it out on Fombertaux and then read it to a meeting on 31 October. It was carried unanimously to cries of 'Vive la République'. It counselled abstention to the people, since the vote would be rigged anyway, and advised citizens worthy of the name to load their rifles and wait for the right moment. In *Choses Vues* Hugo suggested that ballot papers (which would have been pre-recorded with a 'Yes') would make excellent wads for tamping guns.

Thus Hugo had astutely but forcefully stage-managed the declaration, dispensing with objections from others. He asked Madier de Montjau to arrange wholesale abstention in France, and he thought that the two rival groups of proscrits in London would also go for abstention. Sergeant Boichot, who had come over from London to 'rekindle the enthusiasm' of the Jersey proscription, agreed. He in turn was trying to get support for a letter signed by Caussidière, Pyat and himself in London, which Hugo liked though the other Jersey refugees did not.

The declaration was printed by two counts of the old nobility on 1 November. Laurent got hold of a text which he sent to Drouyn, and he warned the sub-préfet of St Malo and the postmasters of Paris, Calais and Le Havre to expect a great number through the post. Letters with English stamps postmarked in Jersey had to be stopped, and they should watch out for tradeswomen and female relatives of sea captains who, not being subject to a *personal* search, would bring in the contraband declaration.

Count X, presumably one of the printers, showed Hugo how one could wrap a copy of the declaration in the leaves of a cigar and pass it through the customs. It was reprinted, Adèle tells us, before dawn on 4 November in all the populous suburbs of Paris.

Laurent pointed out the last sentence to Love, with its bullets for ballots message, as 'a direct provocation to insurrection'. Love replied vaguely that the authorities would eventually take serious steps against the refugees. He asked Jolliffe at the Home Office if it would be possible to pass a law excluding the Channel Islands as a place of refuge, but he was told that he could not interfere until an overt act had been committed. Laurent, meanwhile, learned that English law did not prohibit libel against foreign monarchs: the injured sovereign would have to start the prosecution himself. Laurent continued to press for a prosecution although the declaration was reprinted in full by the official French *Moniteur* of 15 November, another example of Napoleon's relaxed attitude to his enemies and Laurent's obsessive conception of his duty.

Everyone at the meeting of 29 October had supported abstention, but Pierre Leroux, always ready to rock the boat, said that it had not been carried unanimously because of those absent. Hugo's response was that 'if some proscrits failed to turn up, that was their fault' and, with a quick formula, added that those who did attend were 'the real unanimity'. Laurent was quick to exploit the schism, observing that those who did not come to the meeting thought their names had been taken in vain.

A rumour sprang up that Kossuth, Mazzini, Ledru-Rollin and 'a universal man who has sought asylum in Jersey', would be extradited. Victor Hugo tried it out on his watchmaker:

'There is talk of extraditing Victor Hugo.'

'Yes, Sir', said the watchmaker, not knowing to whom he was talking.

'Do you think they will agree to it?'

'Eh, Sir, Victor Hugo will never be expelled from Jersey. It would be a disgrace for Jersey.'

On 22 November the votes were counted: 253,145 against Empire and 7,824,189 (97%) for, with 63,326 spoilt papers, a suspiciously large majority of the sort that the 20th century associates with one-party states. Hugo repeated his charges that the ballot must have been falsified and that the voters had been cowed, slightly contradictory ideas as it would not have been necessary to intimidate voters if the count was going to be falsified.

'So the most abject, vile and shallow will rule', he exclaimed, adding:

> Peace, say a hundred cretins! It is finished, the thing is done
> The three percent is God, Bandit is his prophet.
> He rules. We have voted! *Vox populi* ...
>
> But who voted? Who held the ballot-box?
> Who clearly watched the nocturnal plebiscite? ...
> They have voted!
>
> A flock driven to pasture ...
> Do you think that you are France
> That you are the people, that you ever had
> The right to give us a master, you heap of brutes!

The piece comes from a collection called *Vengeresses*, later *Les Châtiments*, in which Napoleon is continually called a perjured wretch and bandit. One poem starts with the sublime lines

> Ô soleil, ô face divine,
> Fleurs sauvages de la ravine ...

and ends with the rhetorical thrust

> Que pensez-vous de ce bandit?

Hugo's speech at the Polish banquet on 29 November also referred to Napoleon as a bandit, but he was very vexed by a toast to the death of Louis XVI. As a long-time adversary of capital punishment, he thought that Napoleon should expiate the crime. 'Keep the man alive. Oh! What a superb punishment!'

Louis Napoleon was proclaimed Emperor on 2 December 1852, a year to the day since his coup d'état and on the 48th anniversary of Napoleon I's coronation, a date calculated to wound and infuriate his enemies. The same day the proscrits were offered amnesty and return to France, provided they did nothing against the elected government of Napoleon III, as he was now styled.

Laurent had been suggesting to them as early as 15 August that they should apply for amnesty, but Hugo took an unbending stance now and for the remaining 17 years of Napoleon's rule. On 22 October at the Theatre Français in Paris the actress Rachel had gone up to his box and read a piece by Arsène Houssaye called 'L'Empire, c'est la paix'. This echoed a speech made by Napoleon at Bordeaux in which he had said that the Empire means peace because when France is satisfied, the world is peaceful.

Houssaye claimed that he had written this ode to help him obtain pardon for Hugo whenever he chose to return to France. 'That is', wrote Hugo, 'having the goodness to forecast my disgrace, he first disgraces himself, blowing a trumpet.' Remembering those who died on 4 December 1851, just after the coup d'état, he wrote with acid irony: 'Rest in your coffins! Keep silence in your tombs! The Empire is peace!'

He wrote to Louise Colet, Flaubert's mistress, that 'Some are weakening and accepting an infamous return that the Criminal calls an amnesty. Several were dying of hunger. We supported them with difficulty. They leave after acknowledging that they were led astray by treacherous counsels. I pardon and pity them.' Laurent claimed that the *Comité révolutionnaire socialiste* had threatened them with death; there was certainly a proposal to exclude them from the *Société fraternelle* (if that was the same group). Pierre Leroux refused to make a blanket condemnation of those who wished to return, painting a sad picture of life in the penal colonies of Lambessa and Cayenne, the exiles dying of horrible diseases far from their families. Adèle made the good point in her journal that only those who were rich and could afford to support themselves in exile should be judged for seeking amnesty.

After two hours of griping by others at a meeting, a workman interrupted with: 'That's enough about misfortune, misery, of women and children. For God's sake, it's enough. Don't say anything more about it, but don't join Bonaparte either. We've had enough of our miseries, hardships, hunger and thirst, of our women and children and everything, for God's sake.'

Some did, however, go and join Bonaparte. The official *Moniteur* announced in early February 1853 that 4,312 proscrits had been granted amnesty. Fourteen had already returned from Jersey through grace and favour, but 16 more were still in Jersey. Two of them, César Dumont and Benjamin Colin were astonished to find themselves on the list as they had never asked to be pardoned. Colin, a schoolmaster and founder of *La Ligue*, published a sheet with the names of 20 Jersey proscrits who had returned to France (none of whom had played any part in proscrit politics) and added: 'Note: since the amnesty list in the *Moniteur* confuses under the common name of pardoned, men of heart who never asked for it and those who have, whom History will judge, it is necessary for Democracy that this should be made known. Thus everyone is responsible for his acts.' Laurent arranged for Colin and Dumont to be proscribed again and asked for their passports back. A few more Jersey exiles – Serre, Janin and Changobert – were granted amnesty a short time later, in May 1853.

The French were quick to seek British approval of the Empire. On 5 December 1852 the war steamer *Ariel* arrived in St Helier harbour ostensibly to bring despatches for Laurent and to thank the Guernsey captain, Lefebvre of the *Dasher*, for having rescued three French ships only 12 days before. *Ariel* hoisted the British flag and gave a salute of 21 cannon; Elizabeth Castle then unfurled a French flag with a salute; *Ariel* then saluted *Dasher*. Laurent went to see Love, and *Ariel*'s officers dined with him before going to the theatre, where Hugo was in the audience and the 'Marseillaise' played. All this was rather strange for two countries moving towards war. Love surmised that the principal object of the visit was to get the British to salute the French flag. *L'Impartial* called it a farce; Laurent must have known from his superior in London what was in the despatch; why could *Ariel* not have taken the despatch up the Thames to the French ambassador in London?

This démarche in any case amounted to very little, for it was surveillance business as usual. On 5 March 1853 the French added a third steamer to the Jersey station, and Laurent tried to discover, by flattering Lefebvre, precise statistics of Jersey's oyster fishery, hoping thereby to learn obliquely more about the state of the Navy.

'La Marseillaise', the French revolutionary anthem, had been played some time before, when Lord Hardinge visited Jersey at the end of August 1852, as the battalion of St Helier went down to parade on the sands of St Aubin. But when Colonel Le Couteur, the Vicomte, discovered that Hagemann, the master of music of the battalion, had played 'La Marseillaise' to the *Ariel* officers at the theatre on 6 December, he told him to get a written acceptance of apology from Laurent or be dismissed. This Hagemann did. Le Couteur had not recognised the air at the time because, he said, he was not a musician. M. Alexandre, the leader of the French troupe and Le Couteur himself also apologised to Laurent who passed the matter off, saying that it was a compliment to the *Ariel* officers to hear a French tune being played.

Two weeks later, as Le Couteur recounts, 'The Regt called a play in the evg and I was at the theatre punctual to the hour in uniform, with many of the officers. The band on my order played 3 tunes when the Genl [Love] arrived and God Save the Queen was played. A cry for the Marseillaise was raised above us in the upper boxes and a shameful disturbance took place.' Juliette Drouet said it was 'les Jersyais' who called for it, and *L'Impartial* added that the proscrits themselves were quite still. It was in fact a demonstration against Le Couteur for having forced Hagemann to apologise. Le Couteur, under a calm face, was furious. The band played the 'Chant des Girondins', but there were more cries for the 'Marseillaise'. Hagemann consulted Le Couteur. The musicians prepared to leave the stage, and Le Couteur was hissed and jeered as he was forced to follow Love who had left the theatre saying 'I would rather have that tune played twenty times than undergo such an affront'. Alexandre told the audience that he could not play the 'Marseillaise' without risking his licence, but they began to sing it.

Posters, with Le Couteur's 'signature' upside down, soon appeared saying the 'Marseillaise' would be played on 22 December, two days after the incident. An orchestra was specially hired and a great crowd appeared at the theatre, but Sir Thomas Le Breton, the Bailiff, fearing an uproar, closed it down. A travesty of the 'Marseillaise' was sung outside, with the lines:

> They say that pleasing Bonaparte
> Is Le Couteur's only wish

and the refrain

> Allons, braves Jersiais! Aux méchans résistons!

Three groans were offered for Le Couteur, and the crowd sang the anthem again outside Le Breton's house at Quinze Maisons before being dispersed by the police. A proscrit who had taken part in the demonstration was asked to leave the islands. 'Persons receiving a country's hospitality should *use* it, not *abuse* it', intoned the *Jersey Times*, and even *La Chronique* said that life was being made very difficult for M. Alexandre, the leader of the troupe. Le Breton allowed Alexandre to re-open the theatre on 27 December but he had already lost his bespeak night. A subscription was raised for his actors. He played his last evening on 6 January when there were 'two solitary squealing cries for La Marseillaise from the upper boxes.'[1]

Chapter Eleven

Living Fraternally

To help the poorer proscrits and reduce the temptation for them to seek amnesty, a relief fund was set up at the beginning of November 1852. On Christmas Eve a notice in the *Constitutionnel* asked for gifts for a bazaar to be sent to the paper's office, to Le Maout's the chemist or to Mme. Hugo. A letter was sent by a commission of the Société Fraternelle to mistresses of households asking them to come to the bazaar on 10 February 1853 and bring presents, all of which would be acknowledged. The signatories were Hugo, Leroux, Mathé, Roumilhac, Heurtebise, Biffi, Josse, Fournier, Bonnet-Duverdier and others, most of them moderates. On 17 December 1852 Edmond Bacot, who was to teach Charles photography, bravely made the journey from Caen with trunks full of everything from women's fancy-work, jewellery, glassware, knick-knacks and porcelain, to overalls, cotton caps and his own photographs. This generous present, valued at 2,100 francs (£82), had been assembled by democrats in Caen, none too rich themselves, in a week.

The bazaar, to be held at the Queen's Assembly Rooms, Belmont Road, was postponed to 28 February-1 March 1853, and the *Chronique* announced that respectable Jersey ladies would be running stalls. 'The whole population of our island shewed the greatest sympathy and unrestrained enthusiasm for our sale', Mme. Hugo wrote to Julie. 'Knitwear, embroidery and fabrics of all sorts rained down on us. The charity of Frenchwomen is as nothing in comparison with that of the women of Jersey: it only needed a word in the papers to get the fingers of all the women moving, and each would send not one but twenty things, with a kindness matching the lavishness. There were pennants with "Vive Victor Hugo" and "Honour to the Proscrits".' Adèle added in a separate letter to Julie: 'You know how enthusiastic, hospitable and friendly these excellent English people have been to us.'

The second day of the bazaar was rained off, but the first was a great success, netting 4,000 francs (£160). Five hundred people came, and a full band played in the Assembly Rooms. Mme. Hugo and Adèle ran stalls, and Love arrived with some dignitaries and bought an *objet d'art*, though more out of charity than sympathy, Laurent thought. Only the Earl of Limerick and Sir James Reynett, the cynosures of the island, were missing.

It is not surprising that the *Chronique* had referred to the exiles as 'the martyrs of politics', but even the usually crotchety *Jersey Times* recommended charity, adding that the proscrits 'are suffering for what they consider to be a righteous cause'. Mme. Hugo wrote to Mme. Meurice, who had contributed to it, that the bazaar had even stimulated their social life. On behalf of the Commission, Hugo thanked the 'noble and cordial' people of Jersey, regretting that he could not thank them one by one:

Everyone competed in zeal and goodwill; the women, as always, showed that where the heart is needed, they are the first; most of the parcels and gifts were accompanied by letters or notes stating the profound sympathy of free English and free Jersey people for those still struggling against crime and tyranny. The republican proscrits were deeply touched. Such testimony from such a population goes a long way to make up for injustice and suffering. We thank Jersey.

England's hospitality, so proud and great, gives the proscrit security; Jersey's hospitality, more precious still, adds brotherhood to this security.

It was the high point of relations between Jersey and the refugees.

In this open letter Hugo had said that the relief fund was destined for the most needy proscrits. On the next day the moderates came under attack from the 'fanatics' who wanted the proceeds to be shared out then and there. The Commission wanted to invest the money and give work or the means of earning a living, rather than cash. There was a deadlock and the relief fund was abolished by a vote of 45 to 27. That same day Hugo resigned from the Société Fraternelle since conciliation between the factions was impossible. The unwillingness of the Commission to hand out money was understandable; many of the proscrits were improvident. For example, when the fund was resuscitated in 1854, 160 francs was given to Ribot who bought a new suit of clothes and then got drunk. At that time 11 proscrits were on relief, including Déjacque and Bergounioux.

Trouble between moderates and radicals had been brewing for some time. At a reunion on about 14 February 1853 they had discussed a progressive tax on the rich. Hugo seemed to accept this idea of 'applied socialism' and said he would do what he could, inviting others to do the same. With this tax, the bazaar fund and subventions from Goudchaux, the treasurer of the London proscrits, the principle of the bazaar could become permanent. Hugo then went on to say that although the republican idea embraced equality, it also recognised intelligence, and he later said that Proudhon's dictum, 'property is theft', led to anarchy. Fairly hard up himself, Hugo would have preferred to make personal presents or offer a place at his table, but disliked an impersonal levelling tax. Mathé was more outspoken: he said it was not applied socialism but a swindle. Laurent had reported this schism with satisfaction; and the appearance of real money from the bazaar two weeks later made the schism deeper.[1]

Five weeks after the bazaar and Hugo's resignation from the Fraternelle, the split came out into the open. At the age of 38, Louis-Hélin Dutaillis had died of typhoid.[2] Heurtebise and Dr. Barbier, both like Dutaillis from La Sarthe, came to ask Hugo to speak at the funeral. 'I will speak', Hugo replied, 'if others do not speak before me, and if they do not betray democracy; ask my eloquent friend Pierre Leroux.' Leroux at first refused to make a speech, so Hugo consented.

On 9 April the proscrits met at Don Street and moved off to meet the hearse at New Street and go from there to the Green Street cemetery. As Dutaillis had wanted, the red flag[3] came with the procession, and it was draped with black crepe. Laurent imagined, for some reason, that most of the mourners were surprised and disgusted to see this 'hideous' flag instead of the French flag which had been announced. There was to be no priest and no mass. The pall-bearers were French (Dr. Barbier), Polish (Mikulowski), Hungarian and Italian.

At Green Street Heurtebise made a vigorous speech on the suffering and sorrows Dutaillis had been through because of his inflexible devotion to the Republic. The proscrits cried 'Vive la République démocratique et sociale'. After Mikulowski had spoken, Thomy Piquet made a blistering attack not only on Louis Napoleon but also on the parliamentary republicans, the moderates. Hugo refused to speak after this provocation and left Piquet and 15 radicals in the cemetery. Thirty moderates (Hugo, for some reason, not among them) wrote to *La Chronique* to dissociate themselves from Piquet.

This version of events comes from *La Chronique* and French official papers, but Adèle says that Hugo did in fact speak at the cemetery, saying: 'Look at this red flag; it is the symbol of fire and blood, yes, but the fire which illuminates and the blood which breathes life.' It is possible that she was mistaken, and reported what Hugo said after the funeral for, in *Choses Vues* he writes: 'You complain of the colour of our flag. It is purple, the colour of splendour and unity ... is it our fault if ... when we defended it on the barricades of the law it was covered in blood?'

Laurent deplored the absence of the police at the ceremony and the tone of Piquet's speech. Love told him he would ask the advocate general, Jean Hammond, if the matter could be taken to the courts. The Rev. Philippe Filleul, rector of St Helier, wrote to *La Chronique* to say that he neither authorised nor foresaw the events, and he would in future demand that cortèges be accompanied by a Christian minister, and would ban any speeches. *La Chronique* commented that though what had happened was deplorable, the rector could refuse to supply a minister, but not a burial to anyone who had bought a plot.[4]

Only a few days later Hugo went to see another proscrit, 'worn out with suffering', Jean Bousquet. On 17 April, and at the age of only 33, he died. A meeting was held the next day and it decided to avoid a repetition of the events at Dutaillis' funeral by leaving arrangements to Hugo, Charles Ribeyrolles, Jean Colfavru and Felix Mathé. It was agreed that only Hugo would speak and that he would distance the proscription from the vengeful sentiments of Piquet.

Laurent asked Love to do something about the red flag, but he replied that it was used at funerals in London without any official reaction. Nonetheless, he wrote to the Bailiff, Sir Thomas Le Breton, who got the *connétable* of St Helier, Pierre Le Sueur, to ask the 300-400 people assembled at Don Street not to make a political demonstration. The refugees, encouraged by some Jerseymen, objected to this arbitrary intervention and set off, without a priest, behind the red flag. The bearers included a Jerseyman. The procession, attracting the curious to join it on the way up Rouge Bouillon to New St John's Road, went on to Macpela, or the dissidents' cemetery in St John's parish, just outside St Helier's, whose rector had objected to the speeches and lack of a priest at the Dutaillis funeral. More than 150 were reported waiting at Macpela to receive the 250 in the procession. *L'Impartial* reported:

> The corpse, taken from the hearse, was carried to the edge of the grave, and after it had been lowered and buried, citizen Hugo, whom everyone was so impatient to hear, spoke from the depths of the most religious silence to his audience of 400, with that manly voice with which he defended the infant Republic ... in accents of conviction and fixity of opinion.

Hugo's speech was also notable in that he spoke of God and of the French clergy. After an attack on Louis Napoleon and a recital of the agonies of exile, he said:

> We glorify what is immortal and what is eternal, Liberty and God. Yes, God! A grave should never close without this great, this living word being uttered ... Let the religious and free people among whom we live understand well that men of progress, democracy and the Revolution know that the soul's destiny is twofold, and that the self-denial that they practise in this life shows how deeply they count on an afterlife.

He then attacked the Catholic Church in France for serving and submitting to the regime: a message bound to go down well in an island staunchly protestant since the Reformation. He added:

> On behalf of the Jersey proscrits, who have given me a mandate, and I may add in the name of all Republican[5] proscrits (because not a single true Republican with any authority would deny it) ... that we reject all desire, sentiment or idea of bloody reprisals ... the death penalty, gloriously abolished by the Republic in 1848, odiously reintroduced by Louis Bonaparte, remains for us abolished for ever.

He ended by calling Jean Bousquet a martyr in the cause of human liberty.

With a single stone – justice rather than revenge – Hugo had attacked both the reaction of Louis Napoleon and the vengeance of men like Piquet. The speech, directed alike to the proscrits and beyond them, was a remarkable vindication of the fundamental principles which had led the Republicans to oppose the coup d'état. Hugo reported that both factions of the proscription now revered him, and that the treasurers of both the minority radicals and the majority moderates had told him that he alone could heal the rift. To Louise Colet he wrote:

> I succeeded, as you can judge from this speech, in creating some feeling of unity among the proscription which suffers and is thus embittered and divided. At this moment, I think I can say that there is little agreement on the large questions, and most particularly on the most important of all, the redoubtable question of reprisals.

In fact, the disagreement between Hugo and other moderates like J. B. Amiel who also attacked the death penalty at the funeral and, on the other hand, the Jersey radicals and the London Rollinistes, was as great as ever, and it is doubtful whether Hugo's speech achieved more than a truce.

Laurent reported that it would be printed on fly-sheets and smuggled into France by all possible means, probably by the Béghin brothers. This is puzzling since they were mentioned by Sanders as French spies.

For Laurent, the speech was an attempt to show how Christian the refugees were: 'it is now by sweetness that they hope to make conversions.' He thought Love should send a copy to Palmerston who would see that the proscrits were opposed to all governments, not just the French one, as they had shouted 'Vive la République Universelle'. Laurent pointed out to Drouyn that the 'loopholes' in the 'antiquated' laws of Jersey gave libellers an impunity they would not have enjoyed in England. On 29 April Walewski, the French ambassador, showed Clarendon, the British Foreign Secretary, a copy of the speech but without making a formal complaint.

The Paris paper *La Patrie* said that Hugo's speech described France as covered with political gibbets, and that the disgusted people of Jersey had got up a petition to end demonstrations of this sort. Charles Hugo wrote indignantly to another French paper, *La Presse*, quoting from four French-language papers in Jersey to show what his father had actually said and how respectfully it had been received by the inhabitants of Jersey. He reminded *La Presse* that in 1851 P. Mayer of *La Patrie* had retracted an article insulting *L'Événement*, the Hugos' mouthpiece, rather than face a duel. Now that we are absent, said Charles, *La Patrie* starts to insult us again. Adèle records that the courage of *La Presse* in printing Charles' letter had the best possible effect on the proscription who saw it as the start of France's awakening.[6]

Chapter Twelve

Chastisement and Capital Punishment

As the dismal winter dissolved Hugo neared the end of the political poems, *Châtiments*. 'I have spent the winter composing sombre poems. The work will be called *Les Châtiments*', he wrote to Alphonse Esquiros, on 5 March. '*Napoléon le Petit*, being prose, is only half the task. The wretch has been roasted on one side and I am turning the grill.'

On 31 May 1853, at 11 a.m., Hugo finished it. The title was discussed for some time afterwards: Mané Thécel Pharès, Les Indignés, Le Festin de Balthazar, Les Bonapartides, Route de Toulon, L'Empire au Pilori, and César-Mandrin had all been suggested. Hugo thought he would be accused of pride in imagining that his lines could chastise, but he preferred the title *Châtiments*. So did Vacquerie, François-Victor and Mme. Hugo. He admitted to his publisher Hetzel that he did not mind if they shocked the bourgeoisie so long as they roused the people. *Châtiments*, as we have seen, is largely a collection of polemics against Louis Napoleon. For this reason, two editions were published, both in Brussels; one expurgated, and the other, purportedly published by the Imprimerie Universelle in St Helier, complete.

He added some pieces between 31 May and the publication in November, but May really marked the end of Hugo's period of bitterness. To the warmth of his now assembled family was added that of spring, his first in Jersey; 'even for the proscrit, April will be reborn.' Where his winter poems bemoaned the lot of the proscrit and called down execrations on the head of Napoleon, the effect of the vernal weather was to calm him and lead him to contemplate the beauty of nature:

> Oh! leave me! let me escape on the shore
> Let me breathe in the scent of the rough wave
> Jersey smiles, land of the free, in the bosom of the dark seas
> The gorse is in flower, the lamb crops the green pasture
> The foam throws its white muslin upon the rocks.
> For a moment appears, at the top of the hills,
> Giving its scattered mane to the harsh and cheering wind
> A wild horse neighing to the skies.

Hugo would have agreed with his model, Châteaubriand, who had written of a time exactly 60 years before, 'Spring in Jersey preserves all its youth: it could indeed be called *primevère* as it was formerly, a name which has been left for the first flower (primrose) to adorn it.'

The partial withdrawal of Hugo from proscrit politics and polemical writing coincides with a certain relaxation of tension in the summer of 1853. Laurent again failed to get any undertaking from the British government to act against the proscrits: 'unless there are serious disorders, threats to public peace, authority cannot intervene in any assembly or public reunion, whatever the flag or emblem displayed; as far as libel is concerned, only The Queen has the right to prosecute authors. Injured parties, whether public functionaries or others, can only go for civil, not criminal redress', he was informed.

This was precisely illustrated in a singular event on 1 May which foreshadowed something more momentous. François Ribereaut, described as a proscrit and tanner, declaimed in a tavern in Hilgrove Lane that Queen Victoria was the biggest prostitute in England and that when Prince Albert wanted to enter her room, she told him that she was occupied and to come back tomorrow. This was all overheard by François Coutanche, Jean Jaffray, the innkeeper Constant Lerebour and his wife. Ribereaut was seized and held at the General Hospital. He was formally arrested by *centenier* du Jardin on 3 May. Love consulted the judicial authorities and then, on the Bailiff's advice, expelled Ribereaut summarily to England. Laurent hoped that this would be a lesson to the violent among the refugees, but he was disappointed that the same course of action could not be taken when Louis Napoleon was libelled.

Laurent kept up his watch on the refugees, but there was nothing much more to report than the Hugos' visit on 24 June 1853 to Landolphe, one of the few Guernsey proscrits. Love and Sanders seem to have been uncharacteristically silent throughout this summer, to judge from extant Home Office papers. Love, and shortly afterwards, Sir Thomas Le Breton, did go to see Palmerston, the Home Secretary, and it seems that Love also went to dine with General Renault in France. Hugo, who had every confidence in Love's 'loyalty', did not believe that they could have discussed the question of chasing the proscrits from Jersey, though some feared so.

There were some rumblings, nonetheless. Three of those arrested at Neuilly after an attempt on Napoleon's life (the Hippodrome plot) were said to have come from Jersey. One of those implicated, Jules Allix,[1] later told Hugo that the plot had failed only because they lacked pistols. On 13 June Hugo persuaded the proscrit Schmidt, a tailor from Alsace, who was off to Paris on a forged passport, to give up his plans to assassinate Napoleon. 'I forbad him to do it, and gave him all the reasons.' But Hugo was rather ambivalent about these attempts (there was another on 5 July). 'I start by saying that I have a horror of murder and blood, but if I had wished to kill Louis Bonaparte, I certainly would have done ...' Charles proposed an infernal machine in the Opera House, but his father pointed out that it would destroy the Opera and everyone in it. 'For my part', said Hugo, 'this is what I would do ...' But Adèle does not reveal how Hugo would have assassinated Napoleon.

The composition of the proscrits was changing somewhat. A number of moderates, like General Lazare Meszaros, had left Jersey, while some hardliners from London called Rollinistes after Ledru-Rollin, had arrived. One of them, Théobald-Felix-François Cauvert, used his great fortune to keep together the Société des Plumitifs – the Bureaucrats' Club – set up after the dissolution of the Fraternelle. The Plumitifs were in fact open to those who liked to get drunk, and Cauvert was always good for a drink.

At the proscrits' reunion on 24 July the question of capital punishment came up again. The views of the proscrits were all but irrelevant, since their chances of an early return to political power in France were negligible, and they must have known it. It can only have been Hugo's known opposition to the one issue that most clearly and immediately distinguished the moderates from the radicals, that guaranteed its frequent discussion. Now Filhias, a London Rolliniste, was trying to prevent Hugo from speaking at all. Colfavru brought up the burning question, and Martin, another Rolliniste, said he favoured the death penalty, as he favoured all revolutionary ideas. Charles Hugo silenced him: 'So the scaffold is an idea, is it?' Cauvet then claimed that the Jersey and London exiles had opposed Amiel's speech against capital punishment made at Bousquet's graveside; Hugo said it had been accepted unanimously in Jersey. 'Not unanimously', said the Rollinistes. 'Generally, generally by the majority of the proscrits', replied Hugo.

Charles Ribeyrolles, who had sat on the fence between Hugo and the Rollinistes, now made a generous speech asking Hugo, as a universal man and genius, to speak at the grave of another refugee who had died, Louise Julien. Hugo thanked him and turned back to ask Martin if he supported the death penalty. Yes, replied Martin, one has to respect the vengefulness of the people, which no one dares oppose. 'Except me!' said Hugo as the audience stirred, 'Yes, and I have formally undertaken to do so; if necessary, it will be I that stops the people ... Oh, since you are reintroducing the guillotine, I want mine to be the first head to tumble.' 'Bravo! Bravo!', said Charles to his father. 'Citizen Victor Hugo, I am anxious for the honour of climbing the scaffold with you.'

Hugo produced a further sensation when he reminded the meeting that exactly 25 years before he had demanded abolition in *Le Dernier jour d'un condamné*. He accused Filhias of being two-tongued and jesuitical and, swinging the mood of the meeting against the Rollinistes, he said that his vengeance would make Napoleon suffer for the rest of his life. Amid the applause and in the face of Filhias' opposition, Hugo was asked to speak at Louise Julien's funeral.

Louise-Anselme Julien had died on 23 July. Descended from the old Portuguese family of d'Ataïde, she seems to have married a workman called Asbruck. But she was unhappy, and she lamed herself by jumping from a window. In June 1848 she saved the life of her brother's friend, Julien, whom she later married. By the time she came to Jersey she was already very consumptive and as she lay dying at 20 Don Street, Hugo came to see her. (She had once been arrested for reciting his poetry.) 'Victor Hugo, you are the apostle of democracy and the light of mankind', said the dying woman, 'Victor Hugo, my dream was to see you and bless you. Thank you, Victor Hugo, thank you for having come.'

On 26 July, her cortège of about 70 proscrits made its way to Macpela, where she was buried in the same grave as Bousquet. Hugo's speech, 'one long execration of Louis Napoleon and tyranny', in the words of the *Jersey Times*, began:

> Citizens, three coffins in four months. Death hurries on and God delivers us one by one.
> We do not reproach you, we thank you, Almighty God who reopens, for us exiles, the gates of the eternal country.
> This time, the dear and lifeless being we carry to the grave is a woman.

At this point some mourners moved away, and Seigneuret said to Déjacque, 'What dreams is he talking of?' In the crowd someone said: 'God! There is no God, for the Democratic Republic is atheist. Who asked this poet to speak about God at our graves?'

Hugo, though he hardly knew Louise, paid her a fulsome tribute which he extended to proscrites in general. 'It is not a woman that I admire in Louise Julien, but womankind; the woman of today, woman worthy of the name of citizeness ... the 18th century proclaimed the Rights of Man, the 19th will proclaim the Rights of

Woman.' Even the most sincere democrats, he added, refused women equality of rights. He then raised the cry of courage, insurrection and hope and repeated that when victory came there would be no reprisals. At the end Pierre Leroux came to him and said that the proscrits were sincere in their beliefs, the fruit of the 18th century, and that they had decreed, unanimously, that God did not exist!

It seems that Déjacque also spoke, but without forewarning the others. Heurtebise thought he had an absolute right to do so, but Hugo was afraid that those who spoke without a mandate from the proscription could give them all a bad name. If they did not discipline themselves, he would retire from group politics altogether and speak to France on his own behalf.

His speech was soon spirited into France. Ribeyrolles put copies in envelopes which he ostentatiously sealed with his signet-ring, a sort of camouflage reminiscent of Poe's purloined letter. A tanner called Touron found himself up before the magistrates when a cutting with the speech was found in his boots at St Malo; acquitted, he was nonetheless brought before the court at Rennes which was anxious to contain this sort of activity. Shortly afterwards, Charles-Michel Funck landed at Granville with a forged passport and 36 copies of the speech. Funck was given a year's imprisonment, but Laurent failed to get the Jersey authorities to take any action against his collaborators.

If the authorities in France were getting rather alarmed, it is not altogether surprising. Laurent reported that the 76 proscrits had taken lots to decide who would attack 'the tyrant' at the Tuileries at the end of August. 'We shall be in Paris this Winter', Ribeyrolles told François-Victor. The plot fizzled out, but Love went over to France to hear a request for the extradition of some refugees, presumably those thought to be the most dangerous – Lemaout, Colin, Piquet, Seigneuret and Duverdier. At the trial of the plotters on 7 November it was said that they carried papers showing that the Jersey proscrits were planning a landing in France.

A pleasure trip to Chausey by the *Rose* had to be called off when the captain was told he would not be allowed to land, and a detachment of gendarmes was sent to the island as a precaution. More understandably, a trip by the *Rose* to the heavily fortified port of Cherbourg was also cancelled. Lord Raglan, shortly to become famous in the Crimea, came to Jersey to review the militia and a visiting brigade of the Blackwatch and Northamptonshires. He was concerned that the militia's rusty guns often misfired. The manoeuvres were directed at 'the enemy', and everyone knew who that was.

Sanders reported back to London that Hugo presided at nearly all the proscrits' meetings, and that he had been haranguing some of them from the saddle as they wheeled round him in a circle on the beach at St Clement's. From Hugo's own words, we know that he was in fact extricating himself from politics all the time. An emissary of Ledru-Rollin and Mazzini tried to get Hugo to meet them in Southampton in order to arrange sending 100 proscrits to France. Hugo thought the idea absurd and likely to prolong exile by 10 years; the time was not ripe and money would be better spent disseminating propaganda. On 1 September Sanders reported that Hugo was expected to leave for Portugal in October, preparing for a long exile. He seemed to be tiring of the squabbling in Jersey.

The reports from Sanders are rather repetitive and they give the impression that his sources were on the periphery of proscrit politics. Often he is out of date or simplifies. On 13 September, for example, he reported Hugo, Vacquerie, Leroux, Heurtebise and Beauvais as 'fanatics'. A few months later they were 'no longer thought dangerous', but his new danger list had few notable radicals on it either. Dangerous men, he thought, were people like Ribeyrolles, Duverdier, Seigneuret, Cauvet and Vallière, who preached in low public houses for revolution and against revealed religion. The moderates, depleted in the second half of 1853, were men like Hugo, the Polish General Koziell, Sandor Teleki, Colfavru and Felix Mathé. Love, who probably got most of his information from Sanders, was beginning to worry about their intentions. He even saw a threat from the proposed Institut Français de Jersey, which had Hugo as one of its referees. Love implied to Palmerston that it would not be teaching French, as it claimed, so much as spreading hostility to all monarchies and creating 'mischief among the lower orders.'[2]

Chapter Thirteen

The Spy and the Man

On the night of 20 October 1853, Victor Hugo was just returning from posting some letters in St Helier when he ran into a distracted group of four proscrits, Felix Mathé, Rattier, Arsène Hayes and 'petit-père' Henry. 'We are going to execute a man', said Mathé. Hugo who had left the Proscrits' Society and did not live in St Helier had no idea about whom they were talking.

The man was Julien-Damascène Hubert, supposedly a proscrit of 2 December. He had gone first to Brussels and then to London, where he lived in penury. For the first two months he had slept on a flagstone in front of a fireplace where there was no fire, without mattress, covering, or even a handful of straw, in his damp and ragged clothes. He accepted his hardships stoically and in silence. He had reacted with indignation to the offer of amnesty on 5 February 1853, and not having much sympathy for either of the two proscrit factions in London, he left for Jersey in April. As he disembarked in rags he was seen by Eugène Beauvais who took pity on him and put him up at his inn at 20 Don Street. Hubert just asked for a bundle of straw, a corner in the attic and a morsel of bread, but the generous Beauvais offered him a room and dinner. 'How shall I pay you?', asked Hubert. 'When you can', said Beauvais.

Beauvais arranged for Hubert to give grammar lessons, and made him buy himself an overcoat and shoes. Hubert was no trouble to Beauvais, being self-effacing and drinking only water. He was allowed seven francs a week by Gigoux, the treasurer of the Fraternité, but he refused offers of money from François-Georges Gaffney and others because there were some proscrits worse off than himself. Thus he was respected for his self-denial and apparent integrity, though it was known he had extreme views: the Republic, he said, had been betrayed by Louis Blanc, Felix Pyat, Ledru-Rollin and Hugo; after the fall of Bonaparte, a massacre lasting six months would be necessary.

Hubert had made a close friend of Arsène Hayes. One day at the beginning of September 1853 he had taken Hayes aside and, speaking in a low and mysterious voice, told him he was going to Paris the next day. As an amnestied proscrit he had a valid passport and enough money, 20 francs, to get to St Malo, after which he would make straight for Paris, forgoing meals if necessary. In fact he took 6 days to get to Paris by a circuitous route through Rennes, Nantes and Angers. In each place he introduced himself to the leading republicans as a representative of the Jersey proscrits. His own miserable condition was plain to see, and naturally they confided their secrets to him.

Towards the end of September he returned to Jersey on the *Rose*. He took Hayes aside again and said that a coup was planned in Paris; everything – men and money –

was ready but the people trusted only the proscrits and he therefore needed to recruit 10 good men from Jersey to lead them. He said much the same to others, adding 'I'm only telling *you* this'. By this flattering but implausible technique he recruited Hayes, Gigoux and Jego. He also saw Felix Jarrassé, Fameau and Rondeaux. He told them that their expenses would be taken care of when they landed at St Malo. The day of departure was fixed for 21 October.

Hubert's ineptitude was his undoing. Going to Hurel's the tobacconist he found Rattier and asked him to change a 100 franc note. Rattier could not, nor could Hurel. A fact, probably not known to Hugo who gave us this account, was that Hurel was a French spy and it is quite likely that Hubert and he were disturbed in a secret discussion by Rattier's entry into the shop. Hubert must have managed to change his 100 franc note, for he paid his lodging-house keeper with a fistful of shillings and half-crowns. He refused , however, to repay 32 francs lent him by his mistress, Mélanie Simon of 5 Hill Street, instead showing her a portfolio full of yellow and blue banknotes worth 3,500 francs (£140) to tempt her to follow him to France. Mélanie did not want to leave Jersey and said she would denounce him as a spy if he did not pay her back. Hubert laughed: 'Try to make them believe that! Go ahead!' 'My 32 francs!', said Mélanie. 'Not a sou', replied Hubert.

So Mélanie denounced Hubert to Jarrassé. Hubert was still on fairly strong ground: there was no hard evidence against him and no one could believe that this austere and disinterested man could be a spy. But as details began to emerge, the truth dawned on the proscrits. Rattier told about the 100 franc note; people wondered why Hubert had gone to Paris in such a roundabout way; and a Jersey person reported that he had seen Hubert rubbing shoulders with police and customs men at St Malo. Mélanie Simon showed Jarassé a letter from Hubert in France in which he gave his poste restante address in Paris as 30, Rue de l'École de Medicine. Mathé's son saw this and exclaimed: 'But I used to live there. One of the lodgers was a policeman called Philippi'. His friends Hayes and Gigoux warned Hubert that there was gossip that he was a spy, and told him that he should bring the matter into the open with an enquiry. The impassive Hubert eventually agreed.

Thus on Thursday 20 September the Fraternité met and elected Mathé, Rattier, Rondeau, Henry and Hayes to carry out the enquiry. Witnesses and evidence were produced, but there was no proof, only suspicion. Rondeau asked to see Hubert's suitcase at 20, Don Street, which Hubert said contained his personal effects and some socialist and republican literature. Rondeau examined the case, but forgot to look for the writings. Meanwhile a carpenter from Queen Street had come forward to say that he had made a false bottom to Hubert's case. Asked why he had had this done, Hubert replied: 'To hide the democratic tracts, of course', and quietly agreed to another visit, hardly taking his pipe out of his mouth. His laconic manner convinced his friends of his innocence.

Hayes and Henry, assisted by Hubert himself, took the trunk to the carpenter. When the panel was removed, they found copies of Hugo's speeches, *Bagnes d'Afrique* by Ribeyrolles, and *La Couronne Imperiale* by Cahaigne, as well as Hubert's three or four successive passports, the last issued in France at his request, and a collection of papers concerning Ledru-Rollin's society in London, *La Révolution*. They also found a letter, dated 24 September 1852, which Hubert had shown to the proscrits as a testimonial, addressed to the préfet de l'Eure, rejecting his 'shameful' offer of an amnesty, and calling Louis Napoleon a miserable oppressor. But a second letter, dated only 6 days later, emerged. It was addressed to the same préfet for forwarding to Paris, saying that he, Hubert, supported Louis Napoleon and would render great services if he restored to him the 300,000 francs lost through his family's services to Napoleon I.

Hubert continued to smoke imperturbably. Rattier, who was going through the papers, was about to discard a letter beginning 'My dear Mother', when he noticed on the next sheet a letter addressed to Maupas, the Minister of Police, saying that the préfet de l'Eure had not replied to his two letters, that he had not wanted to take advantage of the amnesty before finishing a booklet attacking the republican proscrits in London and again asking for the money due his family. Rattier looked up at Hubert. He had taken his pipe out of his mouth and great drops of sweat glistened on his forehead. 'You are a spy', said Rattier.

That very day the French papers had arrived with news of 300 arrests in Paris alone, and many more in the country, including republicans Hubert had been to see. Gaffney recalled how the police had descended on his mother in Le Havre to search for a copy of *Napoléon le Petit* and could only have been tipped off by Hubert or one other proscrit. It looked as though Hubert had been informing on the proscrits in London and Jersey for quite some time.

Hubert went back to 20 Don Street. He found Pierre Leroux, Philippe Asplet, a St Helier *centenier*, Hayes, Henry, Gigoux, Rondeau, Heurtebise and Beauvais. As Hubert went to collect his room key, Hayes cried 'There he is!' and all fell on Hubert; Gigoux slapped him, Hayes grabbed him by the arm, Heurtebise seized his tie and gripped his neck. Beauvais, his benefactor, would probably have stabbed him, had Philippe Asplet not seized Beauvais's arm. Hubert was set free and some proscrits went off and wept.

This was the story told to Hugo at about 9.30 p.m. It did not deflect him, however, as he went back to Marine Terrace for a session of table-turning. Just before midnight, as he was going to bed, the bell rang loudly. It was Beauvais to ask a reluctant Hugo to come to a meeting in judgement of Hubert. He did not welcome this interruption of routine, but he went off with his sons and Beauvais, collecting other proscrits living at Havre des Pas on the way. Groups of people were talking softly outside Don Street as proscrits continued to arrive from all directions. Nearly all had assembled in the upper room and were whispering together gravely. 'Where is Hubert?', he asked. 'Behind you.' Hugo saw a man of about 50, his face ruddy and pitted with smallpox, with very white hair and a black moustache. His eyes were motionless and from time to time he took off his hat and wiped his forehead with a large blue handkerchief. Hugo had probably met him in Brussels and he had been to Marine Terrace once or twice; but Hugo did not now recognise him. As the room filled up, no one would sit next to Hubert. Nearly all the moderates were present, but most of the radicals stayed away. Jules Cahaigne was asked to preside. He was a man who had been on the barricades, an old conspirator. Young at heart, with his old Cossack's face, his snub nose was framed by a grey beard and white hair.

There was a deep silence. The two feeble gas-jets showed a singular scene: 70 Jersey proscrits sitting, standing, squatting or leaning on their elbows, some on benches, others on chairs, stools, tables and window sills, some with arms crossed and their backs to the wall, but all of them pale, solemn, austere, even sinister. Under the windows looking out on to Don Street there were three tables: one for Hubert, one for Cahaigne and his secretaries Jarrassé of the Fraternité and Heurtebise of the Fraternelle, and one, illuminated by a tallow candle, for the prosecution led by the advocate Rattier. On the mantlepiece, beneath a rack full of pipes, among a mass of large posters – Charles Leroux's advertisement for his bindery, Ribot's for his hat shop – was a placard demanding 'prompt justice', signed by Hubert. The sash windows were open at the top to let out tobacco smoke; here and there glasses of brandy and flagons of beer stood on tables. Glossy caps and hats of straw or soft felt hung from rows of nails around the room. An old draughtsboard, whose black and white squares were almost indistinguishable, hung from the wall above Hubert's head.

Hubert, at last taking off his hat, answered Cahaigne's slightly theatrical questions easily and with precision. The evidence was read out to threats and imprecations from the proscrits. Hubert admitted nothing. When the draft letter to Maupas was read out, there was absolute silence: some clenched their fists, others chewed their moustaches. As Rattier finished 'signed Hubert', there was an explosion of rage and grief. 'These are the criminals who have been betraying us for 20 years', cried the elder Fombertaux.

A large blond man climbed on the table, pointed at Hubert and said 'Death to him, citizens'. The cry was taken up, others adding 'Throw him in the Seine' or 'Throw him in the sea with a millstone round his neck'. Hubert refused to explain the letter, but denied emphatically that he was a spy. He said, with a firm and sincere voice, that he was a republican, that he had nothing to do with the arrest in Paris, and that they had overlooked the first letter to the préfet rejecting amnesty, while the second letter, offering his services to Napoleon, was only a draft which he had not sent; and that his brochure *The Republic Impossible because of the Republicans* was unpublished. When accused of betraying republicans in Paris he replied 'It is you who ruin our friends in Paris, by shouting their names in an assembly where there are obviously spies. I have nothing more to say'. This caused further uproar and cries for his death.

At this point Guay, a shoemaker and communist, a man with a long black beard, pale complexion and deep-set eyes, said slowly and gravely that they were in a country with laws which should be obeyed; instead of executing Hubert, he said, they should shave Hubert's hair and moustache and, when they grew back, cut off a centimetre of his ear. This was a strange notion since mutilation would also have been contrary to the law, and it produced a lugubrious burst of laughter. Avias, a large man with a fierce expression (later to be accused of treachery himself), got onto a table and proposed taking lots to see who should finish off Hubert. Various people offered themselves without a lottery. There was no dissenting voice. Then Victor Hugo got up and said:

> Citizens, the man whom you fed, supported and loved has been found a traitor. The man you took for a brother is a spy ... You are caught by a simmering indignation and grief. I share that indignation, I understand that grief. But beware. What are these cries for death that I hear? There are two Huberts: the spy and the man. The spy is base, the man sacred.

'I see', Cauvet interrupted, 'that's it. Always kindness.' 'Yes', said Hugo, 'kindness. Power on one hand, kindness on the other: these are the two weapons I mean to put in the hands of the Republic.' Hugo continued to articulate but channel the proscrits' anger. Maupas's banknotes and the brotherly mite of the proscrit had mingled in the pocket of a man who 'recruited in Jersey for Cayenne'. But, said Hugo, they should not spoil this occasion when M. Bonaparte had been found in flagrante, by killing a man. 'Touch him, wound him, hit him only, and public opinion will turn against the proscrits.'

When Fillion suggested action not words, he was silenced by cries of 'No violence'. While those extremist proscrits who had attended looked angrily at Hugo, Hubert looked gloomy. He heard Hugo's voice dominating the proceedings and assumed that Hugo and his sons wanted to mutilate or kill him. As the meeting appeared to be breaking up, Fillion came up to Hugo and said that they should not cry from the rooftops that they were going to execute a traitor; four of them should just do it. Before Hugo could reply, the meeting made a decision that moral, not physical, punishment was called for. Even allowing for some *esprit d'escalier* it is clear that once again Hugo's oratory and personal authority had completely moved the meeting.

Cauvet, one of the radicals from London, would not, however, give up. He pointed out that Hubert would now be free to return to France and betray more people. 'There is no need to kill or release him', said Beauvais on an inspiration. 'I have lodged and fed him since April, more or less for nothing. Tomorrow morning M. Asplet will handcuff Hubert and hold him in prison for debt, unless he produces one of M. Maupas's banknotes.' The meeting insisted on searching Hubert, and then prepared a declaration saying he was a member of M. Bonaparte's police. Hugo refused to sign it until all had guaranteed that no harm would come to Hubert. It was not until 11 November that they unanimously adopted a motion on 'l'agent provocateur Hubert'.

Cauvet offered Hubert his pistol. When Hubert refused it, Cauvet offered to shake his hand; Hubert refused that as well. He was led off to prison by Asplet. Hugo got back home just as dawn was breaking and he, Charles and François-Victor finally went to bed at 7 a.m.

The next morning Laurent went to see Asplet to ask for the release of Hubert as an illegally arrested Frenchman. 'For debts', replied Asplet, showing the order signed by George Helier Horman, the Deputy-Vicomte. 'Do you want to pay it?' asked Asplet. Laurent hung his head and left. He pleaded with Drouyn to intercede for Hubert who had been 'maltreated and locked away' by the proscrits, but did not do more. He was not unduly worried that Hubert had been exposed; there were other means of information-gathering, English and French.

La Chronique considered that but for the courage of the Hugos, Hubert would have been defenestrated. Charles indignantly replied that neither he nor his brother 'prevented Hubert from being thrown out of the window. If, incredibly, such an intention had been formed, the whole Assembly would have prevented it'. This is consistent with the account in *Choses Vues* though, strangely, Hugo recorded in *Mes Fils* somewhat later, that his sons had saved Hubert's life. Hubert was not at all grateful to Hugo for his part in the business. In a long and unconvincing letter to *La Réforme* he tried to explain away the evidence, and said that he had heard Hugo's voice dominate the meeting which intended to kill or mutilate him. Was this normal human ingratitude or misunderstanding, or was Hugo's account in some way incomplete?

Hugo wrote that it was Hubert's destiny to be fed by others, for it would cost the proscrits six pence a day to keep him in prison. When Hubert was released on 9 May 1854, because they could no longer afford his upkeep, Hugo said 'I am delighted: I am against prison, even for spies'. He had found a letter from Hubert among his papers with this sentence: 'Hunger is a bad counsellor.'[1]

Chapter Fourteen

The Law of Progress

As winter 1853 drew on, the proscrits became exercised by the Eastern Question. The origins of what became the Crimean War lay in an obscure dispute between Russia, Turkey and France about the right to protect Christians in the Ottoman Empire (and not, as has been said, because Tsar Nicholas I refused to address Bonaparte as 'Mon Cher Frère'). Turkey did not declare war on Russia till October 1853, and the British and French did not enter it on Turkey's side until March 1854. This conflict was to have the greatest consequences for the proscrits.

Sanders reported on 1 September 1853 that they were hoping France would fight Russia and thus remove troops from Paris. The London refugees had decided to offer their services to Turkey but in Jersey, especially among the 'lower class' of refugee, the mood was against it. Those who wanted to enlist in the Foreign Legion in support of Turkey were not opposed, but told that they would receive no help from the relief fund. Xavier Durrieu, on his way to another exile in Spain, consulted the 'chiefs' of the proscrits, but must have found them in two minds. Some were happy to see the Cossacks in Paris, while others felt that Russia was the greater evil and that they should support Napoleon vicariously through his Turkish ally.

The intentions of Russia were very much in mind when the 23rd anniversary of the Polish uprising was celebrated on 19 November 1853. A committee of the captive nations was appointed: Mazzoleni (Italy), Swietoslawski (Poland), Teleki (Hungary), and Fulbert Martin and Bianchi (France). Hugo could not decide whether to go, for he had been very much annoyed by the toast to the death of Louis XVI the year before, and he was afraid people would get drunk and toast the death of Bonaparte. The entry fee for the banquet was one shilling and the tables at the *Hotel de Ville* in Don Street were laid for one hundred and fifty. The numbers of proscrits were eked out by English and Jersey sympathisers. The walls were adorned with revolutionary dates.

Speeches lasted long into the night, and even the most solemn ones were interrupted by the sound of dance music from the ballroom below. Hugo, the Jerseyman Wellman, the Pole Jancewitz and a protestant clergyman spoke, as did Colfavru, Durrieu, Ribeyrolles, Butharyn, Bianchi, Leroux, Cahaigne and Colin. Robert Wellman said that Jersey would always have the honour of keeping the bodies of Bousquet and Julien and that the island, small as it was, knew how to look after her refugees and defend them, even against great nations. This speech, which *La Réforme* called a 'brûlant discours', was received with much emotion and feeling. After Xavier Durrieu and Ribeyrolles, Leroux replied with a heartfelt harangue which the reporter of *L'Homme* could not get down, to be followed by Hugo with an extended attack on the Tsar. The choice was between a Cossack and a republican Europe, but Nicholas

71

would succeed only in uniting the whole of Europe against him, thereby bringing down all thrones and ushering in a United States of Europe. 'No more frontiers, customs posts, wars, armies, proletariat, ignorance, misery.' Like the freedom of Poland itself, it was a noble vision, still 130 years later only partly realised. Bianchi, a Rolliniste, got up and said that Hugo's 'European Revolution' and 'law of progress' was so much rubbish, but this intervention, said Adèle, was a fiasco. Laurent noted that Hugo's speech attacked not only Russia, but also the British and French governments. One hundred thousand copies of the speech were printed for distribution in France.

At this banquet a new mirror of proscrit life made its appearance; the 'Journal of Universal Democracy', *L'Homme*. The title may speak for itself, or it may refer to Bonaparte, 'l'homme tel qu'il est', who features in every edition. The paper seems to have been founded by Ribeyrolles and Luigi Pianciani. On about 10 November Ribeyrolles asked Hugo for a poem from *Les Châtiments*, which had not yet been published, for his fledgling journal. Hugo did not want to take the freshness out of *Châtiments* just to please Ribeyrolles, and did not wish to make the other island papers envious. Nonetheless, pieces from *Châtiments* appeared almost immediately in *L'Homme*, as well as in *La Chronique* and *Le Constitutionnel*. The first issue, dated 30 November 1853, appeared from the presses of the Imprimerie Universelle. There was no difficulty in recruiting foremen, printers and editors for the new paper.

L'Homme included pieces by leading republicans in Jersey and London, accounts of meetings and declarations, extracts from books, advertisements for proscrit businesses, courses and concerts, book announcements and a London newsletter from Philippe Faure. One looks in vain, however, for any reference to Jersey affairs, even those involving the proscrits; the prose is abstract and often bombastic, a series of somewhat lacklustre tirades against absolutism. The Sûreté Generale in Paris got their copy from Laurent; the Home Office from Sanders.

The circulation in Jersey was no more than 100 and the main audience was in France. On 30 November Jean-Pierre Aubin disembarked at Granville and on him were found two copies of *L'Homme* and a letter from the proscrit Roumilhac to Mlle. H. asking her to send the papers on; Aubin, the Jersey papers reported, had a distribution list. Aubin got a month's imprisonment and a 100 franc fine which the higher French authorities thought too lenient. Aubin was also said, by Hugo, to have a copy of *Les Châtiments* in his lining, and the smuggling of the edition, complete or expurgated, created a flurry of correspondence between Laurent, the préfets and the Ministry of the Interior.

The French government in fact kept two spies, probably Héen of *L'Impartial* and Magueraud, by now shunned by the proscrits, in addition to the two kept by Laurent. The Sullivans were still at work too, and would investigate when told by the French authorities of people in France who belonged to secret societies and corresponded with Jersey proscrits. Among the events no doubt reported by the spies would have been the visit to General Le Flô of two other generals, probably Orleanists; the rumour that Pierre Soulé, a French radical who was now U.S. ambassador to Madrid, had sought help in Jersey for an attack on Cuba; and the accusation that the refugee, A. C. Wiesener, was an Austrian spy.

Love, for his part, never told Laurent all he knew, and when he thought he could dispense with Sanders, Laurent asked for the French spies to redouble their activities. London appears to have sent other detectives or agents, named Leise and Larindon, though Sanders re-appeared in Jersey later.[1]

Chapter Fifteen

Truly a Sinner

A series of mysterious fires in Guernsey had culminated, on 18 October 1853, when a man entered the house of Mme. Elizabeth Saujon, murdered her, stole her ring and everything of value in the house, and tried to set light to it. One John Charles Tapner was seen leaving the house; he had no alibi, and an incriminating hair, along with traces of blood, were found on his clothes. The various tapers and resins of the incendiary were discovered at the place where he lived. This was immediately a cause célèbre; the Jersey and Guernsey papers were full of it and for the Jersey proscrits, after months of hypothetical discussion, here at last was the real issue.

Tapner, a 'handsome Englishman, a charming young man who had a position and a good income', according to one description or, in Hugo's words, 'a sort of gentleman', was born into an honest family, his father religious, in 1823 at Woolwich. He had sunk to thievery and murder through debauchery, wine and gin. He lived with two sisters, one his wife, the other his mistress, and he had insured himself and his wife to the hilt, which all seemed rather sinister. He was now a clerk in the Royal Engineers.

After 13 sessions during which they ran up a bill for £19 5s. at the Royal Yacht Club for refreshments, the Royal Court of Guernsey unanimously condemned Tapner to death, the sentence to be carried out on 27 January 1854. Tapner, who had gone through the court proceedings imperturbably, returned to prison and asked for his dinner, a pipe and a pack of cards 'to kill time'. The next day his friends tried to persuade him to ask for a pardon. 'What is the point', said Tapner, 'if my request is granted, what will I get? A commutation! I prefer death to transportation.' After refusing several times, he agreed to petition for mercy, and when this arrived in London, the Home Office asked for more information; the Guernsey court therefore stayed the execution to 3 February. Tapner seemed quite resigned, and even discussed the manner of his execution with his gaolers.

This was the opportunity Hugo was waiting for. His eloquence which saved Hubert from, if not death, violence, would be engaged to rescue the even more detached Tapner. On 10 January he wrote *Aux habitants de Guernsey*, and he wrote it on his own because it was so difficult to get the proscrits to agree any document, let alone one on the most divisive issue.

> Channel Islanders, we proscrits of France ... venerate in you work, courage, the nights spent at sea to feed your wives and children, the calloused hands of the sailor, the sunburnt forehead of the labourer, France whose sons we are and whose grandsons you are, England whose citizens you are and whose guests we are.

He castigated the death penalty as a relic of the idolatrous times when men built cromlechs and dolmens; why, it had even been abolished in Tahiti. He reminded them that a murderer in Jersey, Jacques Fouquet, had been pardoned and came to repent of his crime. 'Guernseymen! What Jersey has done, Guernsey can do.' François-Victor, with his uncritical filial piety, told Hugo: 'I do not know how to tell you of the enthusiasm of the proscrits for your address on Tapner. They were delighted because it exonerates them of murder and impiety in the eyes of France.' Nonetheless, Famot's proposal to make a deputation to thank Hugo was voted down, so the Rolliniste faction were making their views known.

For Hugo, it was a matter of principle too, and he admitted to Louise Colet that he was not interested in Tapner the assassin as such. Tapner knew of Hugo's involvement and asked that he be thanked, and he may have been aware that a petition of 600-700 signatures had been drawn up, and that the issue was dividing Guernsey. In Jersey, Hubert, languishing in the debtor's prison, accused Hugo of hypocrisy in defending Tapner when he had given him such a rough ride. The *Jersey Times* misunderstood Hugo in a rather different way, not realising that his opposition to capital punishment was unqualified. 'We go to a great extent with M. Hugo on the abstract question of the death-punishment but, while the law is what it is, we can not see the slightest ground for commutation of the sentence passed on Tapner – certainly as vile and horrible a convicted murderer as ever passed from dungeon to the gallows.'

Hugo knew, in any case, that his effort was doomed. 'The Guernsey people are very kind; nevertheless Tapner has exasperated them; there have been several fires in Guernsey. All are, rightly or wrongly, attributed to him ... I do not think I will save him.' On 28 January, when Tapner's petition had been rejected, his attitude to visitors, many of them clergymen, changed slightly. He wrote to the Bailiff to protest his innocence, and asked the court to delay his execution; it was again postponed, this time to 6 February. Hugo was inclined to imply that the reprieves were due to his 'epistle' to the Guernseymen, though it seems likely that this was, at most, a weak and indirect factor. He tried to get Paul Meurice in Paris to get it published in *Le Siècle* and *La Presse* to 'touch the honour of the English'. Then he adds, in a telling phrase, 'it should be possible, I think, to save a man's life in England without M. Bonaparte's finding it wrong'.

Even the Guernsey papers did not print the epistle. Tapner's lawyer, Thomas Falla, wrote to Hugo to say 'Your noble, generous and eloquent address to Guernsey has not, I blush for my country to have to say it, had any effect, any happy result ... What has made me most indignant in this affair is that ministers of religion, of whatever sect, have all refused to sign the petition ...' The ministers were already working on him and when, after the second reprieve, Tapner no longer categorically denied his guilt, the Rev. Mr. Bouverie reduced him to tears by asking him to pray that the true culprit be delivered to justice. In reply to a written question from the Rev. Mr. Pearce, whether he was sufficiently implicated in the death of Mme. Saujon to recognise the moral justice of his sentence, Tapner wrote: 'I was'. The Bailiff was not too pleased with an acknowledgement of only the moral justice of the court, but an admission, on the eve of the execution, that he alone was responsible for Mme. Saujon's death, gained Tapner his third and last reprieve, this time to 10 February. Tapner asked whether the executioner was competent and was told that he had proved it by hanging one Béasse in 1830.

At daybreak on 10 February 1854 Mme. Hugo woke up thinking of Tapner and prayed for him. Tapner's last moments with his wife, who condoned his relations with her sister, were harrowing. 'Mais qui donc a sondé tous les mystères du pardon?' wrote Hugo. Tapner had been awake for four hours when, at 7.50 a.m. on 10 February, he left a note for his wife:

Dear Mary,

I feel happier and happier as the time draws nigh. I throw myself on the mercy of God, and hope to be saved by the blood of Christ which was shed for sinners, and truly I am one,

            Farewell,
            John.

As Tapner was led down to the garden where the scaffold was, a group of 150-200 'privileged' spectators gathered. (Mr. Pearce later told Hugo that it was thanks to his epistle that the wretched man was not made to process through the streets first, the cord around his neck.) Supported by Mr. Pearce, Tapner walked firmly with his head held high and behind him came Mr. Bouverie sobbing. Tapner walked firmly up the scaffold steps and helped the executioner, Rooks, fit the rope around his own neck. But as the trap was sprung, a gruesome scene unfolded. After hanging at the end of the rope for a minute, Tapner moved his arms and legs. Then he raised his hands, which had become untied, up onto the edge of the trap and twice tried to lift himself up by the hands and one knee. Rooks pushed him back, but the wretched man did not die for four or five minutes.

The Governor, Sir John Bell, admitted that the execution was 'bungled' and added: 'in execution by hanging according to the usual antiquated and disgusting mode there is no certainty that the criminal will be spared the suffering of protracted struggles even when Calcraft himself is employed.' Palmerston commented that 'a man ought not to be four minutes struggling with Death; the Extinction of Life ought to be instantaneous.'

The execution could hardly have been better contrived if the Guernsey authorities had wished to prove that the death penalty is a barbarity. A long pamphlet published by Brouard on the trial and execution of Tapner ends with some pertinent arguments against capital punishment, still fresh today. The death penalty is monstrous because we should not take away what we cannot give; human judgement is fallible, and the death of an innocent is irreparable; it is useless because it has never deterred – theft was more common in times when thieves were hung, and statistics show that crimes become fewer in countries which have abolished the death penalty; it is absurd because it transfers sympathy from the victim to the condemned man; it is savage because it does not allow the criminal to repent. Hugo's argument, much embellished, is really only the first: that all human life is inviolate.

Hugo brooded long over the execution. Just after the first reprieve he had interrupted his meditations several times to say 'The death of this man weighs on me'. Then he said 'Palmerston will pay dear for it'. Mme. Hugo replied 'He is old and feeble. He does not know what he is doing.' Hugo said 'You are mistaken; he is not more than 68. I dined with him in 1846 at Pasquier's. He was then 60 with white hair, but having all the manners of a young man.' The day after the execution he wrote a long open letter to Palmerston beginning 'Monsieur' and containing these lines:

Once many years ago, I dined with you. The memory of that occasion, I imagine, has gone from your mind. I, on the other hand, retain a vivid memory of it. What struck me most about you was the exquisite way in which your cravat was arranged. I was told that you were famous for your tying of knots. I realise now that you are skilled also in tying knots for other people ...

He asked why Guernsey could not spare a man when Jersey had pardoned Caliot, Thomas Nicolle, Fouquet and Edward Carlton.

Walewski, the French ambassador, had been to see Palmerston on 8 February, and Hugo assumed that the lack of any further reprieve must have been due to Bonaparte's veto. The *Jersey Times*, robust as usual, said that the French Emperor had as little to do with Palmerston's decision as had the Emperor of China or the man in the moon, and Hooker, Hugo's unsympathetic biographer, questions what interest he supposed Napoleon had in hanging a Guernsey convict, and attributes his 'childish supposition' to blind hatred of Napoleon. It is of course true that the French can have had no interest in Tapner as a man, though it is possible that they might have said or hinted that they would be pleased to see Hugo thwarted, and it is possible, and a distressing thought, that Hugo's intervention might have been a factor in the decision not finally to reprieve Tapner. Palmerston might have been provoked by the letter and its didactic tone. Hugo himself thought that Palmerston was 'furious' at being called Sir and not My Lord, a blasphemy in English eyes, and Adèle sees this solecism as the reason why the Jersey papers did not print the letter. The letter seems, however, to have tilted the scales in Canada when a man condemned to death, Julien, is thought to have had his sentence commuted when Hugo's letter was published there. One man who was not impressed by it was Macaulay; he thought Hugo 'a greater ass than Carlyle'.

In December 1855 Hugo went on a pilgrimage to see Tapner's condemned cell, place of execution and grave. He picked a handful of grass from the tomb and placed it in his wallet.

Behind the exaggerations of Hugo's letter to Palmerston was a simple truth; Palmerston was a strong supporter of Napoleon and indeed had been dismissed from the cabinet in 1851 for approving the coup d'état. He was now back in the cabinet as Home Secretary and this was a bad augury for the proscrits. The official *Moniteur* announced that on 19 January 1854 Napoleon had sent the *Ariel* 'to show our flag in Jersey'. The new commander, M. de Beaulieu, met the Governor, and on 20 January officers from the ship helped to put out a fire at the house of Mrs. Bichard at Charing Cross. Laurent said the visit was a success, and *Moniteur* announced that the Bailiff would soon go to Granville to thank Napoleon. *Ariel* made another visit at the end of January, when four officers, de Beaulieu, Letimbre, de Maindreville and Davy, dined at Government House before going on to a fancy dress ball. The *Jersey Times* began to speak of Laurent as 'the respected vice-consul', and there had already been much fraternising with officers from *Ariel* and *Le Daim* when, on 27 March, England and France declared war on Russia.[1]

Chapter Sixteen

Macpela, Spain, America

On 24 February the proscription celebrated the sixth anniversary of the abdication of Louis Philippe, with a banquet at the *Hotel de Ville* in Don Street. The menu was chicken, stew, salad and wine for 1s. 6d. and speeches were again interrupted by sounds of dancing below. There was a certain pathos in the proceedings which could point to no achievements, no hopeful developments. Hugo could only look forward to the United States of Europe and when he asked 'Who wants the Universal Republic?', the audience chorused 'Everyone'. But when Roch Rupniewski wanted to recite some Polish verse, Ribeyrolles would not have it as the French would not understand it, and sharp words were exchanged. Unity was more an idea than an intention.

The proscription was suffering from death, desertion and division. 1854 saw it almost decimated with five visits to Macpela cemetery. Another proscrit was dying of consumption; François-George Gaffney told Hugo, who came to see him in his lodgings in Belmont Road, to go and find somewhere to live in Spain and he, Gaffney, would follow on later. After some more talk he turned to Leroux and said: 'Ah, I was talking to him as one talks in company. Can't you see I'm dying? And I want to die.' On 8 March he did die, aged only thirty-five. About 60 proscrits went to Macpela, Hugo not among them; there were no priests or prayers, and obsequies only from Bonnet-Duverdier. Their flag, 'their red emblem of blood and massacre', said the *Jersey Times*, 'waved in perfect keeping with the miserable scene.'

On 5 May it was the Polish printer Teofil Izdebski, born rich and noble, now finished by poverty and consumption, who took the last journey to Macpela, proceeded 'with the usual bad taste ... by the dirty red flag', as the unrelenting *Jersey Times* reported. Zeno Swietoslawski, who had employed Izdebski as a printer, spoke of his courage in his last days as he struggled to finish setting the type for *Le Peuple Polonais dans l'émigration*. Hugo did not speak, neither did he at the next funeral, Cauvet's, when Ribeyrolles spoke. Cauvet was a rich and generous Rolliniste who had clashed with Hugo over capital punishment. 'A man was buried today who hated me', wrote Hugo, who used to avoid Cauvet but had gone to see him at all hours during his fatal illness of pleurisy aggravated by drink. On one visit Hugo was offended to see pictures of Mazzini, Ledru-Rollin, Schoelcher and others, but not his own which he had presented to Cauvet a while before. 'From now on, I will not give my portrait', said Hugo. After Cauvet's death Hugo immediately agreed to write to Cauvet's family to ask them to spare, from his 'immense' fortune, a pension of 600 francs for the woman who had looked after him devotedly for 10 years. Ribeyrolles came up and said 'What you are going to do, Citizen Victor Hugo, is a very good thing, the more so as Cauvet was not your friend like ours, as you might even have grievances against him, and yet you forget all that in the circumstances.'

Hugo did not speak at the funeral of the mechanic Jean-Pierre Drevet either, when Théophile Guérin did, but at the funeral of Félix Bony, his friend and riding instructor, Hugo finally agreed to make a speech, after trying to get out of it.

> *Victor Hugo* There is a physical obstacle. I have a pain in my knees and I cannot walk, and I have a very important task which I do not want to disturb.
>
> *Charles* What? Writing a speech is nothing. A matter of two hours.
>
> *Victor Hugo* Those two hours will disturb my train of thought.
>
> *Hennet de Kesler* M. Hugo, in spite of what you have just said, I agree with your son that it would be useful if you spoke. No one could do it better than you, and that's what a great number of proscrits are saying now.
>
> *Victor Hugo* No. Ribeyrolles could easily take my place.
>
> *Kesler* He does not have your authority; we've already seen that ... will his voice, like yours, be heard in Berlin, Vienna and St Petersburg?
>
> *Victor Hugo* I have already spoken: I do not want to wear out. There will be more anniversaries in a month and I will be more or less forced to speak. I prefer to keep silent this time.

Bony's friends met at his house in Georgetown, and set off for Macpela. Among them was Teleki who had taken over Bony's riding school to give him an income during his illness. Adèle was alone at home; Marie, who was dressing her, pointed out the cortège following the red flag, as it passed down the road across the fields from Marine Terrace. When Hugo spoke he shouted at the end 'Vive la République', and a Jerseyman added 'God Save the Queen'. A reporter from the *Morning Advertiser* at the funeral told Charles or François-Victor that, but for the particular affection for Queen Victoria, her reign could be the last. Later the Bailiff gathered the 'magistrates' and denounced Hugo's speech.[1]

Though Hugo had spoken defiantly at Bony's funeral, he had only with difficulty decided not to leave Jersey altogether for Spain. He knew Spain well and spoke the language fluently. At first he had regarded Jersey as a temporary stop on the way to pursue the sun in some Iberian land; just after arriving he was talking of Madeira or Tenerife in a year's time. Later it was Gibraltar and perhaps Spain. Sanders reported that Hugo planned to leave for Portugal in October 1853, but then learnt that he would be refused permission to go to Spain because of his insulting remarks about Eugénie de Montijo, Napoleon's Spanish wife. Laurent reported, however, that Hugo would not after all go as he was involved in composing the *Album de Jersey*. Hugo might have opted for Portugal rather than Spain as Schoelcher had been refused entry to Spain and hoped to go to Portugal instead.

Early in 1854 there was a rumour that he would go to Portugal, but he wrote to Coppens that he would not consider it before autumn. Laurent guessed, probably rightly, that he was staying put because he doubted the reception he would get after the suppression of the popular revolt of Saragossa and, as Hugo wrote to Louise Colet, he was loth to leave the sight of France.

A month later Mme. Hugo wrote to Paul Meurice that her husband's dream was 'the Midi, the sun, Spain'. But the Junta of conservative generals, supported by a popular revolt, received a serious check with the defection of the opportunist Baldermero Espartero. On 17 August he wrote to the Junta:

> I would come to Madrid with this letter if I were not held back in Jersey by the trouble of a literary work. As soon as I have extricated myself from this publication, in a very little time I hope, I shall be at pains to take advantage of your gracious invitation which I look on as a glorious call.

Charles was all for going as soon as the Spanish government granted the Junta's wish and gave Hugo asylum. Ledru-Rollin, said Charles, 'would have left immediately if such an honour had been offered him. Ledru-Rollin must be furious that the Spanish prefer you.' Charles continued: 'I will not miss Jersey. I will not be sorry to leave it at all. I will be no more sorry to leave Jersey than I was to leave the Conciergerie (prison). It is a mistake to think that one yearns for the sad times of one's life and the places where one has suffered.'

> *Victor Hugo* You are wrong. I think it is necessary to regret things and learn how to do so. I will miss this house, the Terrace. I will not forget this pleasant life, the great freedom one enjoys here. Here one feels free. To crown it all, we have the sea and the sky.
> *Charles* Jersey may mean freedom, but it also means inactivity. I need to set up barricades, fire guns, go to Spain, make a stir, create a fuss. I don't like Jersey life: it is too calm. Life is pointless if one doesn't use it.

Victor Hugo nevertheless said it was by no means certain he would not go straight away. 'Maman, get ready to pack', he told his long-suffering wife.

Like Guérin and Kesler, Hugo was corresponding with Xavier-Durrieu in Spain. He told Hugo how the Espartero reaction had shattered his illusions and how England and France were putting pressure on Spain to make life difficult for the proscrits there. Since May at least, the consul for Spain in Jersey, Charles Le Quesne, had stopped issuing passports. Advice came to Hugo from many sides: Béranger suggested going to America where at least Hugo would be known; Hetzel reminded him that cholera was raging in Spain. Schoelcher, on the other hand, advised him to go immediately 'while the iron was hot' and become a 'cabeza'. Hugo must have been very tempted by the idea of Spanish sunlight and the offer of a country house on the banks of the Guadalquivir from Enrique de Laza.

Xavier-Durrieu advised Ledru-Rollin, who had condescendingly agreed to place himself at the head of the proscrits in Spain, that all he could do was to wait in Portugal. Hugo had already decided to wait in Jersey and see what happened to 'this quasi-revolution'. He was prepared, as Vacquerie put it to Meurice, to let 'the water flow under the bridge of Spain'. He did not in fact go, and probably no Jersey proscrits other than Xavier-Durrieu, Mathé, Le Guevel and Royer did either.

Many, on the other hand, had asked for a free passage to America. Love considered that 'their departure would rid the island of some of the worst and most violent description of refugees'. The Home Office had no funds for this, but Clarendon, the Foreign Secretary, agreed to their 'removal' using his office's funds. The applications, according to Sanders, caused 'a panic among the Chiefs who are losing some of their best men', and it was only pride that kept the chiefs in Jersey. Fifteen proscrits and their families wanted to leave for America, but by November it was decided that only the most 'dangerous characters' would qualify for a free passage. Ribeyrolles was offered an editorship in New York; General Le Flô applied, unsuccessfully, for a Belgian passport, and Teleki, Jarrassé, Jancewitz and Bulharyn planned to leave as well.

Ribeyrolles, who did not in fact go to the United States, excused those who fled as they could only survive in Jersey on the charity of others. Laurent gloated that the Fraternelle chest was quite empty and that those with neither fortune nor profession were in deepest misery. He noted, as he had after the bazaar in February 1853, that they felt bitter about the rich proscrits who did not practise the fraternity they preached. There is, however, a disingenuousness about Hugo's postscript to the question of further migration. 'As for me, America is fine and if it suits M. Bonaparte, it suits me too.' Hugo, it is true, had suggested a fantastic notion of assembling proscrits in America and attacking France from there, bu he cannot have had any intention of living in America.[2]

The proscription had been deeply troubled by the Hubert affair; how could a man they had tended betray them? Now in 1854 there were two more spy scares. Avias, who had lost a foot at the time of the coup d'état and had set up in Jersey as a dyer, had shown the police the inn where the proscrits amused themselves on Sunday. Avias had known Hubert well, but when Hubert was unmasked he had protested most strongly against him, no doubt as a camouflage. On 17 August he was in the police court for drunkenly resisting arrest, and he said that he had just returned from Guernsey to 'get Victor Hugo's guts'. The judge, Philippe Le Gallais, summed up: 'You had barely disembarked when you expressed atrociously hostile intentions to a gentleman who lives in this island. Such conduct cannot be tolerated.' At the same time Jean Colfavru, journalist, lawyer and professor of philosophy, who had an impeccable republican record, stood accused of being a police spy. Pierre Leroux reckoned that a code-name used by a spy was an anagram of Colfavru, but there the evidence ended. Duverdier, Barbier and Zeno were against Colfavru, and even his friends could not find words to defend him. At one meeting Leroux made a number of insinuations. When Colfavru jumped up and said 'You are an old scamp and slanderer', they had to be separated. Bony and 25 others left the meeting in support of Colfavru and, as Hugo said to his family, 'How can it be proved that one is not a spy?'. He gave Colfavru the presumption of innocence but rather offended him, when they were alone, by saying 'The unjust accusations against you render you interesting'.

The refugees were still riven with dissension, the moderates against the radicals, the republicans against the socialists, the bourgeois against the poor. The bourgeois, who included Hugo, did not want to go back to France at any cost, but then they had money. Le Maout suggested again the idea of a progressive tax, but the bourgeois did not like the idea and Hugo could only suggest an international appeal. Hugo, who mixed mostly with other bourgeois and whose most frequent visitor was the royalist Le Flô, was subject to a sort of whispering campaign. 'Victor Hugo is a peer of France', they said, 'a viscount, a nobleman. Call him a democrat? Listen, he treats princes and the House of Orleans with respect.' There was also a rowdy element among the proscrits who would interrupt him with bursts of laughter or rude comments if he read from his works. At Juliette's, one of them, Charrassin, said that Hugo had taken refuge from the firing during the coup d'état:

> That's not true, said Juliette furiously. I was with him in the streets when he shouted his defiance at the troops. You are lying, Monsieur.
> Be quiet, old girl! Your food is what we want, not your talk.
> Citizen, shouted Hugo, you have gravely insulted the woman who saved my life. Get out!
> All right, Citizen Hugo. You won't see me again and I won't have to listen to your sublime nonsense.

After resigning from the Fraternelle in March 1853, Hugo had tried to keep on good terms with both factions while disengaging himself from both of them. He was annoyed that they never elected him president of a commission. Now he sensed that Ledru-Rollin was trying to take over leadership of all the French proscrits. Rollin arranged a meeting in London for 1 March 1854, but Hugo thought it was very cavalier to have given very short notice. Furthermore, Rollin still supported the progressive tax and possibly the death penalty; these ideas would not only alarm the French nation, but lead to the public washing of dirty linen, which would give comfort to France. Meetings just caused strife: the London proscrits had them and quarrelled, the Belgian proscrits had none and remained united. Finally, Hugo had not been treated by Rollin with deference, he who had sacrificed position, fortune, friends and family. 'What do the Republicans matter! I want the Republic ...' The meeting was postponed for a fortnight, but when Hugo heard that the Belgian proscrits were not going to London, he decided not to do so either.

The Jersey proscription was in a parlous state, and the nervousness of the authorities seems ridiculous. They were worried about Hugo's planned visits to the Ecréhou and Pater Noster reefs, and concerned about the secret society called La Marianne (the Guillotine) which was egged on by the proscrits in Jersey and London, and which aimed to 'put into practice the most insensate theories of communism'. There were rumours that Hugo had spent a fortnight in Paris, and that two of the Opéra Comique conspirators were in Jersey. Laurent, who was spreading the rumour that Hugo got drunk every night, reported to Love and Drouyn that Hugo, as head of the provisional government, was preparing an invasion.

The proscrits had acquired a six-ton boat, the *Amelia*, to smuggle pamphlets into France. Zeno had paid £50 for it, buying it in the name of Seigneuret's wife, a Jerseywoman, and it was to be manned by Seigneuret and Charles Hugo. On 9 May 1854 it left St Helier harbour to anchor in St Brelade's Bay. Perhaps Laurent thought (or hoped) that this was the first move of the provisional government, for he sprang into febrile action, convinced there were arms aboard. The French coast was alerted: *L'Éclair* set out from St Malo, *Ariel* from Granville and *Myrmidon* from Carteret. The whole Breton coast to Morlaix was prepared. Laurent tried to get Jersey ships to give chase, and rumours spread that a 100-gun frigate was about to land a regiment of refugees. Absolutely nothing happened, and Laurent lamely explained that he would not be surprised to learn that the proscrits were fishing from *Amelia* to divert attention and make the maritime watch relax. How he supposed that a boat of six tons and 60 proscrits could land in, let alone invade France, cannot be imagined.

The *Amelia* may have been a damp squib, but the *Rose*, always on the move in the bay of Mont St Michel, was subject to strict surveillance. Heurtebise, who had eluded the French police before, was arrested at Port Bail with a false name and passport. He claimed he had been denounced by Aimée, a former servant of Teleki. Jarrassé, who had unwittingly been carrying 'seditious papers', was arrested on landing at Granville. The *Jethou* was discovered with six cases of *Napoleon le Petit*; the captain, Ferbrache, Jeffroy, for whom the books were destined, and Crepin, who had shipped them from Jersey were all arrested.

The French hoped that their new ally would expel those who were causing so much trouble, but that point had not been reached. The entente was flowering in every other way; *Ariel*, *Le Daim* and *Pelican* made regular visits and in May the Governor raised a toast to Napoleon III. In July the *Jersey Times* reported, but could 'scarcely believe', that Napoleon himself wanted to visit Jersey, and Love visited Granville and went on to Paris to see Persigny, the Interior Minister. In October Hugo was told that his house would be pillaged if he did not illuminate it when, as was expected, Sevastopol fell.

Just as the war retrieved Louis Napoleon's fortunes and popularity in France, so in England he suddenly became the man of the moment. In July Merimée found London decked with dreadful pictures of Louis Napoleon and Eugénie. 'When a foreign dictator suppresses the freedom of the press and imprisons his political opponents without a trial', writes Jasper Ridley, 'the only way in which he can win temporary forgiveness of the British establishment is by becoming their ally in wartime. *The Times* abandoned its virulent campaign against Louis Napoleon and praised him lavishly, lauding the efficiency of the French army and the Emperor's wise policy of alliance with England and his loyalty in the struggle against the common enemy ... For the first time, Louis Napoleon's complaints about the activities of the refugees in Britain were sympathetically received by the British Government and press. They warned and denounced the refugees in Jersey who published incendiary pamphlets against him.'

A visit to England by Napoleon had been in the air since mid-November 1854. The *Leader* reminded its readers of how the *Times*, *Chronicle* and *Daily News* had denounced the coup. It suggested inviting the revolutionary Armand Barbès, who had just refused a pardon, at the same time as Napoleon's visit. Love assumed that Hugo was behind the idea, and told Drouyn that dangerous people had come from London to discuss an attempt on Napoleon's life there. Martin Bernard was expected in Jersey and on 17 December Hugo and some others were on the quay waiting for someone who could only be Barbès. Barbès did not come, and Laurent, who had cried wolf once again, took his worries to Love who said that he was waiting for an inspector from London, who would be particularly welcome as some proscrits had threatened bloody reprisals against Lemoine for something he had written in *L'Impartial*. Love and Sir Richard Mayne, the London commissioner, were vying for the services of Sanders whom they found very useful. Mayne was winning at this point, as Sanders had been back in London since April. Sanders returned on 1 December 1854 to the relief of Love who found the local police 'worse than useless', but Palmerston soon ordered Sanders' recall. Sanders had been trying to discover how the proscrits were smuggling papers through the fishermen of Rozel.

What was certain, however, was that some French merchants in Jersey, Poirier and the Béghins, Prosper and Napoleon, were getting papers to Mme. Macon, a commission agent in Granville. May, the British consul there, was told that papers had been found on the cutter *Princess Alexandrine*. The method must have been successful because Walewski, on 13 March 1855, complained to Clarendon, the Foreign Secretary, that the circulation of pamphlets was getting wider. Love managed to discover, without Sanders' help, that the refugees were still plotting to assassinate Napoleon and form a universal republic. They were still awaiting Barbès and Martin Bernard, and they were greatly agitated by Napoleon's plan to go to the Crimea. Napoleon had decided to assume personal command of his army at Sevastopol, and to become commander-in-chief over Raglan who 'by his delays, his uncertainties, and his resistance to all decisive combinations, is a permanent obstacle to every serious enterprise'. Both French and English ministers tried to argue him out of the idea, and he agreed not to go until he had paid a state visit to Victoria.

At the meeting of 24 February 1855 marking the 7th anniversary of 1848, Hugo again described the universal republic, the crime of the coup d'état and the resulting horrors of the Crimea, but he did not attack English figures by name, rather praising England, with France, as mentors of civilisation. The speech was read to a chartist meeting in London, organised by Ernest Jones, Hugo having excused himself because of his poor health after the rough winter. It must have been plain where Hugo still stood on the question of assassinating Napoleon from a reading of the speech, but Drouyn interpreted it as an incitement to insurrection.[3]

Chapter Seventeen

A Personal Quarrel

The Tapner affair had been the first direct confrontation between Hugo and the English authorities; the next began with his speech on the tomb of Felix Bony which percolated to Palmerston. The third started with the banquet to celebrate the 24th anniversary of the Polish uprising of 1830, when Hugo described the rivers of Crimean blood and the appalling conditions of the troops, all of which he attributed to the coup d'état. In London Kossuth made a parallel attack on the conduct of the war, and his and Hugo's words came to the attention of Sir Robert Peel, son of the great statesman. Referring to France's greatest poet in the House of Commons on 12 December 1854, Peel said:

> This individual has a sort of personal quarrel with the distinguished personage whom the people of France have chosen for their Sovereign, and he told the people of Jersey that our alliance with the French Emperor was a moral degradation to England ... If miserable trash of this kind is to be addressed to the English people by foreigners who find a safe asylum in this country, I appeal to the noble Lord the Home Secretary whether some possible step cannot be taken to put a stop to it.

Hugo's immediate reaction was one of fury. When his wife asked him to pass the bread, he threw it at her. 'Good God, what is wrong with you?', she asked. 'Nothing', said Hugo, turning pale. Then he said:

> This is the end, the son of Robert Peel calling me an individual, but it won't make me waver. Palmerston, furious at having been called *Sir* instead of *My Lord*, has gone to Paris to plot my expulsion with L. Bonaparte ... Little Robert Peel, who is Palmerston's friend, will have spoken of it in the House. Well, let him expel me; I would welcome it ...

The radical paper *Reynold's News*, hinting at Peel's intimacy with Lola Montès, said that it was ridiculous to refer to the coup as a 'personal quarrel'. *Reynold's* would have been nearer the mark if it had said that by referring to a personal quarrel, Peel skated over the question of why Hugo had a political quarrel with Napoleon. Hugo saw Peel as a dummy and responded by turning on the ventriloquist, Napoleon. There was indeed a personal quarrel, he said, the age-old quarrel between the judge and the accused. Peel's remarks he saw as the germ of the prosecution of the exiles. Ribeyrolles too detected in the speech a threat to the proscrits' freedom of expression. If so, he wrote in *L'Homme*, we will make a second exile and bid farewell, saying: 'England is no more!' Not surprisingly, Hugo refused to receive Peel and his wife when they visited Guernsey some years later.

Incensed by the idea of the visit, Hugo penned a long and fustian 'letter to Louis Bonaparte':

> What bait are you going to offer this illustrious and generous nation? What clawing blow are you premeditating against English freedom? Will you arrive full of promises as you did in France in 1848? If you want to know, the alliance apart, what this people think of you, read its real papers, those of two years ago.

In a further attack on the war he said that 'Napoleon III had caused more harm to England in a year of Alliance than Napoleon I did in 15 years of war'. The letter was published in *L'Homme* of 11 April, and in England announced by the bookseller Truelove at Temple Bar with a poster. Truelove's windows were broken and he was threatened, and the poster was torn down though probably not by the 'Paris police' as Hugo, with typical exaggeration, claimed.

Laurent feared an assassination attempt in London, and there was talk of a demonstration at Dover. Love gave orders to prevent any Jersey proscrit from going to England, but some met and were dispersed at Dover, where Prince Albert greeted Napoleon and Eugénie as they stepped off the *Pélican*. Other proscrits were arrested in London, though the leaders there, Louis Blanc, Ledru-Rollin and Pyat had decided to lie low.

The weathervane *Times* had quite forgotten the coup d'état now and greeted Napoleon as:

> the friend and ally. We see the man who has restored order, prosperity, and power to his country in the course of two or three years. We see the man who does what we, with our boasted self-government, our Parliament and all the apparatus of a free constitution, cannot do, whether in the conduct of his armies abroad, or in the execution of great and beneficial works at home.

Napoleon and Eugénie were also well received by the crowds and *Partant pour la Syrie* was heard all along the route. At Windsor they made a great fuss of the children, and the crafty emperor turned his charm on Victoria who found him 'so modest' and 'good humoured and amusing'. The queen found herself 'dancing with the nephew of our great enemy, the Emperor Napoleon, now my most firm ally, *in* the *Waterloo* Gallery'.

Louis Napoleon returned to France with scarcely an untoward incident, but a week later, as he was riding in the Bois de Boulogne with Eugénie, an Italian from the Papal States, Giovanni Pianori, fired a pistol at him and missed. With great sang froid and sense of destiny Napoleon told senators who had brought a message of sympathy that he was not afraid: 'until I have fulfilled my mission I shall be in no danger'. The attack showed, all the same, how precarious his rule was, and made England realise how much the alliance depended on Napoleon's continuing power and popularity. He, for his part, realised what would happen if he was killed in the Crimea, and he abandoned the idea of going there.

A magistrate from La Manche came over to Jersey on the *Ariel* because Pianori was supposed to have spent a few days in the island. A correspondent in the *Jersey Times* suggested an address to the emperor after the 'diabolical attempt on his life' but *L'Impartial*, now run by Lemoine, complained that the attack had been glorified by some of the writers who had taken refuge in Jersey. Indeed, a proscrit had written a verse invocation to Pianori's deed. Laurent asked for the expulsion of the refugees.

Open hostility to Louis Napoleon in France was risky, and it surfaced only in jokes and gossip. Some called him Badinguet – the loafer – thereby risking a prison sentence. Eugénie was La Badinguette, and this was the title of a song supposedly by Henri Rochefort that began to circulate after her wedding. In the poem La Badinguette has five or six hundred fathers and, as a proud Andalusian red-head, will sell herself only for the crown of France. It was published in early 1854 in a Jersey paper, but it was only when it began to circulate in St Helier in July 1855 that the authorities decided that they had got to stop it. *Centenier* du Jardin was sent to seize copies of the song, although there was no Jersey law to prevent its publication and sale. So when one shopkeeper, probably Hurel, who was French though not a proscrit, resisted du Jardin, he was threatened with Love's supposed summary powers to banish foreigners. On the same day, a *centenier*, presumably du Jardin again, was sent to serve an expulsion order on the proscrit Benjamin Colin, who wrote poetry and was thought to have written 'La Badinguette'. Colin denied authorship and added (according to Laurent, ever ready to divide proscrits) 'Why don't you go and see Victor Hugo? He has written much nastier things than I have done'. The seizure of the song was meant as a warning to the proscrits, and it put them on their guard, hindering Sanders' intelligence gathering.

Love did not quite know what more to do. He had assembled Jean-William Dupré the Procureur General, Jean Hammond the Advocate General and John Le Couteur the Vicomte, but they could agree only to pardon the sellers of 'La Badinguette' although Love did 'admonish' one and put him under police surveillance. He found others selling the song openly and thought it 'indiscreet' to act, without further authority, against them all. *Centenier* Philippe Asplet later told Love that 'La Badinguette' had at first provoked laughter but that 'your Government, by prosecuting it, is turning it into something serious'. Sanders, however, reported that the refugees were printing 10,000 copies for posting, which was obviously not a laughing matter for either government.

Sanders had not come to look for copies of 'La Badinguette' but for the brother of the Pianori, who had been guillotined for his attempt on Napoleon's life. Pianori's brother had allegedly come from America to see Luigi Pianciani, an ex-representative of the Rome Constituent Assembly. Pianori's brother's house was watched, though it was said that he never spent two nights at the same place, staying with Pianciani, Teleki and Hugo. Some said he had already moved on to France on 31 July, others that he was still in Jersey on 9 August; and there were rumours that he had been arrested. Sanders left Jersey without even finding him, and it is possible he was never there. The French authorities were nonetheless ready for him, and Clarendon was able to reassure Persigny, the French ambassador in London, that Pianori's brother was not after revenge.

The Pianori and Badinguette affairs gave Love an opportunity for scaremongering. The refugees were demoralising the youth of the island, he wrote to Sir George Grey, thus turning them into republicans and infidels; the refugees would end up by alienating them from England.

> Some of the refugees say that day is not far distant when the islands will again belong to France, that upon the death of the Emperor there will be a democracy and a war with England in which the United States will join. The West Indies will be given to the United States, and the Channel Islands, as a commencement, to Democratic France.

The Bailiff, Sir Thomas Le Breton, was also worried about their effect on the 'middling classes', and he told Love that he, as Governor, could expel any foreigner who, after due warning, threatened 'the peaceable population'. In fact Love got his information from Sanders, who now said that the refugees were 'quite put aside by the Jersey people', and it seems as though Love was looking for any excuse to please the French government, even if it meant standing Sanders' reports on their head.

The British government was abandoning its formal and legalistic stance towards the laws of Jersey because 'it only encouraged the refugees' to do otherwise. The

French authorities were told that Love would take decisive action, and expulsion was on the cabinet agenda for 9 August. Palmerston wrote on 14 August to say that the exiles should be sent away from the Channel Islands where they were making more trouble than they could in London:

> The best way would be to send them off gradually. The most violent first, the rest by instalments afterwards. The identity of language & similarity of Race give them Powers of Mischief in those islands, together with the nearness of the islands to the French coast, which they could not hope for in England.

Love was told to discuss it with the Bailiff and consider warning the 'most obnoxious and violent' refugees to refrain from anything that might give offence and, if they did not, to expel a very few of the 'most conspicuous'. In 1843 the Governor of Guernsey (and author of the *History of the Peninsular War*), Sir William Napier, had expelled a Frenchman, Le Conte, a move which was very unpopular in the island; but no one doubted that Love, given a pretext, could do the same. Unfortunately for him there was no pretext and, what was more, the proscrits were being egged on by Philippe Asplet who, as a Jerseyman, could not be banished on any pretext. Jean Dupré, the Attorney General, did not think that the charge against Asplet – speaking disrespectfully in public of the British government and Napoleon – would even stand up in the Royal Court.

But when Sir George Grey, the Home Secretary, Sir Charles Wood and Sir Maurice Berkeley visited Jersey around 23 August to discuss military matters, Grey complained to Love about Asplet's friendship with the proscrits. On 27 August Love summoned Asplet ostensibly to discuss an incident during a sham fight on St Aubin's sands in which an old man, Bannister, had struck a horse whose rider, trooper Bosdet of the South-West Militia, then hit Bannister with the flat of his sword. At the end of the meeting Love drew Asplet aside to berate him for the behaviour of the proscrits. Asplet immediately counter-attacked:

Philippe Asplet May I further ask Your Excellency this question (let us forget about Victor Hugo). I know several of these gentlemen. They are honourable people who were honoured in their own country. One day, they were driven from their homes without a word of explanation, without any formality; they were thrown out of France, in danger of dying of hunger in a foreign land; now, do you expect these men to admire and praise the present Government of France?

Love (half-heartedly) No.

Asplet These men have always obeyed the laws of the land, and I and my colleagues owe them, as we owe all citizens, the protection of the law. I will not hesitate to exercise the authority confided in me against those who disobey the law, as I have done for the only one who has been charged so far.

Love There is a paper here, *L'Homme*, edited by the refugees, which publishes articles which are wholly hostile to the government of an ally.

Asplet I know it; I even subscribe to it. It publishes articles by Kossuth and other writers which are published in English papers, and no one up to now has imagined that they could be prosecuted.

Love Since you know these men, you would do well to tell them to mind they do not commit a blunder and to watch what they write, or I shall be compelled to take the most rigorous action against them.

Asplet I shall say nothing to them, Your Excellency. If you wish to take police action, you should address yourself to the *connétable* who will take the necessary steps.

John Gardner (Love's secretary) You do realise, *Centenier*, that you are obliged to obey the Governor's orders?

Asplet I have already told the Governor that if his orders are sent to the *connétable* of St Helier, they will be given all the attention they merit.

Love (after a pause) Are you a republican?

Asplet I am a Jerseyman, Sir; and I fully accept the institutions guaranteed by the protectorate of England; I challenge anyone to say that I have ever spoken ill them.

Love I understand, however, that you have criticised my authority.

Asplet I challenge any honest man anywhere to say to my face that I have ever said anything against your authority or you personally. If such a calumny has reached Your Excellency's ears, it was only last Saturday, and I know who said it.

Love You are wrong: you do not know him.

Asplet I could name him; there is only one man in the whole town who could defame me in that way. You can ask all our citizens if I, as a municipal officer, have not acted towards everyone with the strictest impartiality.

Love You should worry less about what the mob thinks of you. You should listen only to those in authority. Furthermore, I would like to give you some advice, and that is to resign.

Asplet (vigorously) I hold my *centenier*'s baton through the suffrage of my fellow citizens, and I shall return it to them when they consider me unworthy of holding it. Whatever I do, I will not drag it through the mud first.

The whole interview had been overheard by Sullivan and du Jardin, the Sergeant Major of the Troopers. Asplet found that custom at his shop suffered, but he became a 'martyr' to the proscrits. As an ironical footnote, the ill-informed Major John Gardner, Love's secretary, was found guilty in 1865 of embezzling militia funds, though on a pension of £167 5s. 10d.

August and September 1855 passed with outward calm, but tension was building up underneath. Surveillance on the French coast was so strict that an Englishman with a valid passport underwent an ordeal at the hands of the police and customs compared to which that of Austria was 'mildness itself', and Jersey passengers going to the Lessay Fair were detained at Granville. Sanders, whom Love had managed to keep for a while, discovered that Le Flô had been over again to see the Orleans family in England. Love told Grey, the Home Secretary, that the headquarters of the Marianne secret society was actually in Jersey, and that proscrits were being invited to send in their mite, as with the Daniel O'Connell fund in Ireland. Its leaders, Hugo, Ribeyrolles, Cahaigne, Pianciani, Teleki and Duverdier convened 'violent' meetings, full of hatred for England, and ending with the cries 'Down with the aristocracy of all nations' and 'Vive la République Démocratique et Sociale'. They planned to assassinate Napoleon, and claimed an alliance with the London Chartists. At the same time they were trying to heal the rift with the London proscrits, Hippolyte Magin acting as courier. Documents were smuggled to France from various places on the Jersey coast by the commission agents Poirier and Beghin.

This was all rather nebulous stuff, nothing to justify expulsions, but steps were taken against *L'Homme*. Since July a stamp duty had hit the paper hard, and in August Love ensured that the only way to get a copy was from the press itself. An editor, Alexandre Thomas, reacted by setting up a reading room at No. 3 Hilgrove Lane where it could be consulted, but he was threatened with immediate expulsion if he published anything against the Emperor or Empress. Thomas was under police watch anyway, since he had publicly threatened Napoleon, incited by Ribeyrolles and a son of Hugo's, Charles presumably. This was not enough for *L'Impartial*, now strongly Bonapartist under the editorship of Lemoine, which suggested that Love fold up all 'political journals', as though it was not such a journal itself.[1]

Chapter Eighteen

The Storm

The libel that Love was waiting for was just over the horizon. On 18 August the Queen and Prince Albert were greeted by Louis Napoleon at Boulogne, on the first state visit of a reigning English monarch to France since Edward II's. They were applauded by the crowds, and Napoleon resumed his calculated flirting with the queen. The visit was a mirror-image of Napoleon's visit to England and a complete success for the alliance. But in London, Félix Pyat, with the nominal help of two other proscrits, Rougée and G. Jourdain, wrote an open letter to the queen which was read at the Scientific Hall, John Street, London, on 22 September, to an audience of French, German and Polish refugees, and two English republicans, Nash and William Jones.

Britain had suffered greatly attacking the Redan Fort of Sevastopol and it was only when the French captured the Malakoff fort that Sevastopol fell. It was a decisive victory. Pyat said that Napoleon welcomed this sapping of English vitals, a prelude to his taking over Europe: Victoria herself would be 'Decembered'. In going to see the tyrant and maker of coups, Victoria had sacrificed everything, 'a Queen's dignity, a woman's scruples, the pride of an aristocrat, an Englishwoman's feelings, rank, race, sex, everything including modesty, for love of this ally'. Victoria had bestowed the Order of the Bath on Canrobert; Pyat said she had 'put him in the bath'. This strained and facetious tone greatly weakened the serious argument underneath.

Pyat's letter was immediately printed in the opposition papers, *Reynold's News* and the *People's Paper*, and reproduced in French on a quarto sheet. The *Times* called it a 'satanic rhapsody' and an 'abominable composition', but it would have been quite forgotten had Pyat not asked Ribeyrolles to publish it in *L'Homme*. At first he did not, for, as G. J. Harney wrote, 'Ribeyrolles was a man of experience, past his hot youth, and was not disposed to print Pyat's philippic ...' but in the issue of 3 October he printed Talandier's speech, made at the same meeting, and, giving way to 'young bloods', promised Pyat's for the next issue. The tempo was quickening: at the Home Office Horatio Waddington had seen Ribeyrolles' article in the 26 September issue of *L'Homme* entitled 'Providence', and thought it justified expulsion, and the article 'Anniversaire du 22 Septembre 1792', a libel 'of the most atrocious description directly inciting the assassination of the French Emperor'. Sir George Grey, the Home Secretary, was more cautious and vague, and he thought that, subject to the opinions of the Jersey law officers, the refugees could be expelled if, after warning, they did anything of which 'just complaint' was made, like, for example, planning to assassinate Napoleon. Palmerston, prompted by Sanders' despatches, thought that this was what the refugees wanted to do, and that they were 'pushed on by Russian agency'. On 12 October he wrote to Grey:

We are not doing Justice by our faithful and zealous Ally the Emperor of the French, by allowing a knot of his mortal Enemies to be plotting within an hour's sail or row of his Shore ... I think they ought all and every one without exception to be sent out, and that the misconduct of their Fellow Refugees should be assigned as the reason.

On 10 October, *L'Homme* printed Pyat's letter. Ignored in London, it raised a storm in Jersey, though no more than 100 people, mostly proscrits, in the island bought it. That afternoon, *centenier* John Thomas du Jardin 'was seen going about, from house to house, with a newspaper in one hand and a dictionary in the other, trying to explain some detached sentences of that document, purposely to excite public indignation against the Proscripts residing in Jersey. Being no scholar, but having a deadly hatred of all political and social freedom, he succeeded in making it appear to many persons, that the private character of the Queen, as a woman, was grossly calumniated!' Du Jardin must have remembered arresting Ribereaut in May 1853 for saying that Victoria was the 'biggest prostitute in England'. One of the Asplets had told Hugo that every liberty is allowed in Jersey except speaking ill of the queen. Then as now, the English monarch was revered in the Channel Islands, both as 'Duke' of Normandy and as the apex of Britishness, as proof against France on which the islands had so long and so resolutely turned their backs. Laurent, Lemoine, Love and Sanders must have sensed that this was possibly the last great opportunity to get the proscrits expelled.

The enemies of the proscription also promptly 'translated' the letter into English, with an introduction pointing out the 'gross and infamous' attack on Victoria, and had it printed as a poster by 6 a.m. on 12 October. If in doubt, and even when not, the more extreme or coarse English word was used in the translation which was peppered with exclamation marks. Pyat had said that Victoria had sacrificed her 'pudeur' for the alliance, but it was anglicised not as 'modesty' but as 'chastity' and this, combined with Pyat's feeble puns about her putting General Canrobert 'in the BATH' and kissing Jerome (Bonaparte), told the English-speaking population that Pyat was calling Queen Victoria a courtesan.

If the translators exaggerated the letter's malice and salaciousness, the proscrits and their allies tried to play it down. For Vacquerie it was just 'two or three puns'; Mme. Hugo said people 'believed it was an attack on the Queen'; and Ernest Jones, the Chartist leader in London, claimed it was not personal. Hugo himself, who first described it as 'a prank', 'shrill', 'awkward' and 'clumsy' though fundamentally right, later asserted that it was 'eloquent, ironical and witty'. Pyat's letter may have been ironical, but it was insulting and meant to be so.

The proscrits had long caused annoyance by refusing to stand and uncover their heads when 'God Save the Queen' was played. Thus, on 20 January at the *Hotel de l'Europe* (where Marx was to stay 25 years later), various Jersey and English people had wished to toast the proscrits at a dinner. M. Beaufils, not one of them but a French teacher at Victoria College, suggested a toast to Victoria and Bonaparte which the Jerseymen prudently refused. One of them, Robert Wellman, normally a supporter of the refugees, upbraided them for their ingratitude in not singing 'God Save the Queen'. Charles replied that he was no more grateful for English hospitality than he would be to an innkeeper whom he had paid. A quarrel developed which was reported to Love, and Wellman was so annoyed that he refused to attend the proscrits' banquet on 24 February 1854.

To avoid compromising principles or the possibility of being hissed at the theatre or even ejected from it when they failed to stand or take off their hats for 'The Queen', the proscrits ceased to go to plays or, like François-Victor and Teleki, would hide in the boxes. Hugo saw that a snare had been set:

> The exiles have done well to avoid this trap by not going to the play, for it is evident that if they had, there would have been a quarrel between them and the Jerseymen; and from that to an expulsion from the island is but a step ... The old English pride is opposed to turning us out openly, but they seek a pretext for showing us the door. Let us not fall into the trap.

François-Victor and a Jerseyman, John Godfray, being men of good sense, averted an unpleasant scene in October 1854 by drinking to each other's country, not head of state. But now, a year later, the trap had been sprung and the pretext provided, possibly unwittingly, by Pyat and Ribeyrolles.

The reaction to Pyat's letter, if orchestrated, was fully blown. Those who had been waiting for the pretext greeted it with a mixture of relief and indignation. Laurent denounced it as a 'violent libel' and the *Jersey Independent* called it a 'contemptible attempt at assaults'. In the Home Office, Waddington wondered if this 'execrable band of ruffians' could be endured much longer, and Grey wanted to prosecute *L'Homme*. Sir Richard Mayne, the London Police Commissioner, wanted the proscrits expelled or punished, while a Jersey 'magistrate' had a better idea: put them in an old boat and sink them in the tide.

In St Helier, posters sprouted everywhere. On the evening of Thursday 11 October, Sanders, Vatcher, an employee of the French consulate, and most of the members of the Jersey United Club, worked themselves to a pitch, agreeing to Lemoine's resolution that the president, Charles Bisson, should ask the *connétable* of St Helier, Nicholas Le Quesne, to hold a public indignation meeting. These meetings were an American idea, usually held to protest against those proposing the abolition of slavery. Later that evening Sanders, Lemoine, Vatcher and du Jardin produced their handiwork, a placard saying:

OUTRAGE

fait à la reine d'Angleterre par des
mécreants, des républicains révolutionnaires
Allez au meeting

A BAS LES ROUGES

This led to a heated argument. Sanders agreed to omit 'A bas les Rouges', but it was still there when the poster appeared on Saturday 13 October. Two other placards had already appeared, on 11 or 12 October:

HABITANTS DE JERSEY!

A quelque nation que vous apparteniez,
natifs ou étrangers, vous tous qui
respectez le sexe auquel vous devez le
jour, et dont

LA REINE VICTORIA

est l'ornement, accrourez au meeting qui
sera tenu demain soir, samedi, dans les

QUEEN'S ASSEMBLY ROOMS
sous la présidence de M. le connétable
de Saint Hélier.

It went on to say that it was effrontery to carry on selling *L'Homme* (at 32 Roseville Street); that the proscrits, who had been so warmly welcomed and helped were ingrates; and that Jerseymen, who for centuries had distinguished themselves for loyalty to their sovereign, should assemble and demonstrate that they had not degenerated. The second placard, in English, asked Jerseymen if they wished to see the First Lady insulted with impunity, and told them to save Jersey from the shame of being a focus of treason.

On 12 October Love summoned the law officers, Dupré and Hammond, and Le Quesne, du Jardin and Sanders. Either Dupré or Hammond told Love that Pyat's letter was not a misdemeanour and so Love, who claimed that the indignation meeting was his idea, decided to wait for its resolutions before acting.

Colonel Pianciani, whose house at 32 Roseville Street had been wrongly described as an outlet for the paper, wrote to Le Quesne to ask for police protection in the face of what looked like incitement to attack his house, and Le Quesne immediately sent officers to guard it; but Pianciani had not expected such a prompt reaction and was, with François-Victor and Théophile Guérin, already at the offices of *La Chronique*, whose editors were the proscrits Rattier and Rondeaux and which was the only paper which still defended the refugees. As they arrived, Le Quesne's secretary was leaving. Rattier told them that he was no longer in effective control of the paper, and that people had been sending in insulting notices since midday. *La Chronique* could not print the letter from Pianciani to Le Quesne, even among the advertisements, so Pianciani had it printed on *L'Homme's* presses and posted on walls next day. Rattier and Rondeaux resigned the next day, leaving the proscrits with no friends in the fourth estate.

Their few Jersey friends were carried like corks on the wave of indignation. Philippe Asplet told a proscrit's wife: 'What can we do, Madame? They are sixty thousand, we are twelve.' The other 11 were probably Charles Asplet, John and Philippe Binet, Elie Derbyshire, Robert Wellman, George Vickery, François Aubin, George and James Picot, and Messrs. Rols and Ouless. Derbyshire was only a *connétable*'s officer, Philippe Asplet and John Binet *centeniers*, but ranged against them were the ardent *centenier* John Thomas du Jardin and, above him, the *connétable* of St Helier, Nicholas Le Quesne. In vain did someone put up counter-posters asking Jerseymen to think again. 'Is it a question of the *Honour*, the *Modesty* of a woman, a queen? What is in question is honour and modesty in a *political* sense, in connection with a political visit ...'. It was too late; the enemies of the proscription had touched two tender nerves, and the reflex could not be damped.

Charles tells us that the meeting, first planned for Monday 15 October, was brought forward to Saturday 13th to allow less time for reflection and because it was the day when unenlightened country folk came into St Helier and some of them got drunk. To make sure there was no backsliding, two more placards were put up on Saturday; one was Sanders' 'A bas les Rouges' poster, the other an English version without any 'Down with the Reds'. *L'Impartial*, now financed by the French Empire, printed at least one of the posters. Lemoine had done all he could and, like Love, waited for the indignation meeting.[1]

Chapter Nineteen

Lynch Law

Queen's Assembly Rooms in Belmont Road was a long gallery lit by branched candlesticks and gas chandeliers. It was here that the proscrits' bazaar was held, and here above the ballroom that anniversary banquets took place. At one end was a platform with a balustrade and an armchair for the president of the indignation meeting. Between 1,500 and 2,000 people, perhaps a tenth of the adult population, were crammed in, with more on the steps or outside in the drizzling rain. At 7.15 p.m. Edward Sullivan, the somewhat eclipsed spy, proposed that Nicholas Le Quesne, the *connétable* of St Helier, should occupy the presidential chair, and this was approved with acclaim.

Nicholas Le Quesne Gentlemen, this meeting is no doubt aware that a most scandalous and outrageous publication, containing the grossest and vilest remarks against the honour, dignity and virtue of our most Gracious Queen has been circulated among our loyal and devoted community. I feel confident that there is not a single Jerseyman or Englishman who could have read the villainous calumny without feeling the greatest indignation against the authors and propagators of this foul and treasonable production. It has been observed to me that it would have been as well to have treated the scandalous publication with silent contempt; but I do not think so ... It is a duty we owe ourselves as well as our Sovereign to protest against the dastardly publication that has assailed the honour of Britain's Queen. We cannot punish the culprits; that is the duty of the authorities, but we can and will let these scoundrels know how they stand in public opinion (*Hear, hear*). We have by far too many French refugees and although I do not mean to say that there are no exceptions, I do not hesitate in saying that the Island would be much better without them. We have succoured and relieved them in time of need, and how did they testify their gratitude? By dragging in the mire the character of our virtuous and well-beloved Queen (*Groans*). Under these circumstances, I think that everyone present would agree with me that it behoves the men of Jersey to express their feelings on this occasion, and to show that they are animated by the same sentiments of loyalty which so eminently distinguished their forefathers (*Immense cheering*).

Advocate François Godfray then complained that the resolutions of the meeting had been prepared in advance and that the culprits could have been sent before the Royal Court. Le Quesne admitted that he had asked a friend to prepare the resolutions, and the first was read out by William le Vesconte Le Quesne who said that it was right that Jersey should at all times give asylum to political and religious refugees, but that they should submit to the island's laws; to act otherwise was an abuse of the most ungrateful character and gross violation of hospitality.

J. C. Rumball (seconding the resolution) The meeting should not throw the mantle of iniquity on all the refugees ... I honour the man who, for the sake of honest principle or conscience, has left his country to live in exile; but the author of the scandalous libel on the Queen cannot be a man of that description. I will not read to the meeting the scandalous article in question, but will leave it in the mire from which it emanated.

Rumball ended with a sketch of Victoria's life from her tender years up to the present day, which was interrupted with cries of 'Business! Business!', and his speech was greeted with prolonged applause and cheering. The resolution was accepted.

George Bertram read out the second resolution:

> The meeting learns with regret that for more than a year some political refugees have been publishing in the island the weekly *L'Homme*, which has for its objects the suppression of Christianity, the propagation of Socialism, the destruction of all Thrones, including that of the Gracious Sovereign whose loyal and devoted subjects it is our pride and privilege to be.
>
> *Captain William Childers* (seconding the resolution) Those proscrits involved in producing *L'Homme* should be expelled and if the refugees refuse to obey the laws of the island, it must be shown that the place is no longer safe for them.

This was followed by cries of 'Swing 'em! Cross-cut 'em!' Childers went on to recall Jersey's links with the Crown and Victoria's visit in 1846.

> *François Godfray* Gentlemen, I consider this meeting to be completely useless. (*Hisses, groans, murmurs and whistling*) I am not to be put down by noise. (*Whistling redoubled*)
>
> *Le Quesne* Everyone has the right to express his opinions. Let Mr. Godfray speak.
>
> *Godfray* Do you suppose that I would countenance anything directed against the First Lady of the land? No. But I still say that this meeting ought not to have been called (*Hisses*) because the act of calling upon us to protest against the paper called *L'Homme* is giving the editor of that journal more importance than he deserves. But how can we condemn that paper? There are no more than TEN persons in the room who have read more than one number of that paper. Let us, therefore, condemn the article we have read, but not those we have not seen. It is alleged in the resolution that during upwards of a year some political refugees have hebdomadally published in this Island a journal called *L'Homme*, which has for its objects the suppression of Christianity, the propagation of Socialism, and the destruction of all Thrones. Now, if that be true, why has our loyalty allowed it for so long a time? Why were not the offenders apprehended on Wednesday, and taken before Mr. Judge Le Gallais, and afterwards before the Royal Court? (*No, no, Lynch Law for such fellows!*) I do not understand what Lynch-law is; I know only constitutional law. I propose, as an amendment to the resolution, that our censure be limited to the article which has appeared in the last number of *L'Homme*. (*More cries of 'Lynch Law! Lynch Law'*)

Lemoine got up to say words to the effect of 'Messieurs, je ne suis pas comme M. Godfray, le bruit m'effare', when he was drowned in shouts of 'Speak in English, Down with the spy' and 'Go and dance with naked women in Pier Road'.

> *Godfray* Mr. Chairman, are others than British subjects allowed to take part in the proceedings of this meeting?
>
> *Le Quesne* This is a meeting of the inhabitants generally and I conceive that everybody has a right to speak on the occasion.
>
> *Lemoine* Messieurs, do not allow yourselves to be held back by the admittedly honourable scruples of M. Godfray. (*Silence for the police*) Messieurs, the journal which published the article ... (*What the Devil has he got to do with it?*)
>
> *Le Quesne* I beg you will allow M. Lemoine to speak.
>
> *Lemoine* Messieurs, the journal does not cease attacking all which is great and virtuous.

He was interrupted by a cry of 'Enough! Cut it short! I recognise you; you are Lemoine and everyone knows of your contacts with the French Consulate. We don't want spies here.' Lemoine then sat down.

> *Philip Le Feuvre* (of La Hougue, St Peter) This is the first *L'Homme* article I ever read, and I would do better to abstain from voting.

Le Quesne asked for a show of hands, and it appeared that a third or half of those present preferred Godfray's amendment merely censuring Pyat's letter to Bertram's motion censuring *L'Homme*. Bertram's motion was recorded as being carried unanimously, but there was so much confusion that the outcome of the vote was quite unclear.

Dr. Joseph Dickson (moving the third resolution) This assembly protests in the most solemn and emphatic manner against the doctrines preached by the above-named socialist journal which not only advocates unbelief, incites the upsetting of all authority ... and shamelessly assails the great and cordial Ally whose efforts in cementing the union between England and France entitle him to the respect and attachment of the people of this country, but extols political murderers, inculcates regicide and basely and wantonly insults the Queen of this Realm ... This meeting considers its publication here as a misfortune for the Island, and earnestly trusts that immediate measures will be adopted by the authorities to suppress it. (*Cheers and applause*)

Captain C. Bisson seconded the resolution but thought suppression was going too far; and Godfray was overruled when he proposed an amendment that it was enough to prosecute the publisher. The resolution was nonetheless adopted 'unanimously' with loud cheering. Sullivan proposed a fourth resolution that a copy of the three resolutions should be conveyed by Le Quesne, Col. Hemery and Dr. Dickson to the Governor: this was seconded and adopted.

The meetings then gave three cheers for Victoria, three for Napoleon and three for Eugénie, and three groans for *L'Homme*. In the gallery behind the President, John William Godfray, *denonciateur* of the Royal Court, lit the offending issue of *L'Homme* to general hilarity, literally burning his fingers in the process. The meeting broke up at 8.30 p.m.[1]

Before the end of the meeting Colonel Katona, worried by its ugly mood, had gone to Pianciani's house which was a possible target for attack. There he found 18 proscrits, many armed, though protected by two policemen with batons sent by Le Quesne. Dr. Barbier had his surgical instruments ready, and the women were making bandages. At 9 p.m. General Le Flô, the monarchist, appeared to tell Pianciani that he did not agree with any of them, but added 'If you are attacked, permit me to defend you'. Barbier replied: 'General, we will never forget what you have just done.' Teleki left Pianciani's and went to Marine Terrace to warn *centenier* Philippe Asplet that the Imprimerie Universelle in Dorset Street was threatened. Asplet had come to reassure Mme. Hugo that he would follow any rioters wherever they went and interpose his municipal authority if Marine Terrace came under attack. Hugo had refused to take any precautions whatsoever.

When the meeting had broken up English officers from the garrison rushed about the streets with drawn swords, stopping a man with a long beard only to discover that he was English. Among the officers was Captain Hedworth Liddell of the 81st Regiment, and they were joined by some Jersey 'dandies' and a mob of about 60-100, many of them drunk. The Imprimerie Universelle was in darkness except for a single gas light; three policemen with batons paraded in front. Inside, in complete darkness, workmen and proscrits waited on the stairs with bars and implements in hand. Zeno, the absent owner of the press had told them that the English house is inviolable and that they should defend themselves if anyone broke in, blowing the house up if forced to retire.

Liddell and his rioters arrived at the press and offered a sovereign to a man called Mitchell to throw the first stone. A newly appointed night policeman, George Henley, told them to move on. One of the soldiers told him to move aside and allow them to take down a shutter and break down the presses. Henley refused and the rioters started chanting 'Down with the Reds'. Another officer offered Henley a handful of guineas. Henley responded: 'I shall do my duty as long as I am stationed here and if any of you attempts to force his way into the house, I shall arrest him.

What would you think, you who are British officers, if a soldier deserted his post when on duty?' A third officer tried to break in through the window. 'I am responsible for this window as much as this door', said Henley firmly, 'woe betide the man who touches it.' The officers discussed what to do and one of them, Childers, said they would be back with 400-500 people to destroy the press. An old woman, probably Zeno's mother-in-law, who was rather deaf, said: 'That's right, very proper too, to protect us from such blackguards' to a roar of laughter at the expense of the officers. Had the officers attacked the press, it is quite possible that the neighbours, who admired Zeno, would have protected it. The officers may have secretly felt relieved as they beat a retreat still shouting 'Down with the Reds!'. When they got to the Queen's Assembly Rooms, they found it deserted. Liddell retired to his club.

At about 10 p.m. Le Quesne, du Jardin, and Philippe Asplet arrived at the press. Le Quesne told the embattled proscrits not to be afraid. 'We are in a civilised country.' Dr. Barbier replied with sad irony: 'We scarcely doubted it.' Le Quesne, obviously rather abashed about his role in the indignation meeting, offered to escort any proscrit home. As he left by himself, *centenier* du Jardin stepped into the press to be greeted with jeers and a furious Asplet. 'You helped to light this fire, and now you pretend to put it out. Get out of here!' The proscrits spent the rest of the night at the press, but saw no more of the mob whose enthusiasm had been somewhat dampened by the rain.

The calling of the disgraceful indignation meeting was an attempt, successful as it happened, to get round the fact that the staff of *L'Homme*, let alone the proscrits as a group, had broken no criminal law. One person who deserves particular obloquy is Captain William Childers. At the meeting he had said that if the proscrits refused to obey the laws of the island, they should be shown that it was no longer safe for them. It is fair to surmise that Captain Childers's knowledge of Jersey law, a very complicated distillation of the *Grand Coutumier* of Normandy and English Common Law, was rudimentary, but even he must have realised that no law sanctions the destroying of other people's property. More pathetic, perhaps, is Captain Liddell, who spoke French and claimed to admire Hugo's poetry, and had unsuccessfully sought an interview with him a short time before. The only people to come out of the affair with credit were Philippe Asplet, François Godfray and above all the admirable George Henley of the St Helier night police, who doubtless averted an extremely nasty and, for the authorities, highly embarrassing incident. It is true that Le Quesne had posted policemen at Pianciani's house and at the Imprimerie Universelle, Henley among them, but it was he who allowed the meeting to get out of control in the first place and who, by failing to silence those baying for the lynch law, encouraged them to think that the authorities would condone violent and summary action.[2]

Chapter Twenty

The Jersey Vespers

At 8 a.m. the next morning General Love, freshly shaved and wearing his uniform and insignia, was waiting for Le Quesne, Hemery and Dickson as they called with the resolutions. He told them that he was taking immediate steps to respond to the wishes of the meeting. In fact he had persuaded the law officers to agree that he could banish the staff of *L'Homme*, Ribeyrolles, Pianciani and Thomas, although they were not happy about the convening of the indignation meeting. The next day Le Quesne and *centenier* John Ching called on Pianciani to say that the Governor could no longer tolerate his presence in the island. The same message was given to Thomas, and to Ribeyrolles who asked in vain for a copy of the expulsion order. On the same day, a deputation of lawyers and merchants, 'real Jerseymen', called on Pianciani to urge him to resist the government and to promise him the means to do so. Emboldened by François Godfray, presumably one of the delegation, some of the proscrits wanted to test the legality of the expulsion in the Royal Court, others thought it too risky, for if the action failed, the *L'Homme* staff would stand as condemned men. In any case, thought Charles Hugo, the French Revolution was above the Jersey constitution, and he did not care what the Royal Court felt. In the event, Pianciani and Ribeyrolles left on 17 October, Thomas on the 19th.

On the eve of Pianciani and Ribeyrolles' departure, 25 proscrits, accepting that they could not resist the expulsions, met at Marine Terrace and nominated Victor Hugo, Cahaigne and Martin Fulbert to write a declaration. In fact, it seems that Hugo had already written one without consulting the others and that it had been printed at the Imprimerie Universelle as Captain Childers had bought a printed copy with 27 names attached at 2.45 p.m. that afternoon.[1] The declaration stated:

> Three proscrits – Ribeyrolles, the intrepid and eloquent writer; Pianciani, the generous representative of the Roman people; Thomas, the courageous prisoner of Mont St Michel, have just been expelled from Jersey.
>
> The act is serious. What is on the surface? The English Government. What is at the bottom of it? The French police. The hand of Fouché can wear Castlereagh's glove. This proves it.
>
> The coup d'état has just made an inroad into England's liberties. England has come to the point of proscribing the proscribed. One more step and England will be an appendage of the French Empire, Jersey a canton in the arrondissement of Coutances.

The declaration went on to say that Louis Napoleon Bonaparte had been condemned for high treason by the High Court in Paris, and added a list of his crimes, ending:

> The French people has for its executioner and the English Government for its ally, the crime-emperor.
>
> That is what we say.
>
> That is what we said yesterday, and the whole English press said so with us; that is what we shall say tomorrow, and posterity will agree unanimously.
>
> That is what we shall always say – we who have but one soul, the truth; one word, justice.
>
> And now, expel us!

The majority of the meeting thought it unwise to treat the Governor on equal terms and to end by inviting expulsion. Rattier and Colfavru repeated the argument that they should go to the Royal Court. Hugo was obdurate: he would make his protest even if he was alone. Charles says that the declaration was unanimously approved though he does not mention that it had already been printed. It was posted up on 18 October, collecting 9 further signatures. This was another example of Hugo's ability to persuade the proscrits to do something against their better interests: it might have been relatively easy for him to earn a living elsewhere, but what about the ordinary proscrit who had laboriously carved a niche for himself by giving lessons or adopting a trade? It is also strange that Hugo, who had urged his sons not to invite expulsion when, in early 1854, they refused to stand for 'God Save the Queen', should now ask to be expelled. Was he tired of Jersey?

About 500 copies of the declaration were printed. Albert Barbieux plastered it over the walls of Havre des Pas; Charles Hugo and J. B. Amiel around St Helier. They guarded the posters while the glue dried, as the police would tear the posters down as fast as they were put up. A friend of the proscrits, Mr. Rolls, went out to St Ouen, St Peter and Trinity, pot of glue in hand, and posted up the declaration wherever he could. The chemist Robert Wellman showed it in his window. Le Quesne ordered 12 copies and a French steamer took 10 away.

Support for the declaration came from the London refugees, Schoelcher, Louis Blanc, Greppo and Deville. Schoelcher disowned the Pyat letter, but called the expulsions 'an act of violence'. Louis Blanc wrote to *L'Impartial* to deny that he was 'ashamed of the excesses of the French refugees', adding that the only excesses had been committed by 'certain parties (who) have worked themselves into a delirium of anger against a letter, of which they knew only some passages, and those misunderstood, and some words ingeniously detached from their context '. He might have been thinking of the *Illustrated London News* which said that the refugees deserved to be deported to France, and that if they fell into the hands of the French authorities, the fate of Pianori, whom they pretended to regard as a martyr, that 'would be no inappropriate one for them'.

There was a strange calm in Jersey for the week after the expulsions; few letters in the papers and no placards or meetings. It was as though the declaration had been ignored. Charles Hugo, writing some time after the events and without access to official despatches, reckoned that during that week the Bonapartist police were arranging for the extradition of the refugees. An agent of the French consulate, Vatcher, had advised the *Ariel*'s commander to wait for the arrival of the Southampton packet on the 20th. Could it be that Love was already waiting for orders from London to expel the refugees? Charles thought that another packet, the *Sir Francis Drake*, which left Jersey on the 19th, carried copies of the declaration, one of which would have got to the cabinet on 20th and to Paris on the 23rd; on 24th, Napoleon would have telegraphed London with an order of expulsion which would have arrived in Jersey on 25th.

Charles' guess was inspired, but the facts are slightly different. The refugee question was discussed in cabinet on the 15th and on the 16th Clarendon, the Foreign Secretary, wrote to Waddington:

> The good sense and right feeling of the people of Jersey are coming to our aid & I only wish they would take the law *into their own hands* and settle the refugee question in the island. I hope the law officers may be animated by similar feelings and venture for once to look libel in the face.

All Dupré and Hammond could tell Love, however, was that neither the Sovereign in Council nor the local legislature had ever made any statute affecting libel. 'We have only the Grand Coutumier de Normandie – which treats of (oral) slander and not written or printed libel – and providing only a civil remedy for slander.' Seditious libels affecting those in authority or incitement to assassinate Napoleon could be prosecuted criminally, and indeed the *Gazette de Jersey* had been prosecuted in 1803 for reproducing an article 'liable to disturb the understanding between England and France'. Dupré and Hammond advised not prosecuting for libel against Napoleon, but they agreed that Love was right to have used his powers to banish Ribeyrolles, Pianciani and Thomas.

Love preferred to rely on an Order in Council of 2 June 1635 which ruled that foreigners could not live in the island without the Governor's permission, and he was determined to deny the refugees that permission. The cabinet was thinking along the same lines, for on 23 October Palmerston wrote to Grey:

> Governor should be *ordered* to exercise the powers which it is clear that he has, to expel foreigners by sending away many signers of the insolent Declaration. The question now is whether these islands belong to us or to Victor Hugo and Co. I would, if anything, not leave it to the discretion of the Governor, and we can take the responsibility ourselves.

On the 25th Love was told by Grey that his expulsion of Ribeyrolles, Pianciani and Thomas was fully approved, and that it was therefore unnecessary to give him special instructions for the future. Unambiguous secret instructions to expel the signatories were probably added, but Love preferred to say that Sir George Grey had sanctioned his decision.

Persigny and Walewski of course wanted this expulsion, but they were careful with their words. Persigny wrote to Clarendon on 20 October that the French government did not intend to demand that the British government should suspend the right of asylum, but only to bring to their attention recent serious events. They had also suggested introducing an Alien Bill for getting rid of unwanted strangers, but there was no question of them 'giving orders' to Palmerston. Charles was right in seeing the week's silence as a sign that decisions were being made and orders given, but wrong in the overriding influence he attributed to France. If Walewski had had his way, the signatories would have been removed from the British Isles altogether, whereas most of them went on to London, or to Guernsey which is not much further from France than Jersey is. Hooker is therefore right when he says that the expulsion was a punitive rather than a preventive measure.

Thus on 25 October, Love told Le Quesne to order each signatory to leave and on 26th Le Quesne, as *connétable* of St Helier, with his *centeniers*, started to tell the proscrits living in St Helier that they had to go. The Jersey correspondent of the *Moniteur* wrote on the 26th that Hugo would be expelled, although Hugo himself, who lived in St Clement, was not told until the 27th and by John Le Neveu, the *connétable* of the parish. This led Charles to suggest that Paris had known of the expulsions even before the refugees themselves, which it may have done, but this was not proved by the supposed inconsistency in dates.

When a St Helier *centenier*, probably Pierre-George Prialx, told Cahaigne to leave, he said 'I am not at all satisfied that your message is genuine; show me the written order '. 'Sir, it is not the custom', said Prialx. As with the expulsion of the *L'Homme* staff, the St Helier authorities did not want to give the proscrits written proof of a dubious action. François Godfray, who had defended them at the indignation meeting, managed to do so in this way. He was *connétable* of St Saviour where four proscrits lived: Théophile Guérin, Hennet de Kesler, H. Préveraud and the Austrian A. C. Wiesener, and he refused to order them out of the island. Meeting Guérin in St Helier, Le Quesne therefore told him to go, and he tried to give the same message to Préveraud through his wife who refused to pass it on. When he met Godfray, Kesler said he had still heard nothing. Kesler told Godfray 'I am not proposing to be difficult about it, but I do need to be told officially'. 'I am very angry about it', said Godfray, who asked Kesler to stay and fight a court case. Kesler replied that he did not recognise the court and was leaving anyway. Godfray even invited Hugo to seek asylum in St Saviour's. Hugo replied rather sententiously: 'I live at Marine Terrace and I will not move. I do not recognise your governor or the Jersey law; I know only of England and M. Bonaparte. I shall sit and wait; my parish is the Republic.'

Kesler was never officially told to go, but Godfray did write an ironic letter to Wiesener to say that His Excellency the Lieutenant-Governor considered the declaration seditious, defiant of England, compromising of the peace, and threatening (if such a thing were possible) to relations between Great Britain and France; and that the Governor had ordered Wiesener's expulsion.

The proscription took the expulsion calmly; Mme. Hugo found more happy than sad faces. True it was only the signatories, perhaps half the active proscription, who were being expelled, but they had to dig up their roots and face an uncertain future. Dr. Barbier, who lived up to the high reputation of French doctors in the island, was begged by his patients to stay. 'Nothing is more painful than to have to give this order to a man as justly respected as you', Le Quesne told him.

Hugo lived in St Clement's and it was therefore *connétable* Jean Le Neveu who came to order him away. They had met before when Hugo had readily contributed to a fund for the Crimean wounded. It is not quite clear what passed next as the account which follows, probably due to the Hugos, was strongly contested by Le Neveu. According to the account, Hugo failed to get a written order of expulsion, and then said:

> It is not you whom I hold responsible for this act; I will not even ask you your opinion concerning it. I am convinced that in your heart you are sorrowfully indignant at the task imposed upon you this day by the military authorities.

Le Neveu and the two people with him, presumably *centeniers*, made no reply but remained seated with downcast looks. Hugo continued:

> I do not wish you to tell me your sentiments – your silence speaks. There exists between the consciences of honest men a bridge of communication by means of which their thoughts meet and are interchanged without requiring the service of lips.

Hugo asked Le Neveu what he would say if the Governor had behaved as Louis Napoleon had, and described the coup d'état and its aftermath. The *connétable* listened in 'profound silence and with visible embarrassment', but made no answer. Hugo insisted on a reply, and finally the *connétable* answered 'I would say that the Governor was wrong '.

Hugo then persuaded Le Neveu that it was not just wrong, but a crime, and asked him if it was not the duty of a people's representative driven from his country to promulgate the history of the crime, and placard the decree of the court which found the Governor guilty of high treason. Hugo got him to agree that it was a duty and asked him what he thought of a government which would expel the person performing that duty, adding quickly: 'But on this point I will be content with your silence. You are here three honest men, and I know – without your telling me – the reply your conscience gives.' One of the *connétable*'s officers then said timidly: 'M. Victor Hugo, there is something in your declaration besides the crimes of the Emperor.' Hugo replied: 'You are mistaken, Sir, and to convince you I will read it to you.'

When Hugo got to the clause saying that with another step England would be an appendage of the French Empire, Jersey a canton in the arrondissement of Coutances, he said to his visitors, 'That step has been taken'. At each clause he repeated 'Did I have the right to say that?', and at the end he asked: 'Is there anything there which is not the plain truth?' 'It is not always good to tell the truth', replied Le Neveu, who asked 'But you disapprove of the expulsion of your friends?' Hugo said 'I disapprove of it in the highest degree, but had I not the right to avow it? Does your liberty of the press not extend so far as to admit the criticism of an arbitrary act of the authorities?' Le Neveu replied 'Certainly, certainly'. 'And it is on account of this declaration that you are here to intimate to me the order for my expulsion? On account of this declaration, which you acknowledge it was my duty to make, and the terms of which you admit do not exceed the limits of your local liberty, and which you in my place would have published, as I have done?', Hugo continued. 'It is on account of the letter of Felix Pyat', said one of the officers. 'I beg your pardon', said Hugo 'have you not told me that I am to quit this island on account of my signature appearing at the foot of this declaration?' The *connétable* drew the Governor's order from his pocket and said: 'In truth, it is solely on account of the declaration, and for nothing else, that you are expelled.'

Le Neveu pressed Hugo to say when he planned to leave.

> If I could leave in a quarter of an hour, I would. I am eager to leave Jersey. The land which has lost its honour burns my feet ... Now, M. le *connétable*, you will render to your superior, the Lieutenant-Governor, an account of the execution of your mission, who will render his account to his superior the British Government, which in turn will render its account to its superior, M. Bonaparte.

Le Neveu protested to the *Daily News*, which published this account, that 'It is not true that M. Hugo addressed me in the set speeches which you have published, and which have evidently been got up for publication and effect; nor is it true that in answer to any summons from him I acknowledged anything that was derogatory to the Emperor or the Lieutenant-Governor. I positively deny having seated myself "with downcast eyes" to enter into any controversy with him, or listened to his words "with visible embarrassment", or submitted to be catechised as your imaginative correspondent states ...' Douglas Jerrold, commenting on the interview, said the *connétable* was fortunate 'that he was not painted sucking his thumb'.[2]

Chapter Twenty-one

A Line in History

The signatories had been told to leave Jersey by 2 November, 'a day of disgrace for Jersey, if not indeed England', wrote Swinburne, Hugo's adoring disciple. Sandor Teleki and Dr. Franck were among the first to leave on 29 October. On the 31st, Victor and François-Victor Hugo, Juliette Drouet, the inseparable Guérin and Kesler, and a few others left. François-Victor records:

It was six in the morning; dawn was just breaking and the gun of Elizabeth Castle which announces daybreak to the inhabitants of Jersey had not yet gone off. In spite of the thin and penetrating drizzle, my father wished to go on foot by the road that leads from Marine Terrace to Port Victoria, where we were to embark. The road is charming, in fact; one avoids the town, which is already an advantage, and then one follows the coast through a settlement of fishermen called Havre des Pas and loses oneself under trees along a steep hillside.

It was seven. The ship's bell tolled its last stroke. My father and I climbed down onto the deck and found our friends G[uérin] and K[esler] who were coming with us. The *Dispatch* cast off her moorings and turned on herself to head through the harbour mouth separating the Victoria and Albert jetties. We wished to have a last look at those who remained ... they all saluted our departure with the shout of release.

We were already under way. The steamer carried us with all the speed of its one hundred horsepower. In a few minutes we were opposite Elizabeth Castle, its tall Louis XIII chimneys faintly visible in the growing daylight. We said goodbye while passing this old fort which the Ocean fortifies at every rising tide, and which had sheltered behind its cannons the proscrit Charles Stuart. We could no longer see St Helier except for a few houses, quickly hidden by the Mont aux Pendus. The land was rapidly slipping past at the rate of twelve miles an hour, and each turn of those paddle-wheels brought a new swarm of memories to mind.

Here was the road which skirts St Aubin's Bay where once, on a lovely autumn day, we had passed with the author of *Lady Tartuffe* and the *Lettres Parisiennes* [Delphine de Girardin]. And there at the end is the little port of St Aubin, where we used to ride: Do you remember, Sandor [Teleki]? Here is Noirmont Point, a sombre rock fending off all shipping, where Paul Meurice had admired the sunset with us.

Here, at the end of the cliff, little Portelet Bay; at the far end, behind [Janvrin's] Tomb which is isolated at high tide, is the small thicket of woodbine and creepers where I feel I can still hear the laughing voice of Margaret [Allen], charming young woman carried off by scarlet fever at 19, fresh apparition of exile whose death has already cast its shadow. Scarcely had we time to wipe away a tear than the boat has brought us, with rapid contrast, more happy memories. Here was the Bay of St Brelade, inevitable rendez-vous for picnics and English jollity and there, on the left, in front of the bay a rock which dominates the old romanesque church on one side, and on the other, the fort of St Brelade which we used as a dining-room more than once.

At last, here is La Corbière Point with its row of serrated rocks which we assaulted more than once with the valiant General L[e Flô]; La Corbière, a terror to mariners, a dreadful reef, colossal granite watch-dog guarding this corner of the island which the storms toss a ship's carcase from time to time.

Having turned the point of La Corbière, the *Dispatch* headed north ... The sea, which had been as smooth as a pond, brusquely changed its appearance. Everywhere on the horizon we saw waves topped with foam. At first we did not pay much attention to this burst of violence, we were so absorbed with the view. Just at that moment my father pointed his finger to St Peter's Bay [sc. St Ouen's] with its baleful hills of sand and its long bay covered with dunes, where we had had an amazing steeplechase a few weeks before. But the Ocean, instead of calming itself, grew very angry. Our steamer thrust right into the wind which was against us and whistled impertinently in the rigging and spat great drops of rain into our faces. The crossing was getting really rough ... The steamer advanced inexorably.

We looked back to where Jersey should have been. In fact, we could just see, through some cloud, a whitish line, far away, floating on the waters. It was the coast of the island. It became effaced and disappeared under the waves. Jersey seemed to have sunk in the storm ... We turned round and saw in front of us another white line piercing the storm-cloud ... it was the coast of another island, Guernsey ... after an hour, in fact, the *Dispatch* came to rest in front of a charming town, climbing the hillside picturesquely ... It was St Peter Port ... The very name was a good augury, for St Peter, as we know, keeps the doors of Paradise.

Hugo, who enjoyed a good storm, provided a terser account:

Left Jersey at 7.15 a.m. Arrived in Guernsey at 10. Heavy seas, Showers. Squalls. Jersey: rock, then cloud, then shadow, then nothing. Difficult boarding. Huge waves. Small boats full of men and baggages. Crowd on the quay. The proscrits Bachelet, Dessaignes, Thomas, Fruchard etc. The consul [Loyeux] (Guernsey's Laurent) with a white tie. All heads bared when I went through the crowd. This reception is not a bad sign.

> It was in the month of October, the year '55
> That, having chased Ribeyrolles from Jersey
> A certain Love, thus named I swear
> From the top of Fort Regent, crowned with gunners
> Burst on us the order to go elsewhere.
> The proscrit is forever young
> I'm little troubled by this 'expioulcheune'
> And I laughed at this English thunderbolt.
>
>   October.
> The proscriber is strong, the expeller only vile
> This cowardly expulsion tries to outrage
> It is not hatred; madness only.

Englishmen! I grasp each of your liberties in turn, and every time they are taken away, I find a bleeding fragment under my nails.

A page in my life. A line in History.

Love, more perplexed than angry, was not far off in writing, on 30 October: 'Mr Victor Hugo is most violent against me and threatens to hand me down to posterity as an enemy of the human race.'

In Guernsey the steamer (in fact the *Courier*, not the *Dispatch* as François-Victor says) had had to moor off the White Rock, and people and cases were transferred to small boats pitching up and down. Hugo looked in dismay as his trunkful of manuscripts was slung down a gangway and perched in the bows of a rocking boat. He hated to let the trunk out of his sight (though he had allowed his disciple Préveraud to remove it from Marine Terrace for safekeeping at the time of the indignation meeting). 'It was dreadful', wrote François-Victor, 'for some minutes the trunk wobbled on the waves ... I could just see *Les Contemplations* disappearing under ten feet of water. But luckily there is a Providence which watches over Poets.'

At midday, the proscrits left in Jersey went to Macpela cemetery to pay their respects to Hélin-Dutaillis, Bousquet, Julien, Gaffney, Courtès, Izdebeski, Cauvet, Bony and Drevet who had been buried in a common grave, now marked by a granite stele. Love had forbidden any showing of the red flag:

The exiles entered and made a circle around the tomb. For ten minutes, the expelled proscrits of Jersey remained bareheaded before Death. It was dark and misty, the countryside deserted. No ceremony was ever so touching, so profoundly religious and austere.

Two days later, on a beautiful morning, the rest of the signatories, 22 without Guiseppe Rancan who was ill and Piasecki who was in hiding, assembled on the quay. Many other proscrits were there, and one of them had a small red flag reading 'À bas Bonaparte' snatched away by the police. This was probably Bourillion who had been nipping in and out of the crowd trying to persuade other proscrits, who had not allowed him to sign the declaration, to shake his hand. Perhaps he was suspected of *mouchardise*, spying. As they parted, some proscrits embraced and kissed each other, a few declaimed in theatrical voices that they would soon be back with artillery and the glorious red flag. A market woman bounded up the gangway after Teleki's wife to claim a £3 debt; Philippe Asplet stopped her and put her back in her cab.

At 8 a.m., as the *Dispatch* sailed through the harbour mouth, the proscrits on board and on shore threw their hats in the air and shouted 'Vive la République'. Charles Hugo, who was on the *Dispatch*, called it a 'veritable ovation', but mingled with it were cries of 'Vive l'Empereur', and when someone shouted 'Down with the bloody Reds', Vacquerie and Dulac asked him to repeat it. He stammered and went pale and denied saying anything. Du Jardin approached, and Vacquerie said 'Since this gentleman denies it, he is a liar and a coward and what he says counts for nothing'. Vacquerie reckoned that the Jersey population was unhappy about losing the proscrits (and their money) and had wanted only the suppression of *L'Homme*.

Vacquerie had not signed the declaration, so he was able to stay behind and help Mme. Hugo, Adèle and Mme. Bouclier pack up while Hugo was looking for lodgings in Guernsey. Mme. Hugo was paying off tradesmen and replacing what was lost and damaged to avoid having to pay Mrs. Rose all she claimed. Charles, from Guernsey, asked his mother to pack the geraniums, the cuttings and the delicate little contraption from Saunders's nursery which was in the grotto. There were 40 boxes in all. Vacquerie took a few photographs of the conservatory where they had spent so much time and then, on 8 November, he left Jersey with Mme. Hugo, Adèle, Mme. Bouclier and Dulac on the *Dispatch*. Mme. Hugo was sad to leave. She told Julie: 'We had a delightful three years there, and I finished by liking even the bad bits.' Hugo, of course, had not asked her whether she wanted to live in Guernsey just as, three years before, he had not asked her views on Jersey. Mme. Hugo thought, however, that she would prefer Guernsey to Jersey. François-Victor was thrilled with it, and Vacquerie found their new house at 20 Hauteville Street charming. Hugo thought that Guernsey was altogether preferable to Jersey, and he was very pleased with his reception at the White Rock. Only days after arriving in Jersey in August 1852 he had said 'My dream would be to live in Guernsey in a room overlooking the sea, so that I could watch boats and ships pass beneath my eyes '.[1]

Chapter Twenty-two

The Aftermath

About half the proscrits – at least 41 – had now left Jersey. The storm was over but there was still some tension to be discharged. Bourillion, who had been disowned by the proscrits on the quay, tried to make up for it by attaching a poster to the base of the statue on the Royal Square, accusing the Governor of being an accomplice of 'Bonapendre'. Bouillard, whose name had been added to the bottom of the original declaration without his knowledge, now wrote to the *Nouvelle Chronique*, to say that he adhered to the declaration minus the last few words (presumably 'Et maintenant, expulsez nous'), but he would leave anyway. Léon Goupy the watchmaker accosted du Jardin in the market on 13 November and demanded to know why he was saying offensive things about him. Du Jardin replied 'Yes, I have said that I have been told that you formed part of a plot to assassinate; and I consider that to be true'. There was a scuffle and du Jardin felled Goupy, who nonetheless found himself in court for insulting and menacing du Jardin. In spite of François Godfray's vigorous defence, Goupy was fined 10 shillings. So raw were du Jardin's nerves that when, on the same day as the scuffle, Alavoine said to a boy who was maltreating a dog, 'Watch out, little fellow' (*moutard*), du Jardin, on the other side of Beresford Street, thought Alavoine was calling him a spy (*mouchard*).

The next morning, as Pierre Louis Lemoine, editor of *L'Impartial*, was emerging from the *Cock and Bottle* café, he was attacked from behind by Philippe Asplet. Asplet knocked him down, snatched away his cane – which was supposed to be a sword-stick – and broke his 'very tough' English spectacles. Lemoine, who was twice Asplet's age, lost a lot of blood. 'These are the men', commented *L'Impartial*, 'with the baton of peace in their hands'. Godfray, who said that *L'Impartial* had been provoking Asplet, agreed to defend him and boasted he would get off with a 10 shilling fine. The trouble, as Sanders reported to the Home Office, was that the Bailiff was in his second childhood, and the law officers, Dupré and Hammond, were afraid of Godfray. The case was sent by the Tribunal de Police Correctionelle to the Royal Court, and it then dragged on for two years. In 1857 Engels wrote to Marx from Jersey:

> The battles are fought out in the Royal Square, where the grocer cut down the editor-in-chief of the Jersey Impartial, a bonapartist spy by the name of Lemoine, on account of which a trial has been going on for a year [*sic*], and which will be decided next Monday.

Battles were also fought out in the papers. *L'Homme* reminded its readers how the *Illustrated London News*, now calling the proscrits dangerous madmen, had attacked Napoleon just after his coup d'état in December 1851. *The Times*, now alternately sneering and raging at them, had criticised Napoleon in August 1852. Charles Hugo recorded that when they arrived in Jersey, 'the island's papers, copying those in

England, had opened their columns to the proscrits' writings, and added their indignation to ours ...'. The Jersey papers and the Guernsey *Comet* now turned on the proscrits. For the Jersey *Nouvelle Chronique*, Love had merely ratified the will of the people in expelling the *L'Homme* staff, but the signatories of the declaration had not learned their lesson. Its faith in the proscrits had been shaken on the day they 'refused to toast The Queen'.

The Sheffield Free Press, referring to Napier's expulsion of Le Conte from Guernsey, considered that 'Justice would have been answered by the legal trial, and the certain punishment of the offender', a line similar to that of François Godfray (though he might have demurred at the idea that a *legal* trial necessarily entails *certain* punishment). Many English papers were, however, very critical of the expulsions, including *The Daily News* (which termed it the 'Jersey coup d'état'), the *Morning Advertiser*, the *Daily Telegraph*, the *People's Paper*, the Chartist *Reynold's News* and several provincial papers. 'The incident caused so much controversy', Hooker informs us, 'that several papers predicted that the Government must immediately fall.' He considers that some of the pro-proscrit comments were motivated by genuine sympathy for them, but most were simple challenges to Palmerston's government. This is possible, but he does not explain, any more than did *The Times*, the *Illustrated London News*, the *Globe* or the *Patriot* at the time, why the things which Napoleon did in December 1851 were condemned then, but condoned in 1855. His coup d'état can scarcely have been vindicated because of the tone of Pyat's letter, still less by the refusal of some Jersey proscrits to toast the queen.

It is difficult to gauge the English reaction to the expulsion. Guille says it was 'immediate and violent' and that walls carried placards proclaiming 'Victor Hugo forever!'. There were, it is true, protest meetings in London, Newcastle, Glasgow and Paisley, but it is not clear how well supported they were. The meeting at St Martin's Hall on 12 November was organised by Ernest Jones, editor of the *People's Paper*, and former leader of the Chartists. But the chairman, Edward Miall of the Manchester School, was a member of the Peace Party which was much more concerned with stopping the war than with the Jersey expulsions; they were even accused by the *Morning Advertiser* of having pro-Russian sympathies. Nonetheless, the meeting carried almost unanimously a motion deploring the expulsion, and declaring that foreigners should not be exposed to legal penalties without trial by jury. *The Times* suggested that the Peace Party wanted an end to the war with Russia so that England could start another one with France, 'to be conducted by meetings, and newspapers, under the discreet and temperate generalship of M. VICTOR HUGO and some other gentlemen of his class '.

The day before, the Newcastle Foreign Affairs Committee, former Chartists, had organised a meeting there. Joseph Cowen and Thomas Gregson of the committee sent a message of support to Hugo protesting against the violation of the 'sacred right of asylum'. It was presented to Hugo in Guernsey on 23 November by the ex-Chartist George Julian Harney. Harney spoke no French, and Hugo's only English was 'thank you' and 'very velle', so François-Victor acted as interpreter. Hugo wrote to thank Cowen and Gregson, saying that it was impossible that the further proscription of the proscrits would not raise public indignation in England. 'England is a great and generous nation where all the live forces of progress palpitate; she understands that liberty is light. But what has happened in Jersey is an experiment in night, an invasion of shadows ...' The meeting at Glasgow City Hall on 27 November heard from Harney that Alexandre Dumas was to be tried in the Imperial Court for writing to a friend that 'My body is at Paris, but my soul is in Jersey', and that a relation of Hugo's was told by Walewski, the French foreign minister, that Palmerston intended to submit an Alien Bill to parliament which Walewski had no doubt would pass.

At this time, some German papers said that the language of the refugees had caused England to promise to renew the Alien Law or some such measure, and the French had been pressing for it for some time. On 12 October, Walewski asked Persigny to show Pyat's speech to Clarendon, adding that the need for the Alien Bill had never been better demonstrated. Persigny could only reply that it was a bugbear to English ministers and would only be enacted by parliament in the sort of dire circumstances of 1848. In the event, Palmerston discreetly dropped the idea. Schoyen suggests that the outcry at the expulsions blocked the cabinet, and the *Daily News* thought that Palmerston 'will have too much prudence to risk the damaging debates to which the introduction of such a measure would give rise. Neither he nor his Imperial masters will court the renewed publicity that would be given to the transactions of 1851 ...'. A simpler explanation would be that there was now no need for the Bill, and the Act could not have justified the summary expulsions, and certainly not retrospectively.

In Jersey the law officers, never very happy about the expulsions, were hoping to justify them by an old Order in Council of 1635. They asked the Home Office for a copy of the order for the expulsion of Le Conte from Guernsey in 1843. Love told Waddington that 'an attorney' – presumably François Godfray – wanted to apply to the Queen's Bench to serve a mandamus or other process on him. Someone, probably Grey, has overwritten on the letter: 'I am much amused by the notion of proceeding in the Queen's Bench against General Love.' Persigny, too, had great hopes for the Order in Council. 'In the arsenal of Jersey laws, some disposition or other from the 13th [sic] century has been found which empowers the Governor to send away from the island all strangers who have not requested and been granted permission to remain there ...' In fact, as a vigorous pamphlet by 'Justitia' (probably Messervy) showed, the Order in Council says only that strangers have to get permission from the Governor to stay in the island, it was enforced only in times of war and it included Englishmen among strangers. In any case, the order was a dead letter and it had been trumped by Letters Patent from Charles II who, in return for Jersey's hospitality when, as Prince of Wales, he was exiled in the island in 1646 and 1649, gave to the Bailiff and Jurats '... full, entire and absolute authority' to judge all kinds of law cases.

Dupré and Hammond would have liked to ignore the matter and what they wanted above all was to prevent the case coming to the Royal Court, where they would not have been able to defend Love's action very wholeheartedly, and where their opponent, François Godfray, a man of passion and determination, dominated. He would, for example, tell others in court to hold their tongues and he boasted that he could always get a decision in favour of his clients; he had managed to delay the hearing of the case against the captain of the *Superb*, who had run it onto the Minquiers reef 5 years before, drowning twenty.

The expulsion was never brought to court, but it was debated in the States assembly. On 19 November 1855, Judge David de Quetteville presented a motion that no stranger should be expelled by the Governor without the consent of the Royal Court which must first try the case. François Godfray immediately rose to ask why the *connétable* of St Helier, Nicholas Le Quesne, had reported to Love that the indignation meeting unanimously censured *L'Homme* (and by implication, all proscrits), whereas it had only voted for his and Dr. Dickson's amendment that Pyat's letter should be censured and the editor and printer brought before the Royal Court. Le Quesne replied:

> My opinion is that the majority was for the resolution. We all know that they insulted us. Have they not carried their red flag in our streets? ... We have only acted in this affair as loyal subjects; and had we brought the offenders before the Court, it would only have been acting a comedy, which would never have had an end. I regret that the Lieut-Governor thought such power resided in him. I am aware the Court would never finish the affair were it brought before it.

The proposition was lodged *au greffe*, and redebated on 26 January 1856 but, owing to de Quetteville's illness, his motion was adjourned *sine die*. That was the end of the matter.

It is rather strange that Godfray made an issue of whether the resolution for censure was carried or not for, even if it had been carried unanimously, that would not have empowered the Governor to order the expulsion. Either he had the power in law or he did not, and it cannot have depended on the voting of a group of self-selected people at a meeting. Le Quesne's back-tracking is also curious; he let the indignation meeting get out of control and then obviously felt enough contrition to go to protect the Imprimerie Universelle. The day after, he took the meeting's resolutions to Love, but here in the States he seems to regret that the Governor ordered the expulsions.

The expulsion may have been regretted by many in the island as an overreaction, but it remained in force. When Eduardo Biffi, one of the signatories, returned to Jersey in 1856 with his English wife and child, he was promptly arrested by the old bulldog du Jardin and taken to court. Godfray went over old ground, saying that the 1635 Order in Council applied to strangers – English subjects not born in England – and not to foreigners, and that it had been negated by Charles II in 1674. Dupré said that the order applied to foreigners *a fortiori*, that it had been incorporated in the 1771 Code of Laws, and that it had been used in Jersey in 1824 and 1843 and in Guernsey in 1843. Judge de Quetteville, critical though he had been of the expulsions at the time, now seemed persuaded they were legal. Biffi was imprisoned, but in November 1857 we find him in London, petitioning to be allowed to join his wife and father-in-law, John Gartrell, in Jersey. Love said that Biffi was a disreputable character, a deserter from the Pope's guard, and the least deserving case.

On 14 August 1859 Napoleon offered amnesty to the refugees. Hugo of course refused it, though Laurent reported that some Jersey refugees wanted to go back to France. An article in the *Jersey Independent*, presumably by George Julian Harney, sensibly pointed out that if Napoleon was 'not alarmed by (the proscrits') appearance in Paris, he could not object to their presence in St Helier'. Thus Benjamin Colin, who had been amnestied, reckoned he could return to Jersey, but the Home Secretary, Sir George Cornewall Lewis, thought otherwise; the amnesty was all the more reason for maintaining the exclusion from Jersey. But General Godfrey Mundy, the new Governor, told Colin, arrested by du Jardin, that unless he applied officially to stay in Jersey, he would be expelled, which means that it was the manner of his return, rather than his presence, which was objected to.

The *Jersey Independent* article goes on:

We suppose that by this time there is not one Jerseyman possessed of common sense, and having regard for 'national' honour, but must wish that the page which records the 'expulsion' of the glorious poet and patriot, VICTOR HUGO, could be effaced, or torn, from the history of the Island. Certain it is that the spirit of bitter hostility which animated a portion of our population nearly four years ago had long since died out; and if VICTOR HUGO would return to Jersey he would be received with all the demonstrations of respect and regard which his genius and greatness unquestionably entitle him to. We do not expect anything of the kind. We think it exceedingly improbable that VICTOR HUGO will ever again set foot on the soil of Jersey.[1]

Chapter Twenty-three

Garibaldi's Gift

The *Jersey Independent* was quite wrong; Hugo returned to Jersey the next year. On 24 February 1860, at Philippe Asplet's suggestion, the Jersey proscrits sent a letter to their friends in Guernsey commemorating the 12th anniversary of 1848. Asplet now asked Hugo to come to Jersey to speak in favour of Garibaldi who had just captured Palermo.

> It would be a double triumph for you to see this people who, scarcely five years ago so ignobly drove you out, now recognise their mistake and run to hear your powerful voice speak for those suffering in the cause of liberty. It would be the best day of my life, because I have shed torrents of tears thinking of what my compatriots did in chasing you from among us. I would gladly give my life to be able to wipe this stain from the history of my sorry country. You alone, my noble and generous friend, can do it, and all that in serving the cause of humanity, a cause which you have championed and for which you have suffered so much.

Harney seems to have had the same idea as Asplet, for Hugo wrote to say he was sorry Harney had not thought of it sooner. He could not, however, come at short notice as he needed at least 1,200 or 1,500 signatures to efface the famous indignation meeting. 'I cannot enter Jersey by a side-door, it must be the front door, and wide open; it is a question of dignity ...' It would take a week to gather the signatures, and if a considerable part of Jersey's population was invited, he would speak; if Harney could not get the signatures, the meeting would have to go on without him.

The next day Asplet dined with Hugo, bringing a request that he speak at the Garibaldi meeting. Hugo presumably told him to go back and get the signatures, and on 12 June, Asplet and Picot returned to Guernsey with 427. The signatures were too few, but Hugo was persuaded:

> Gentlemen, tell the Committee, tell the honourable signatories of this address, how deeply touched I am. I love Jersey. Jersey was for me, in a way, the first station of exile. I spent three years there, one of the sweetest and most soothing memories of my life. It is a beautiful place, with great-hearted people. I forget the misunderstanding of 1855 entirely and blot it out to the limits of my ability. In shaking your hand cordially, I shake the hand of all Jersey. I shall go to the meeting and speak there. You are welcome.

Juliette and Suzanne left for Jersey that day to stay at the *Hotel Southampton*, and Hugo arranged to leave the day after. But the sea was so rough that the packet from Southampton had to put into Alderney. The Jersey-Guernsey telegraph had broken down, so Hugo sent a telegramme to Asplet via London, Calais, Paris and Granville (cost 10s. 6d.) to say that the meeting would have to be put off for a day. Juliette waited on the quay in Jersey all day, beside herself with anxiety. She heard a cab driver say 'telegraiphique message stimear Alderney to moro Jersey', but still she slept poorly. The next morning she was again pacing between the *Southampton Hotel* and the quay, so worried that she forgot to buy a toothbrush (she had left hers in Guernsey).

Then on 14 June 1860, at 2 p.m., Victor Hugo and his sons, Bonnet-Duverdier, Hetzel, Hugo's publisher, and Émile Deschanel, arrived at St Helier. Juliette impatiently came out to meet Hugo in a small boat, but he seemed rather put out by it. Laurent the clumsy but tireless consul was waiting and he thought Hugo and his party could be arrested but the new governor Mundy was, like the English public, very favourable to Garibaldi and Laurent could do nothing. The arrival was, in Hugo's words, 'an immense success, the whole town clamorous and welcoming'. The walls were covered with enormous posters:

Victor Hugo
has arrived!

Hugo wrote to his wife 'The welcome of this fine little community is charming', and he only regretted that the two Adèles were not with him to enjoy it. He promised his friends in Jersey to return with the Adèles.

That evening Hugo gave a resounding speech in praise of Garibaldi at the Queen's Assembly Rooms, helping to raise £120 for the cause. It was here that the indignation meeting had bayed for lynch law, but now even more people, 3,000, were crammed in as the hall shook with applause. Harney and others spoke, probably most of them in English, and the pastor N. Martin-Duport gave a vote of thanks. Hugo, who seemed tired, was moved to hear a French voice, an echo of his country. After the meeting, he wrote to Vacquerie, now in France, and Meurice with copies of his speech for publication. 'Would you believe it, Jersey is on its knees, crying *mea culpa*. The ovation equalled the expulsion.'

On the 15th Hugo and Juliette went on a hot and dusty omnibus tour, but the next two days it was raining. They lunched with Hetzel at the *Pomme d'Or* and supped with Charles Asplet. There was time to have a photograph taken by Henry Mullins, revisit some of their favourite places, and make a pious journey to Macpela cemetery, 'our Westminster and Saint-Denis', where they saw the mother of Philippe Faure on her daily visit, prostrated before his grave.

On the 18th, a magnificent banquet was given for Hugo at the *Pomme d'Or*, with representatives of the English press and Belgian bar present. With champagne, Martin-Duport got up and spoke of Lamartine, Musset and other poets, but said that Hugo was greater than them all. He spoke of Hugo's genius as a thinker, republican and proscrit. When he had finished, the whole audience was on its feet. Victor Hugo, leaving his place and followed by his sons and some proscrits, came up to Duport and embraced him. Obviously moved, he told the company that the best way to thank them was to say that he loved Jersey:

I left Jersey with regrets, I find it again with happiness. Liberators have the marvellous and charming gift of sometimes achieving more than they intended. Without a doubt, Garibaldi has killed two birds with one stone: he has removed the Bourbons from Sicily, and caused me to come back to Jersey.

Your applause and hearty interruptions at this moment touch me more than I can express. I do not know how to respond to a welcome so universal and everywhere so friendly, to so much cheering and sympathy. I would almost say: spare me. You are many against one ...

I will tell you what I love about Jersey; I love it all. I love this climate where Winter and Summer are always mild, flowers which seem always to be in April, trees of Normandy, rocks of Brittany, the sky which reminds me of France and the sea of Paris. I love this people which works and struggles, all these good people that one meets continually in your roads and fields, whose faces combine English liberty and French gracefulness, which is another freedom.

When I came here, eight years ago, at the end of the most prodigious political struggles of the Century, I, shipwrecked and still dripping from the catastrophe of December, quite bewildered in the tempest, disheveled in the hurricane, what did I find in Jersey? Something sacred, sublime, unexpected: peace ... I found, I repeat, peace, repose, a pure and deep tranquility in the softness of your countryside, in the warm-hearted greeting of your labourers, in these valleys, in these secluded places, in these nights which, above the sea, seem more amply filled with stars, in this ever-moving sea which seems to throb directly with the breath of God. And it was thus that, while nursing sacred anger against the crime, I felt immensity mixing its serene fulness with this anger, and what growled within me was stilled. Yes, I give thanks to Jersey. I thank you. Beneath your roofs and in your towns I found human goodness, and in your fields and seas I discovered divine indulgence. Oh! I shall never forget nature's majestic calming in those first days of exile! Pride no longer prevents us from saying what we say today, and none of my companions will deny that we all suffered in leaving Jersey. We all had roots here. Fibres from our hearts penetrated your soil and held fast. It was painful to tear them up. We all loved Jersey. Some loved it because they had been happy here, some because they had been unhappy. Suffering is no less a bond than joy ...

Gentlemen, I reply to your toast by a toast to Jersey. I drink to Jersey, to its prosperity, its enrichment, its industrial and commercial expansion, and still more to its intellectual and moral improvement.

There are two things which make a people both great and attractive, and these are liberty and hospitality; hospitality was the glory of ancient nations, liberty is the splendour of modern nations. Jersey wears both these crowns; let her guard them ...

Be always hospitable. Let this sacred role of hospitality always honour this island; and allow me to add Guernsey, her sister, and all the archipelago of the Channel. It is a great country of asylum, great not in size, but in the number of refugees from all parties and countries which for three centuries it has sheltered and consoled. Oh! Nothing in the world is more beautiful than to be a refuge ...

We who are here, all proscrits of France, we have wronged no one, we have carried through our mandates and listened to our consciences, we suffer for what is just and what is true ...

One day it might be – for all events are in the hands of God, and the divine hand is inexhaustible – it could be that, among those whom the great storms or great tides of the future throw up on your shores, there will be the man who proscribed us, driven out in his turn and wretched. Good! Show him clemency as you showed us fairness; if he knocks at your door, open it and tell him: 'Those whom you proscribed asked us to give you refuge which we now do.'[1]

Epilogue

The man who proscribed Hugo offered him amnesty in 1859, the year before this visit. Hugo turned it down contemptuously: 'When freedom returns, so shall I'. But after the débacle of Sedan in 1870 – the nemesis of his coup d'état – Napoleon was driven out of France and offered asylum, not in Jersey, but in England, and for the third time. On his return to France that same year after 19 years of exile, Hugo was received rapturously. He had become almost a national monument of France. Yet he was not at ease in the new order, and indeed he returned for a whole year in 1872-3 to Guernsey. 'The rock on which the great poet moaned', as Renoir called it, was not easy to abandon.

In his 'last words' in *Les Châtiments*, Hugo had written 'If there remains but one, it will be I'. This was borne out in two senses. He was one of the last proscrits to return to France, and he was abandoned by, or lost, members of his family one by one. In 1858 both Adèles had revolted and gone to France for a long stay; in October Charles had lost his temper with Hugo and François-Victor accused him of being a tyrant; and by Christmas Vacquerie had left. In 1861 Charles left Guernsey for good, in 1863 Adèle. Then in 1868 Mme. Hugo died, followed by Charles in 1871. The next year the poor demented Adèle returned from the New World having failed to marry Albert Pinson; exactly half way through her life, she was to spend another 43 years, never speaking, in an asylum. François-Victor, who never left his father's side, died in 1873; Juliette in 1883. When Hugo died in 1885, survived only by his daughter, the rather etiolated bachelor Vacquerie, and Charles's children, he was given a hero's funeral, the only Frenchman to lie in state under the Arc de Triomphe before the First World War.

In the Guernsey years, 1855-70, Hugo forgot politics and concentrated on imaginative writing and travelling. He still retained an affection for Jersey, which he showed at the Garibaldi meeting of 1860. In 1866, in an echo and reversal of the Tapner affair, he tried, from Guernsey, to save a convicted murderer in Jersey named Bradley. Writing to Alfred Asseline, he said:

> Jersey, the little island, is ahead of the great peoples. She is free, honest, intelligent, benevolent. It seems that Jersey, finding that the world is retreating, wants to retreat as well ... What a rebuff for God who has done so much for this charming place! What ingratitude towards its soft, serene and kindly nature! A gibbet in Jersey! Alas, he who is fortunate should be clement.
> I love Jersey; I feel this deeply.

Hugo was to see Jersey again en route for Brussels and France in 1870, and on his way to spend a year at Hauteville House in 1872 he passed some days in the island which had first sheltered him:

114

Je la revois après vingt ans, l'île où Décembre
   Me jeta, pâle naufragé.
La voila! c'est bien elle. Elle est comme une chambre
   Où rien encore n'est dérangé.

Oui, c'était bien ainsi qu'elle était; il me semble
   Qu'elle rit, et que j'aperçois
Le même oiseau qui fuit, la même fleur qui tremble,
   La Même aurore dans les bois;

Il me semble revoir, comme au fond d'un mirage,
   Les champs, les vergers, les fruits mûrs,
Et dans le firmament profond, le même orage,
   Et la même herbe au pied des murs,

Et le même toit blanc qui m'attend et qui m'aime,
   Et, par delà le flot grondeur,
La même vision d'un éden, dans la même
   Éblouissante profondeur.

Oui, je la reconnais cette grève enchantée,
   Comme alors elle m'apparut,
Rive heureuse où l'on cherche Acis et Galatée,
   Et l'on trouve Booz et Ruth;

Car il n'est pas de plage, ou de montagne, ou d'île,
   Parmi les abîmes amers,
Mieux faite pour cacher les roses de l'idylle
   Sous la tragique horreur des mers.

Ciel! océan! c'etait cette même nature,
   Gouffre de silence et de bruit,
Ayant on ne sait quelle insondable ouverture
   Sur la lumière et sur la nuit.

Oui, c'étaient ces hameaux, oui, c'étaient ces rivages;
   C'était ce même aspect mouvant,
La même âcre senteur des bruyères sauvages,
   Les mêmes tumultes du vent;

C'était la même vague arrachant aux décombres
   Les mêmes dentelles d'argent;
C'étaient les mêmes blocs jetant les mêmes ombres
   Au même éternel flot changeant;

C'étaient les mêmes caps que l'onde ignore et ronge,
   Car l'âpre mer, pleine de deuils,
Ne s'inquiète pas, dans son effrayant songe,
   De la figure des écueils;

C'était la même fuite immense des nuées;
   Sur ces monts, où Dieu vient tonner,
Les mêmes cimes d'arbre, en foule remuées,
   N'ont pas fini de frissoner;

C'était le même souffle ondoyant dans les seigles;
   Je crois revoir sur l'humble pré
Les mêmes papillons avec les mêmes aigles
   Sur l'océan démesuré;

C'était le même flux couvrant l'île d'écume,
   Comme un cheval blanchit le mors;
C'était le même azur, c'était la même brume,
   Et combien vivaient, qui sont morts![1]

Notes and References

Abbreviations

AM	Victor Hugo, *L'Archipel de la Manche*.
Ang.	P. Angrand, *Victor Hugo raconté par les papiers d'État*.
BSJ	Le Bulletin de la Société Jersiaise.
BN	La Bibliothèque Nationale, Paris.
CH	Charles Hugo, *Les Hommes de l'Exil*.
Chat.	*Les Châtiments*.
Cont.	*Les Contemplations*.
Corr.	Victor Hugo, *Correspondance* (Albin Michel).
CV	Victor Hugo, *Choses Vues* (Gallimard).
DC	A. De Chêne, *Les proscrits du Deux-Décembre à Jersey*.
EC	Victor Hugo, *Oeuvres*, Edition Chronologique (ed. Jules Massin).
FO	Foreign Office papers, series 27, Public Record Office, Kew.
HO	Home Office papers, series 45, Public Record Office, Kew.
JAH	Adèle Hugo, *Le Journal d'Adèle Hugo*.
JDMS	Juliette Drouet, MS letters to Hugo in the BN.
M-D	N. Martin-Duport, *Victor Hugo anecdotique*.
Miettes	A. Vacquerie, *Les Miettes de l'histoire*.
MVH	MS letters in La Maison de Victor Hugo, Paris.
NAF	Nouvelles Acquisitions Françaises (MSS) in the BN.
NI	François-Victor Hugo, *La Normandie inconnue*.
PLE	Victor Hugo, *Actes et Paroles. Pendant l'Exil*. (Albin Michel).
TM	Victor Hugo, *Les Travailleurs de la Mer*.

(In the better known works of Hugo, which run to many editions, the chapter or section rather than a page reference to a particular edition are noted.)

Jersey Newspapers

Chr.	La Chronique.
Const.	Le Constitutionnel.
JI	Jersey Independent.
JT	Jersey Times.
LH	L'Homme.
LI	L'Impartial.
NC	La Nouvelle Chronique.
Pat.	La Patrie.
Ref.	La Réforme.

Les journaux y abondent, en anglais et en français ... Tel est le puissant et irréductible instinct anglais. Supposez une île déserte; le lendemain de son arrive, Robinson fait un journal, et Vendredi s'y abonne. (AM 13.)

Notes and References

'JERSEY'

1. From *Les Quatre Vents de l'Esprit*. Le Creux de la Touraille is the proper name for Le Creux de Vis which, by a false etymology, is now called the Devil's Hole. Hugo's reference elsewhere to a rock at Plemont as 'the Headless Monk' and the mention of Plemont in this poem suggests that it was written at Plemont not at the Devil's Hole. The reference to 'laurier rose' may be a play on the two political parties of the island, Rose and Laurel.

CHAPTER 1

1. Grant.
2. Ang. 41, Claretie 9.
3. VH, *En voyage* (letter to Adèle, 30 June 1836).
4. Corr. 2. 93-4; Gaudon, S. 203; JAH 1. 166, 196.
5. Corr. 2. 102-3.
6. Corr. 2. 118-9; Ang. 43; JAH 1. 235.
7. JAH 1. 225, 230; Hazard 391-2.
8. PLE, 1852, i. *En quittant La Belgique*; JAH 1. 236ff; *JT* 6 August 1852; Ang. 42; *LI* 7 August 1852.
9. Ang. 41; Corr. 2. 123-4; JAH loc. cit.
10. Corr. 2. 123; Miettes 415.
11. JAH loc. cit; Hazard 393.
12. This is probably Pasajes, near St Sebastian, which Hugo visited in 1843.
13. Hazard loc. cit; JAH 1. 242ff; Seché 252; Miettes 368; VH, *William Shakespeare*, introduction.
14. Corr. 2. 127; JAH 1. 262; Seché 252; Hazard 393; *Rose of Jersey*, see *BSJ* 1977, 110-11.
15. VH, *William Shakespeare*. Henri Houssaye noted in 1884 that the walls of Marine Terrace were dark grey and the shutters harsh green.
16. JAH 1. 261ff; Laurens 678.
17. *LI*, cited by *JT* 17 August 1852; JAH loc. cit; Corr. 2. 127, 187; Seché 252; Hazard 393.
18. VH, *William Shakespeare*; JAH 1. 262; Laurens 678.
19. Miettes 369.
20. From Océan in VH Poésie (Seuil) vol. 3, 754.
21. JDMS, 1852, 207-10; Guimbaud; Barbier 123-4, 127.
22. Barbier 139; Guimbaud; VH, *Lettres à Juliette Drouet*, ed. Pauvert 131-2 (Hugo

wrote to Juliette at 'inn rich Land' but this was probably Richard Landhatherland's inn, the *Green Pigeon*).

23. Corr. 2. 120; 4. 216; Maurois, *Victor Hugo*, 340; Maurois, *Three Musketeers*, 200; Guille 83.
24. Hazard 395; CV 29; Portefeuille poetique in EC.
25. JAH 319; Guille 85; Clément-Janin 70; Maurois, *VH* 340-1.
26. VH, *William Shakespeare*.
27. EC viii, 1039-41. On Hugo's heart condition see Claretie, *Revue de Paris*, 1894.
28. Barbier 150-5; MVC. Vacquerie to Meurice 'fin 1852, jeudi' but probably 6 January 1853.
29. Maurois, *VH* loc. cit; Barbier loc. cit.
30. Barbier, loc. cit; MVH Vacquerie to Meurice, idem.
31. MVH Charles Hugo to parents 6 January 1853.
32. Clément-Janin 69-71.
33. Idem 66-8; Seché 261; Guille 81-7.
34. JAH 2. 15, 447; CV 236, 282, 328; Seché 257; Hazard 398; Daudet 135. Simon 310 mentions another servant, Olive.

CHAPTER 2

1. Seché 253; Laurens 684, 688-9. Laurens says that Hugo worked sitting on his bunk but Barbou (*VH et son temps* 255) says he worked standing up. He certainly stood at his desk in the lookout in Guernsey.
2. Seché 256-7.
3. MVH Mme. Hugo to Mme. Meurice 14 October 1852, 8 November 1852.
4. Mme. Hugo to Asseline 13 October 1852 in Asseline, *VH intime*; Seché 325.
5. *Chr.* 18 February 1854. The ball is described in *Const.* 25 February 1854, while Mme. Hugo's letter is dated Sunday 19 February. This must be 1854, not 1853 as Seché suggests.
6. Seché 258; Jean Hugo 168; JAH 3. 64.
7. Asseline; JAH 2. 457ff (Cahier intime); 3. 13-67. According to the Rose sepulchre in St Clement's churchyard, J. W. Rose died in England and was buried on 12 July 1853. Before this the Roses had four surviving sons and it is possible to match them with initials used by Adèle in her cahier intime, with the exception of 'P' who may in fact be Albert Pinson:
Thomas Rose, father, aged 50, whom Adèle called Père Rose.
Sarah Rose, his wife, 41, whom Adèle called Mme. Rose.
John William Rose, about 23, whom Adèle called J.
Thomas Henry Rose, 18, whom Adèle called T., Tom.
G. B. Rose, 16, whom Adèle called G., 'le petit de 15 ans'.
Frederick Ernest Rose, 4, possibly referred to by Adèle as 'le petit Pr.', 'cet enfant de 7 ans'.
8. Seché 261.
9. Seché 324.
10. JAH loc. cit.
11. Vacquerie, *Depuis* 65; JAH 1. 67ff; 3. 13-67.
12. Maurois, *VH* 394; Clément-Janin 79-80.

13. Vercel 56-8; Seché 322, 328; Daudet 135.
14. Laurens 680; JAH 3. 172; Seché *Revue de Paris*; M-D 98; Guillemin 7.
15. MVH, MS account sheet. A date of 1855 has been suggested for this account sheet which refers to an 'accumulated debt' over four years.
16. Lacassagne 258-62; M-D 164. On Leroux's personal pathology, no doubt related to his interest in recycling sewage ('Circulus'), see the story in JAH 1. 317. Ang. 126 claims that Mme. Hugo was extravagant but cites no source.
17. JAH 3. 289. On Hugo's supposed avarice, see Guillemin 44-50 and M-D.
18. Daudet 135; Barthou 107-8; Souchon 444, 454, 456; Guimbaud 431.
19. JDMS, 1852, 233-50; Barbier 138-9.
20. Berret; Maurois 341; Souchon 443.
21. Barthou 107-8; Daudet 135; Barbou, Guimbaud, Barbier.
22. Daudet 137.
23. Barbier 123.
24. Guimbaud 427.
25. Laurens 667-89; Seché 322.
26. Hazard 398; CV 236-7; *JT* 5 April 1853.
27. Corr. 2. 210; *JT* 6 June 1854; *Chr.* 27 June 1855; JAH 3. 250.

CHAPTER 3

1. *Writings*. Vacquerie, *Profils* 390; Hazard 397; JAH 1. 307; 2. 23, 290-2, 404, 440, 470-2; 3. 76, 94, 104-5, 126-8, 210, 553; Seché 323; *Chr.* 26 October 1853, 7 April 1855; Ang. 100; Guille 93; MVH Vacquerie to Meurice 'Tuesday' 1854.

2. *Conversations*. M-D 163-5; Guillemin 7; JAH 1. 253, 281, 300; 2. 74, 101, 116, 124, 171, 191, 283-4, 387; 3. 146, 150, 270, 347, 354, 447-9, 542.

3. *Theatre*. Seché 253; JAH 1. 270, 311, 334; 2. 447, 455; Guimbaud 427. On 20 November 1852 *Chr.* stated that *Angelo* would be played on the 22nd and that the 'savant auteur' would no doubt be there, but it seems that the first performance was not until the 26th – see *Chr.* 1 December 1852. Hugo was also at the Theatre Royal on 6 December 1852 (*JT* 10 December 1852) and probably on 23 August 1852 (*Chr.* 21 August 1852 and JDMS 1852, 233-4); *Const.* 24 December 1853; *JT* 20 January 1854; JAH 3. 83-5, 95; Miettes 389.

4. *Music*. Miettes 373; JAH 1. 271; 2. 19, 180, 303, 338, 414, 430; 3. 331, 349, 424, 562; *Chr.* 16 April 1853, 9 November 1853, 12 December 1853, 16 December 1853, 9 September 1854, 4 October 1854, 18 October 1854; Seché 254-5; *Const.* 16 September 1854, 18 October 1854; *LH* 11 October 1854; Lazar 179. See Schoyen 248 for other visits of Remenyi to Jersey.

5. *Fencing etc.* Miettes 405; Rivet 101; Barbou *VH et son temps* 255-6; Laurens 682; Seché 331-2, who wrongly dates this letter to 1853, when it must be from 1855.

6. *Photography*. JAH 1. 335; 2. 23, 56, 290, 305, 478-9; 3. 96. Guille suggests the name 'Rageot' in JAH 2. 305 but it must be Bacot. Hazard 396; Guimbaud 430;

Seché 260; Barbier 129; MVH Charles Hugo to his parents about 17 March 1853 and 31 March 1853; Corr. 2. 158, 169.

7. *Gardening*. VH, *William Shakespeare*; Clément-Janin 67; JAH 1. 261-4; 2. 72-4, 98-9; 3. 256; Seché 323-324. Seché suggests 1854 for this letter but the similarity with JAH 2. 72-4 makes 1853 much more likely; Laurens 685; CV 282.

8. *Dogs and cats*. JAH 1. 273; 2. 72; 3. 231-2, 416, 463; Cont. v.11; Miettes 417-29, 448-54; Vacquerie, *Profils* 393-4; CV 282, 288, 327-8, 492; Corr. 2. 215; Seché 256, 323; M-D 93; MVH Mme. Hugo to Mme. Meurice 9 July 1854. Lazar 178 says that Teleki gave the Hugos Chougna, but Mme. Hugo says that Chougna came from a 'vilain fermier'. In Corr. 2. 215 footnote, Carton is said to be a dog, but Mme. Hugo says that Carton, formerly 'le sauvage', is a cat.

9. *Swimming*. Souchon 459; Miettes 405; JAH 3. 145-6; Claretie 31; Barbier 137-9; CV 327.

10. *Riding*. Miettes 405; Vacquerie, *Profils* 389; NI 16; Guimbaud 459; *LH* 28 December 1853; JAH 2. 145; Corr. 2. 200; HO 4816; Guillemin 7.

CHAPTER 4

1. JAH 3. 196.
2. JAH 1. 242-3, 248, 274; 2. 136, 267; MVH Vacquerie to Meurice, n.d.
3. JAH 1. 275, 365; Cont. v.24. This verse seems to have been composed at Boulay Bay in 1852 not, as in some editions, in Sark in 1855.
4. JAH 1. 276; Souchon 439. There is some confusion in JAH about dates and itineraries: an advertisement in *JT* 31 August 1852 says that the *Rose* would sail round the island on 1 September 1852 and stop at the Fancy Fair.
5. VH, *Les Quatre Vents de l'Esprit* iii. 14; VH, *Quatre-vingt treize* i. 2.
6. AM 22; JAH 1. 331, 365-6; 3. 369; Miettes 366.
7. JAH 1. 136-9, 282; AM 14.
8. Chat. vi. 4; Cont. vi. 2, 3, 26.
9. Cont. vi. 18, 22, 23, 25; AM 6, 22; JAH 2. 347.
10. TM i. 6. 1; iii. 1.1; VH, *L'Homme qui rit* i. 2. 15; VH, *Quatre-vingt treize* i. 2. 1; NI 15; JAH 1. 312.
11. VH, Océan. Tas de Pierres (Albin Michel) 466; JAH 3. 288. There was a J. Humphry, R.E., in Jersey *c*. 1811.
12. AM 14, 16; JAH 3. 190.
13. Cont. v.23. *Pasteurs et Troupeaux* is dated in the edition 'Grouville 1855' so the 'vallon' is probably Queen's Valley.
14. Ang. 91; Souchon 453; Vacquerie, *Profils* 10; JAH 3. 19.
15. Laurens 677.
16. JAH 1. 243-4; AM 1, 6, 9; Miettes 464; VH, *Les Quatre Vents de l'Esprit* iii. 14; PLE Ce que c'est que l'exil, iii.
17. TM i. 6.1; Corr. 2.189; AM 11, 16, 22; Cont. v.20.
18. JAH 1. 244; Corr. 2. 126-7; Seché 252; Hazard 393.
19. Miettes 362, 373.

CHAPTER 5

1. Corr. 2. 228; JAH 1. 244; AM 9.
2. Vacquerie, *Depuis* 67; Miettes 361, 416-7.
3. TM i. 2. 3; AM 14, 15; Corr. 4. 154.
4. HO 4816; *Chr.* 27 December 1854.
5. Wace, born *c.* 1090 in Jersey, reputedly at La Ville-ès-Normans, was author of the *Roman de Rou.*
6. NI 104.
7. Seché 252, 323; TM i. 3. 1.
8. Miettes 375, 405; VH, Océan. Tas de Pierres (Albin Michel) 252. cf. Alexander Herzen 'The refugee in England vegetates in safety. He cannot be followed, nor can he be moved. He finds no enemies, and makes no allies.'
9. Océan from VH Poésie vol.3 (Seuil) 727.
10. *Reasoner* 6 January 1856; R. Lesclide 284; JAH 2. 52-4; VH, Océan. Tas de Pierres (Albin Michel) 253; Mineka and Lindley eds. *The later letters of J. S. Mill.*
11. PLE Historique 502; VH Océan. Tas de Pierres (Albin Michel) 252.
12. JAH 3. 396-7; AM 12, 17; TM i 3.2.
13. AM 12; TM i. 6. 2.
14. AM 13.
15. JAH 2, 115.
16. TM i. 5. 3; AM 22.

CHAPTER 6

1. CV 235; Claretie 36.
2. Hazard 395; Claretie 15.
3. Seché 254.
4. Béranger (letter to Mme. Hugo 21 September 1852); Seché 253, 323-330; Mercié 63-4; JAH 2. 470-2.
5. Miettes 375-82; JAH 2. 271ff; NI 15; Lesclide.
6. *Table turning.* The version of the first seance comes from Vacquerie (Simon 32-7) but the phrases marked * have been added from JAH 2. 272-8. Grillet; Miettes 381-9; JAH 2. and 3. *passim*; Guillemin *VH et les fantômes*; VH, Océan, vers sans date (Seuil Poésie vol.3. 717).
7. Seché 253; Corr. 2. 129, 159, 173, 179, 191, 198; Chat. ii. 5, vii. 13; CV 275; VH, Océan. Tas de Pierres (Albin Michel) 251, 254; Flaubert 539; JAH 3. 353.

CHAPTER 7

1. Brock 180; Lazar 177; Ang. 45-50; HO 4013, 4547A; *JT* 20 August 1852; *Pat.* 7 and 28 August 1852 and Jersey newspapers *passim*; PLE 1852, ii, En arrivant à Jersey.

CHAPTER 8

1. Ang. 50-2, 56, 102-3, 108; Biré; HO 4008, 4547A; Malmesbury 346; Stevens *Victorian Voices* 124, 128-9; *Chr.* 11 September 1852; *JT* 10, 15 and 24 September 1852; Corr. 2. 128-9; M-D 39; CH 180-2; JAH 3. 288, 292; Vercel 69; Seché 254; Chat. iii. 2.

CHAPTER 9

1. Angrand says that Laurent heard the story on 25 September and reported the French sloop's arrival on the same day. *Chronique*, however, says he went to St Malo on 26 September for the day. It is difficult to reconcile these dates: one or more may be wrong or Laurent may have made two visits to France. Laurent is not actually named in the *Times* report of 9 October 1852 as the man who was tipped off by the man present at the dinner and who warned the authorities in France, but it must have been he.
2. Ang. 57-61, 77-80; HO 4013, 4547A; *Times* 29 and 30 September 1852; *Chr.* 13 October 1852; *JT* 15 October 1852; Ridley 318; Brock 179-183.

CHAPTER 10

1. PLE 1852, iii, Declaration à propos de l'Empire; Ang. 63-73; JAH 1. 231-2, 327-8, 337; NAF 24778, ff 515-9; Corr. 2. 131-2; HO 4547A, 4907; Chat. i. 4, ii. 4, iii. 4; Ridley 318; CV 231; PLE, Historique 496; BN Lb. 56. 3237; *Chr.* 8, 22, 24 and 29 December 1852, 20 April 1853, 14 May 1853; *Times* 7 February 1853; *JT* 7, 24 and 28 December 1852, 7 January 1853, 15 February 1853; *Const.* 11 December 1852, 5 February 1853; *LI* 4, 8, 11, 24, and 29 December 1852; *Pat.* 11 December 1852; John Le Couteur, MS Diary 20 December 1852; *Illustrated London News* 8 January 1853.

CHAPTER 11

1. *Bazaar*. Ang. 75-7; MS letter to households (priv. coll.); MVH Mme. Hugo to Mme. Meurice 6 January 1853; PLE, Historique 496-7; JAH 2. 37-9, 41; 3. 81, 109, 310; *Const.* 24 December 1852; Barbier 127-9; CH 184; *Chr.* 23 February 1853; *JT* 22 February 1853; Seché 260-1.
2. According to *Chronique* Dutaillis died in his wife's arms, but Adèle says he was separated from her.
3. Angrand says that Gornet carried the flag, but *Chronique* says that a 'noble Hungarian' (?Teleki) did.
4. *Dutaillis*. JAH 2. 54-5; *Chr.* 13, 16 April 1853; Ang. 82-4; CV 238.
5. The word 'Republican' was added by Seigneuret: JAH 2. 65.
6. *Bousquet*. JAH 2. 129-30, 162, 482-6; PLE 1853, i, Sur la tombe de Jean Bousquet; Ang. 84-8; HO 4816; Corr. 2. 152; DC 21, 64; Chat. vii. 13.

CHAPTER 12

1. Jules Allix was implicated in the Hippodrome plot, though Guille (JAH 3. 151) suggests he was not.
2. CV 239-40, 267, 282;   Corr. 2. 138-9; Chat. vi. 5; Chateaubriand *Mémoires d'Outre-tombe*; HO 4816; PLE 1853, ii, Sur la tombe de Louise Julien; *Chr.* 7 May 1853, 27 July 1853; *JT* 6 May 1853, 14 June 1853, 1, 15 and 29 July 1853, 30 August 1853, 6 September 1853; Ang. 90-4, 112; *Const.* 15 June 1853, 2 and 6 July 1853, 24 August 1853, 14 June 1854; *Ref.* 25 June 1853, 2 July 1853, 6 September

1853; *Times* 11 and 14 June 1853; JAH 2. 90-2, 120-2, 139, 145-50, 157, 161, 168-70, 178, 212, 487; 3. 151; Leroux 43, 147; Ridley 352; Stevens *Victorian Voices* 129-30.

CHAPTER 13

1. *Hubert*. CV 242-73; JAH 2. 294-303, 310-22, 488-90; 3. 218, 528-9; Rivet 107-17; *Chr.* 22 October 1853.

CHAPTER 14

1. HO 4816, 5180; Ridley 355 ff; JAH 2. 359; 3. 132; PLE 1853, ii, 23ème Anniversaire de la Révolution Polonaise, Historique 500; DC 7, 13-6; Ang. 98-101, 113-4; *JT* 13 December 1853; *Chr.* 14 December 1853.

CHAPTER 15

1. *Tapner*. 'Procès de Jean Charles Tapner'; 'Execution of J. C. Tapner'; JAH 3. 81-3, 88-9, 115-6, 118, 127, 531, 541; CV 295-317; PLE 1854, i, Aux habitants de Guernesey; ii, À Lord Palmerston, Historique 501-2; HO 5871, 5194A; Corr. 2. 181-3; *Const.* 25 January 1854, 4, 15 and 25 February 1854; *Macaulay's letters* ed. Pinney, Macaulay to Ellis 20 February 1854; *JT* 20 and 24 January 1854, 17 and 24 February 1854, 3 March 1854; *LI* 31 January 1855; Hooker 108-9; Ang. 120-1.

CHAPTER 16

1. *Macpela*. Ang. 123-4; PLE 1854, iii, Sixième anniversaire; v, Sur la tombe de Félix Bony; *JT* 3 and 14 March 1854; JAH 3. 129-33, 168, 199, 264, 374-6, 387-9, 398-9, 409, 422, 548, 556-8; *LH* 14 March 1854; *Chr.* 11 March 1854; Leroux 40; Brock 184; *Const.* 8 October 1854.
2. *Spain, America*. JAH 3. 157, 247, 304, 316, 329, 336, 342, 354, 358-61, 383-7, 396; CH 188; Ang. 125-6; *Chr.* 7 June 1854, 26 August 1854, 25 October 1854; HO 5180; PLE 1854, iv, Appel aux Concitoyens.
3. JAH 1. 307; 2. 33; 3. 76, 78, 134-5, 138-45, 178, 217, 230, 258, 263, 267-9, 278, 286, 310-5, 331, 537, 556-8; NAF 24778, f 542; CV 265-6, 290-1; Corr. 2. 152; Daudet 136; *Const.* 3 and 17 May 1854, 14 June 1854, 28 October 1854, 15 November 1854; *Chr.* 24 May 1854; *JT* 16 and 30 June 1854, 21 and 25 July 1854; HO 5180, 6188; Ang. 129-31, 143-6; Ridley 374-6; PLE 1855, i, Septième anniversaire du 24 février 1848.

CHAPTER 17

1. JAH 3. 520-1, 551; Hooker 110-2, 135; PLE 1855, ii, Lettre à Louis Bonaparte; Ang. 136-40, 146-53, 155-6; *JT* 24 April 1855, 4 May 1855, 31 July 1855, 7 August 1855, 7 and 14 September 1855; Ridley 376-81; *LI* 5 May 1855, 1 and 8 August 1855; *NC* 28 July 1855; HO 6188, 6721; CH 191-5; *LH* 15 August 1855; *Chr.* 29 August 1855, 1 September 1855; *JT* 25 August 1855; Miettes 441-2; Stevens op. cit. 117; M-D 67.

CHAPTER 18

1. Ridley 384-6; HO 6188; *Times* 5 and 17 October 1855; Ridley, *Palmerston* 479-80; Hooker 113; PLE, Historique 506; Harney, *Athenaeum* 20 June 1855; *LH* 26 September 1855; Justitia, 34-5, 65-6, 104; JAH 2. 81; 3. 92, 110, 124, 131, 535-6; *Chr.* 13 October 1855; *Reasoner* 14 November 1855, 17 February 1856; Miettes 446; CH 204-6, 212-3, 227; M-D 64; Pelleport 46.

CHAPTER 19

1. *Indignation meeting.* DC 12, 76; CH 214-6, 222; Miettes 447; *Chr, NC, Times* of 17 October 1855; Justitia 36-42; *Reasoner* 20 January 1856.
2. *Dorset Street.* CH 241, 245; Miettes 448-9; *Const.* 27 October 1855; Payne 10; Justitia 42-4; *Reasoner* 17 February 1856; M-D 40-1.

CHAPTER 20

1. The sequence of events would suggest that they met on the 15th, but Martin-Duport says that Hugo had written the declaration before the meeting without consulting the others; further, Mme. Hugo wrote to Mme. Meurice (MVH) on the 16th: 'It is this evening alone that the proscrits are meeting'. This all suggests that Hugo presented the declaration as a fait accompli on the 16th.
2. CH 185, 236, 251, 253, 258, 275ff, 281-9, 294; Ang. 166-71; HO 6188; Payne 11; PLE 1855, iii, Expulsion de Jersey; Miettes 453-7; Vercel, *Esquisses*; *Const.* 27 October 1855; Charles Hugo, *Putnam's Monthly*, July 1869; *LI* 31 October 1855; FO 1094; Hooker 117, 123; Seché 229-30; Justitia 45-50.

CHAPTER 21

1. NI 11-20; CV 294; *NC* 31 October 1855; CH 298-302; HO 6188; Hazard 401; MVH Mme. Hugo to Mme. Meurice, 'Dimanche' – probably 4 November 1855; Seché 332; *Chr.* 3 November 1855; DC 88, 104; Guille 106; Simon, *La vie d'une femme* 331-2.

CHAPTER 22

1. *NC* 3 and 17 November 1855; DC 90, 94-7, 101, 103; HO 6188, 6406, 6333; *Chr.* 21 and 28 November 1855; Marx-Engels *Briefwechsel*, vol. 2, 196; Hooker 118, 120, 124, 128-31; *LH* 31 October 1855, 17 November 1855; CH 184; *NC* 3 and 21 November 1855; Harney papers 115; Corr. 2. 229; Justitia 51-61, 67; Guille 106; *Reasoner* 18 November 1855; Schoyen 243; *JT* 30 October 1855; Ang. 158, 168-9, 194; *Times* 26 November 1855; Brock 187; *JI* 30 September 1859.

CHAPTER 23

1. Richardson 161; Harney papers 125-7; PLE 1860, i, Rentrée à Jersey.

EPILOGUE

1. Richardson 151, 154, 211, 216; PLE 1866, ii, Le condamne à mort de Jersey, Bradley; CV 437; Corr. 4. 555; *Toute la Lyre*, v.37.

Bibliography

Angrand, P., *Victor Hugo raconté par les papiers d'État*, Gallimard, 1961.
Asseline, A., *Victor Hugo intime*, Marpon & Flammarion, 1885.

Barbier, J. P., *Juliette Drouet: sa vie, son oeuvre*, Grasset, 1913.
Barbou, A., *Victor Hugo et son temps*, Charpentier, 1881.
Barthou, L., *Les amours d'un poëte*, Conard, 1919.
Berret, P., *Victor Hugo*, Garnier, 1939.
Biré, E. *Victor Hugo après 1852*, Perrin, 1894.
Brock, P., A Polish 'proscrit' in Jersey, *BSJ*, 1954.

Carré, A. L., Victor Hugo in Jersey, *BSJ*, 1953.
Claretie, L., *Correspondance entre Victor Hugo et Paul Meurice*, Charpentier, 1909; Les causeries de Victor Hugo, *Revue de Paris*, 1 July 1894.
Clément-Janin, N., *Victor Hugo en exil*, Éditions du Monde Nouveau, 1922.

Daudet, L., *The tragic life of Victor Hugo*, tr. Whitall, 1939.
De Chêne, A., *Les proscrits du Deux-Décembre à Jersey* (1852-5), extracted from *Études* 1917, Dumoulin.

Execution of J. C. Tapner (Broadsheet), 10 February 1854.

Flaubert, G., *Lettres*, Club de l'Honnête Homme, 1974.
Fleischmann, H., *Une maîtresse de Victor Hugo*, Libraire Universelle, 1912.

Gaudon, J., *Les Tables Parlantes*, in Édition Chronologique, ix, 2.
Gaudon, S., *Correspondance entre Victor Hugo et Pierre-Jules Hetzel*, Klincksiek, 1979.
Grant, E. M., *The career of Victor Hugo*, Cambridge, Mass., 1946.
Grillet, C., *Victor Hugo spirite*, Vitte, 1935.
Guille, F. V., *François-Victor Hugo et son oeuvre*, Nizet, 1950.
Guillemin, H., *Hugo*, Seuil, 1951; Victor Hugo et les fantômes de Jersey, *Revue de Paris*, September 1952.
Guimbaud, L., *Victor Hugo et Juliette Drouet*, Blaizot, 1914.

Harney, G. J., *The Harney Papers*, ed. F. G. & R. M. Black, Van Gorcum, 1969; Victor Hugo in Jersey, *The Athenaeum*, 20 June 1855.
Hazard, P., Avec Victor Hugo en exil, *Revue des Deux Mondes*, 15 November 1930.
Houssaye, H., De Marine Terrace à Hauteville House, *Journal des Débats*, 15 September 1885.

Hugo, Adèle, *Le Journal d'Adèle Hugo*, ed. F. V. Guille, Minard, 1968, 1971, 1984.

Hugo, Charles, Victor Hugo and the constables, *Putnam's Monthly*, July 1869; *Les Hommes de l'exil*, Lemerre, 1875.

Hugo, François-Victor, *La Normandie inconnue*, Pagnerre, 1857.

Hugo, Jean, *Le regard de la mémoire*, Actes Sud, 1983.

Hugo, Victor, *Actes et Paroles*, vol. 2, Pendant l'Exil, Albin Michel, 1938; *L'Archipel de la Manche*; *Les Châtiments*; *Choses vues. 1846-1869*, ed. Juin, Gallimard, 1972; *Les Contemplations*; *Correspondance*, Albin Michel, 1947-52; *Édition chronologique*, Jules Massin; *En voyage*, Ollendorff, 1910; *Lettres à Juliette Drouet*, ed. J. Gaudon, Pauvert, 1964; *Océan. Tas de Pierres*, Albin Michel, 1942; *Poésie*, l'Intégrale, vol. 3, Seuil, 1972; *Les Quatre Vents de l'Esprit*; *Quatre-vingt treize*; *Les Travailleurs de la Mer*; *William Shakespeare*, introduction.

Justitia, *To His Excellency Major-General Love*, 1856.

Lacassagne, J. P., *Histoire d'une amitié: Pierre Leroux et George Sand*, Klincksieck, 1973.

Laurens, Jules, *La Légende des Ateliers*, Carpentras, 1901.

Lazar, André, Les emigrés Hongrois dans les Îles de la Manche, *BSJ*, 1978.

Leroux, P., *La Grève de Samarez*, Dentu, 1863.

Lesclide, R., *Propos de table de Victor Hugo en exil*, Dentu, 1885.

Malmesbury, J., *Memoires of an ex-minister*, Longmans, Green, 1884.

Martin-Duport, N., *Victor Hugo anecdotique*, Storck, 1904.

Marzials, Sir Frank, *Life and writings of Victor Hugo*, n.d.

Maurois, A., *Victor Hugo*, tr. Hopkins, Cape, 1956; *Three Musketeers*, tr. Hopkins, Cape, 1957.

Mercié, J. L., *Victor Hugo et Julie Chenay*, Minard, 1967.

Payne, de V., *Victor Hugo in Jersey*, Jersey Society in London, 1930.

Pelleport, A., *Tous les amours*, Charpentier, 1882.

Procès de Jean Charles Tapner, printed by Brouard, Guernsey, 1854.

Richardson, Joanna, *Victor Hugo*, St Martin's Press, 1976.

Rivet, G., *Victor Hugo chez lui*, Dreyfous, 1883.

Schoyen, A. R., *The Chartist Challenge: a portrait of George Julian Harney*, Heinemann, 1958.

Seché, L., Lettres de Mme. Hugo à sa soeur Julie, *Les Annales Romantiques*, 1912, 1913.

Simon, G., *Chez Victor Hugo. Les Tables Tournantes à Jersey*, Conard, 1923; *La vie d'une femme*, Ollendorff, 1914.

Souchon, P., *Mille et une lettres d'amour de Juliette Drouet à Victor Hugo*, Gallimard, 1951.

Stevens, Joan, *Victorian Voices*, La Société Jersiaise, 1969.

Vacquerie, A., *Depuis*, Calmann Lévy, 1882; *Les Miettes de l'histoire*, Pagnerre, 1863; *Profils et Grimaces*, Calmann Lévy, 1897.

Vercel, R., *Les Îles Anglo-Normandes*, Albin Michel, 1956; *Esquisses Anglo-Normandes*, Fayard, 1947.

Index